New Testament
Disunity

NEW TESTAMENT

John Charlot

DISUNITY

*Its Significance
for Christianity
Today*

E. P. Dutton & Co., Inc.

New York

1970

Published simultaneously in Canada by
Clarke, Irwin & Company Limited,
Toronto and Vancouver

Library of Congress Catalog
Card Number: 79-92617

Designed by The Etheredges

SBN   0-525-16527-4

[04]

For Dominique

Abbreviations

FRLANT   Forschungen zur Religion und Literatur des Alten und Neuen Testamentes

HNT   Handbuch zum Neuen Testament, founded by Hans Lietzmann

Meyer   Kritisch-exegetischer Kommentar über das Neue Testament, founded by Heinrich August Wilhelm Meyer

NCR   *The National Catholic Reporter*

ZTK   *Zeitschrift für Theologie und Kirche*

Contents

I THE PROBLEM

VARIETIES OF CONTRADICTIONS
Successive Contradictions
JESUS AND AFTER / THE DELAY OF THE PAROUSIA:
CONSEQUENT PROBLEMS AND SOLUTIONS /
FROM PALESTINE TO HELLENISM / TOWARD EARLY
CATHOLICISM / ATTITUDES TOWARD THE STATE
Contemporary Contradictions
GROUPS IN EARLY CHRISTIANITY /
CONTRADICTIONS BETWEEN AND WITHIN SCHOOLS,
FORMS, AND INDIVIDUAL THEOLOGIES / NEW
TESTAMENT CHRISTOLOGIES
THE LOGICAL STATUS OF THE CONTRADICTIONS IN
NEW TESTAMENT THEOLOGY

II ATTEMPTED SOLUTIONS

CRITERIA FOR VALUE JUDGMENTS
CRITERIA BASED ON A CERTAIN LEVEL OF
TRADITION OR ON A CERTAIN TEACHER
CRITERIA BASED ON A CERTAIN TEACHING

I
THE
PROBLEM

"Let those
who think I ought
to be answered,
those Catholics,
first master
the great difficulty,
the great problem,
and then,
if they don't like
my way of meeting it,
find another.
Syllogizing
won't meet it."

JOHN HENRY NEWMAN

1
Introduction

Unity of doctrine has always been a principle of Christian teaching. St. Paul writes: "But even if we or an angel from heaven should proclaim a gospel different from what we have proclaimed to you, let him be anathema" (Galatians 1:8).

Also, unity of doctrine has always been considered to be the basis of the unity of the church. Leo XIII mentions this point as a universally accepted presupposition: "Just as for the unity of the Church . . . unity of faith is necessarily required, so . . ." [1]

A modern theologian such as Stephen Pfürtner can express this principle with equal conviction: ". . . any difference in doctrine which is not properly cleared up will eventually reveal its latent power to create divisions in the life of the Church, even if at first it seems unimportant." [2]

Finally, orthodox Christian theology has always based itself on the Bible, and in particular on the New Testament, as its authoritative source. Some Roman Catholics consider tradition to be an equal source, but, theoretically at least, this in no way devalues the central importance of the Bible. Christian theology was, and often still is, considered to be an *interpretation* of that which was revealed in the Bible. Creeds were and are considered official interpretations, more or less guaranteed by the church.

Precisely because of the place of the Bible, and especially of the New Testament, in this general view, its unity has always been assumed. Texts from many different parts of the Bible were used as if they were single propositions of some unified theological system. A later theologian would consider his system to be latent in the different Biblical statements.

Theories of inspiration were formulated to explain how God could speak unfettered through the medium of men. Scripture was, of course, without error; that is, it did not contain untruth. Truth, of course, was one. Any observed inconsistencies within the Bible were somehow explained away. In no case could a theological teaching of the church *contradict* the Bible.

Even today, many theologians speak of *"the* teaching of the New Testament" or *"the* message of the Bible." Often ecumenists propose *the* theology of the New Testament as a basis on which all churches could unite.

These positions and attitudes are indicative of a certain view of theology which I would formulate in the following way: the unity of the church is based on the unity of theology which is based on the unity of the Bible, and especially of the New Testament. Visser 't Hooft illustrates this view when he states: "To deny the unity of the Bible is to deny the unity of the Church." [3]

This view can be called the theory of unity and considered an important part of a general theory of theology. It is, roughly, the theory of any Christian orthodoxy.

Of course, unity means different things to different people and churches. Some tolerate much greater differences than others within their framework of "unity." But the great majority would not consider fundamental differences on basic questions as unity. Unity can be defined then, very roughly, as fundamental agreement on basic issues, and disunity as the opposite. Paul would not allow that Christ was not the Lord. Leo XIII would not consider Roman Catholic anyone who did not accept the infallibility of the Pope. Luther could not be reconciled with anyone who did not believe in justification by faith alone. Although the Christian churches seem now to be testing the extent to which the bounds of the theologically allowable can be stretched, unity remains the ideal. Creeds are still employed; claims of infallible teaching authority are still being made. Intercommunion is still being delayed until doctrinal agreement has been reached. In all these cases, Christians are still adhering, however unconsciously, to what I have described as the theory of unity.

That theory has however been rendered questionable by the progress of several sciences. Historians have long held that the history of Christian theology displays no observable unified tradition. Newman rejected as historically indefensible the criterion for church teaching proposed by Vincent of Lerins: "Christianity is what has been held always, everywhere and by all." [4] No teaching of Christianity could satisfy that criterion.

Bible scholars have been in some difficulty to find any unity in the New Testament. Philosophers are questioning whether the kind of unity demanded by the theory is in fact possible or even desirable. The less empirical a statement, the less real agreement and mutual understanding are possible.

The ordinary Christian knows he is living in a time of theological upheaval. As he reads the many accounts of disagreements to be found in the papers, he might well ask whether the church enjoys theological unity and, if it does, of what sort it could be.

Some theologians, taking account of these disturbing factors, have begun to speak of the "variety" of theology, of different "schools," and of "development." These theologians would most often however want to set some limits to that variety. They would not in principle want to accept, say, a theological position which would contradict the New Testament. They would often prefer to speak of the "real meaning of the Bible message."

The theory of unity is therefore far from being a dead horse. Not only is it still presupposed in church practice, but one can also ask, in the words of Ogden and Richards: "How far is our discussion itself distorted by habitual attitudes towards words, and lingering associations due to theories no longer openly held but still allowed to guide our practice." [5]

Clearly, the intrinsic importance and growing actuality of the question as well as the relative newness of the pertinent evidence, suggest that the question of the theory of theological unity should be reopened in some conscious and scientific manner. A theory is tenable only insofar as it is confirmed by the pertinent phenomena. One may ask: does the phenomenon of New Testament theology confirm or disconfirm the theory of unity?

Certain religious theories, it can be claimed, do not admit of empirical testing. One cannot investigate the phenomena which they claim to explain the way one can physical, psychological, or historical phenomena. But the theory in question can be confirmed or disconfirmed by a phenomenon which can be investigated by an appropriate science: historical, philological research can determine whether New Testament theology constitutes a unity.

Some Christians may object to my speaking of religious views as theories. But John Henry Newman considered his momentous work a *theory* of the development of Christian doctrine. He writes: "In my own book . . . 1rst I laid down what I conceived to be a *fact*. 2nd I said that that fact was a *difficulty*. 3rd I said it required a *solution*. 4th I offered a solution in a theory of *doctrinal development*." [6]

Those who object to my treating Christianity's claim to theological unity as a theory to be confirmed or disconfirmed, modified or rejected, most often ignore the fact that the idea of Christian theology has already undergone several profound changes.

Galileo was condemned on theological grounds. To hold that the earth went around the sun was thought to contradict Christian teaching. If a difference arose between theology and another field, the faithful Christian was to adhere to theology. That Christians can accept Galileo's findings today implies a profound change in their theory of theology. Theology is no longer considered the arbiter of all the other sciences. The field of competence of theology was severely restricted. Christians were forced to modify their theory of theology.

Many dismiss the implications of the Galileo case by saying that the theologians of the time had an erroneous view of theology. The motions of the earth are not a theological question. Those theologians did not however have merely an erroneous view: they had *the* view of theology. Christians have a different idea today because they have *changed* their view; they have modified their theory of theology.

Similarly, Darwin's theory of evolution was contested because it contradicted the Biblical version of creation. Christians felt that the inspired Bible could not be proved wrong on such an important question. That Christians can now accept evolution indicates that they have once again changed their view of theology: the inspired Bible is no longer thought to be correct in all fields.

Finally, I might mention the great change in the theory of theology brought about by Newman's theory of development. His historical research convinced him that differences could be found between early and later Christianity. This created a difficulty for the view that the Christian tradition was a unity. Newman attempted to solve this difficulty by his theory. In the process, he changed the usual static view of theological tradition.

The generally accepted view or theory of theology has therefore been definitely changed on a number of occasions. These changes became necessary when the progress made in related fields rendered the old view untenable. Since progress is still being made in such fields, one need not be surprised if one's view of theology must change once again.

The *need* for change is today especially apparent. The theological quarrels that divide many churches are due, not merely to different conclusions, but to completely different approaches to theological questions. The ecumenical movement is in an impasse because theological unity appears ever more clearly unobtainable. As a result, churchmen are turning increasingly away from theological problems to others which seem more hopeful of solution. Theology has ceased to provide a way for human progress—it seems indeed incapable of reflecting the progress made in other fields. This, I would argue, is due in large part to unexamined and unreconstructed attitudes and practices in theology. A new theory of theology could possibly be a very practical aid. However, before a new theory can be formulated, the old one must be criticized.

I propose to apply the recent, established findings of New Testament studies to the theory of theological unity. This procedure is not new. From the very beginnings of scientific New Testament research, grave objections have been raised against that theory. It has, in fact, been modified on several occasions to meet those objections, just as the general theory of theology has been modified to account for findings from other fields. A brief survey of some of the most important modifications of the theory of unity would, therefore, be helpful in putting this work in perspective.

Notes

[1] Henricus Denzinger and Adolfus Schönmetzer, *Encheridion Symbolorum Definitionum et Declarationum de Rebus Fidei et Morum* (Freiburg: Herder, 1963), No. 3306. See also, e.g., No. 870.

[2] Stephen Pfurtner, *Luther and Aquinas on Salvation* (New York: Sheed & Ward, 1964), p. 24. See also pp. 25 f.

[3] Quoted in NCR, February 16, 1966, p. 2.

[4] John Henry Newman, *An Essay on the Development of Christian Doctrine* (London: Longmans, Green, 1894), pp. 9–27. Newman's words.

[5] C. K. Ogden and I. A. Richards, *The Meaning of Meaning, A Study of The Influence of Language upon Thought and of The Science of Symbolism,* with essays by B. Malinowsky and F. G. Crookshank (London: Routledge & Kegan Paul, 1960), p. xi. For interesting examples, see John B. Cobb, Jr., "Faith and Culture" in James M. Robinson and Cobb, ed., *The New Hermeneutic,* New Frontiers in Theology, Discussions among Continental and American Theologians; 2 (New York: Harper & Row, 1964), pp. 219–231, pp. 228 f.

[6] Charles Stephen Dessain and Vincent Ferrer Blehl, ed., *The Letters and Diaries of John Henry Newman,* Vol. XV, *The Achilli Trial, January 1852 to December 1853* (London: Nelson, 1964), p. 372. Italics Newman's. See also pp. 373 f.

2

The Textual
Disunity
of the
New Testament

The seventeenth-century scholar Richard Simon offered the first great challenge to both Protestant and Catholic theories of unity.[1] He attacked the received texts of the time.

Among scholars, both Protestant and Catholic, the Masoretic text of the Old Testament had been accepted with exaggerated respect. The consonants of this text, as is well known, had been gradually established by Jewish scholars during the first millennium after Christ. Divergent traditions of the vowels of the text had not been assimilated until the fourteenth century. This did not prevent the greatest Protestant Oriental scholars of the time from claiming that these vowels and even the slightest accent or sign of the Hebrew text were inspired and had been miraculously preserved through the centuries.[2] For this reason, they spoke of "the divine Masoretic text." [3]

Similarly, Protestants and Catholics accepted religiously the text of the New Testament which Erasmus had sloppily assembled. The text had first been published in Spain in 1514 and then in 1516 in Basel by Erasmus, who had used bad manuscripts and worked with little or no critical care. Nevertheless, from 1633 on, this text was accepted as inspired, and the least correction of it was forbidden. The reason for this was that Scripture was considered by Protestants to be the sole basis of doctrine, and, by Catholics, to be one of the two bases; to cast doubts or raise difficulties in any way about that basis was to endanger the doctrines which the Protestants and Catholics had reared upon them; [4] both their theories demanded "the absolute immutability of Revelation." [5]

To these extreme attitudes, the Catholics added an exaggerated respect for the Vulgate, Jerome's Latin translation of the Bible. The Council of Trent had declared this translation to be "authentic," and, in Spain, those suspected of not properly respecting it were actually persecuted by the law.[6] Cardinal Ximenes, on seeing the Latin text printed between the Hebrew and the Greek, declared: "They have placed it there like Jesus Christ between the two thieves!" [7]

The Catholics had constructed an enormous doctrinal system on the text, which they considered stable. They had regarded the whole Bible as furnishing them with dogmatic propositions and arguments, the meanings of which were clear and which were all logically consistent. A text was taken from this book to support this theological point; another was taken from that book for another point. As a modern exegete was heard to say: "For the major, they take Jeremiah; for the minor, Mark; and for the conclusion, Apocalypse!" To do this, of course, they were compelled to force the sense of their texts absurdly. All of these proof texts passed with their theological points into the manuals of theology, where they were considered sacrosanct. ". . . just one proposition less in the vast catalogue of what they considered theological truths, and all orthodoxy seemed to them in danger." [8]

Richard Simon was the first to study these texts scientifically. He compared the best manuscripts he could find; he compared translations into several ancient and Oriental languages. He found that no text was absolute, simply because the original manuscripts no longer existed. Each text had to be approached critically and compared to other texts. Additions, subtractions, reworded phrases, sentences, and sections were found. Throughout its long history, the text had suffered changes. In sum, an immense scholarly effort, following a strict scientific method, was necessary before one could even establish the text upon which such vast theological systems were being constructed. An equal effort had to be made to distinguish the various layers of composition within the authentic text itself: the longer additions that had been made in the course of history; the various parallel stories that had been gathered and edited by ancient redactors.

Simon used the Septuagint, the ancient translation of the Old Testament into Greek, to discover readings prior to the systematization of the Masoretic text, thereby offending its extreme adherents. But the Septuagint was itself only a translation, and he had found that every translation had its advantages and disadvantages; the Septuagint suffered, especially, he said, from a tendency to translate Hebrew words into the very different terms of Greek philosophy.[9] Simon thereby offended those who, like the English Protestant scholar, Isaac Vossius, held the Septuagint for divinely inspired.[10] The Vulgate was also a mere translation, and, after criticizing its failings at length, Simon remarks that "one would have to lose one's senses to fall into such passionate exaggerations" as had its dogmatic defenders.[11]

The text was considered inspired and immutable; it could not admit of change.[12] But, Simon asked, "on what basis [one] admitted a special Providence to watch over the manuscripts of the Bible and all the copies that one has printed from them."[13] By his textual criticism, Simon had introduced "a principle of change and relativity . . . into the history of the more or less contingent forms of Revelation."[14]

Simon had proved that the understanding of Scripture, at the most basic level, was difficult. This had serious consequences for both the Protestant and the Catholic theologies of his time.

Against the Protestants, Simon argued that Scripture was neither so clear nor so sure that they could base all of their doctrines on it without some recourse to tradition.[15] He challenged those who thought "that the infused light can supplant knowledge of grammars and that such and such a doctor does not need 'to catch the sense of the original words.' "[16] To understand Scripture, one needs "all the resources of scientific exegesis."[17]

It is important to see that this challenge to a particular

theory arose from the discovery of evidence which, until that time, had not been known. For, as Margival, the essayist on Simon, concludes:

> To show . . . that Scripture was neither constant enough in its text, nor clear enough in its statements, nor, in the end, independent enough of tradition to be able to serve as the sole rule of faith; this was not to depart from his completely historical subject. It was rather to formulate one of the most obvious consequences of the simple exposition of the facts." [18]

Simon's conclusions were equally critical of the use that Catholics made of the Bible. Catholics had supported their theological points on texts that could not bear the weight. They had believed the sense of most Hebrew words to be clear. They had founded some proofs not only on just a single word, but sometimes even on the position of that word or on the punctuation of a phrase. Their method of reading meanings into texts had made them ridiculous in the eyes of their adversaries. As we have said before, such dubious interpretations had prevailed only because they had become habitual, enshrined in the manuals of theology.

Simon traced these faulty methods to a certain dogmatic mentality, the first mark of which was the tendency to set up certain theories as immemorial and irreformable traditions. Opinions, such as that God had revealed the Hebrew language to Adam, that the text of the Bible had been miraculously preserved, that Moses had written all of the Pentateuch, had been raised to this honorable status. Simon countered by beating the traditionalists at their own game. He showed that the "immemorial traditions" which they professed had all been rejected by the Fathers of the Church and originated, in point of fact, in later rabbinical traditions.[19]

Another method used by theologians possessed of this dogmatic mentality was to consider purely scholarly questions as theological ones, to transform possible opinions into articles of faith. Simon challenged such theologians by using his findings to disprove one of their most important "articles of faith": that the letter of Scripture was incorruptible.[20]

Finally, Simon attacked the manner with which Catholic dogmatic theologians dealt with their proofs, accepting them uncritically from their predecessors without examining either their truth or their power of convincing. In fact, for such theologians, almost any "proof" would do, if it helped to support their system. By refuting through his researches a number of these alleged proofs, which had been used from time immemorial to support doctrinal constructions, Simon opened the way, by creating the necessity, for a new methodological approach to theology: a return to the investigation of the ascertainable facts. From then on, theologians had to weigh their proofs as well as count them.

Simon would have agreed with his contemporary, the Abbé le Camus: "It is a strange thing; the Huguenots, who say that Scripture is clear, do not cease to work to clarify it, and the Catholics, who maintain that it is obscure, do not even try to explain it." [21]

Simon's contribution is well summarized by Margival: "His genius is a combination of dialectic and intuition: the former to overturn the opinions accredited by a vague tradition, the latter to substitute for them some truths as fruitful as they were original." [22]

Simon was, of course, attacked by both Catholics and Protestants. Bossuet led for the Catholic side.[23] He attacked the principles of the new scientific method, its dependence on linguistic phenomena: Simon, he charged, "believes that to know languages and grammars is to know everything"; "the critic who professes to weigh words by the rules of grammar and believes himself able to overawe the world with the Greek or with the Hebrew on which he prides himself." [24] Bossuet, basing himself on the Council of Trent, condemned Simon's attitude toward the Vulgate: "It is to think too basely of this decree to make of it a simple decree of discipline; this is a question of faith, and the Council of Trent had the intention of assuring Catholics that this ancient edition, the Vulgate, represented perfectly the fundament and the substance of the sacred text." [25]

He criticized Simon's translation of the New Testament from an equally dogmatic point of view. Simon should not have translated the article, "ho" (=Greek for "the"), in John 1:21, although it stands incontestably in the text—where the priests and Levites ask John the Baptist if he is *the* prophet." Bossuet argues: "St. John could well have denied that he was a prophet, in the sense of someone who must predict the future, but he could not in good faith deny that he was the prophet whom one must expect, as another Elias, before Jesus Christ, and who must act as his predecessor." Similarly, Bossuet would translate "houtos" as if it were "touto" in "the words of consecration" because this word is "appropriate to the transubstantiation, which is the real and natural sense of this passage . . ." These and many other examples[26] show that, where theology was concerned, facts were no obstacle for Bossuet, especially if they had been established by scientific scholarship. His mind was completely absorbed by the theological system which he had inherited, and Simon could be for him only " 'a secret partisan of the heretics, of the schismatics, of the unbelievers' [who], even while giving the appearance of refuting them, wanted only 'to put in their hands weapons against the doctrine of the church.' " [27]

Protestant scholars also sprang to the attack, but revealed only "How much in this science the Lutheran theologians were still behind." [28] One complained that, according to Simon, "one can secure almost nothing as certain in Religion, if one does not join Tradition with Scripture to decide questions of faith." [29] Another, bridling at Simon's method of comparing one book of Scripture to another, asked the fundamental question: "Are there then two kinds of truth and is that which is true at one time false at another?" [30]

Simon, however, enjoyed polemic too much to refrain from replying.[31]

Bossuet had been forced to admit that Moses had not written the account of his own death and that perhaps a few small changes or additions had been made by Joshua or Samuel.[32] "It little matters," Simon rejoined, "to know if Joshua or Samuel are the authors of these additions, or if they came from the hand of Esdras. It is enough that there are prophets who, after the death of Moses, continued his history, who completed a genealogy begun, explained the name of a village changed by time or some other similar thing." [33] Bossuet had admitted the principle; Simon was able to argue from it to his own conclusions.

He remarks of the Protestant scholar Camerarius:

"He blames the indiscreet zeal of some Protestants who believe that all is clear in Scripture and that there is nothing obscure and equivocal; because God gave it to men to use as a rule, not having the appearance that he wanted to fool them. But his whole work, in which his main application is to clarify a great number of equivocal terms, proves evidently the contrary. Equivocations and ambiguity being common to all languages, there is no reason to exempt from them the Sacred Writers; not to mention the fact that it is ridiculous to oppose a truth that leaps to the eyes." [34]

This appeal to observable phenomena against widely held, but unexamined theories was often to be heard in the history of New Testament scholarship. The later Biblical scholar, Johann Salomo Semler, in his *Abhandlung von freier Untersuchung des Canons* (1771–1775), wrote: "One would have to speak deliberately and, as it were, against the light of day, if one denied the real difference of circumstance of a teaching which was Jewish or regulated according to Jewish-Christians; and if one wanted to consider all the concepts and types of discourse that are found in these so different books as equally appropriate to an equally good instruction for all men of all times." [35] Similarly, Johann Philipp Gabler, one of the first scholars to notice the mythical elements which are to be found even in the New Testament, wrote in 1800: "If one wanted still to defend as true history such myths, which contain in part, or certainly presuppose, very unworthy concepts of God; that would be the direct way to make the whole Bible ridiculous in our day." [36]

In any case, the theory that supported the received text as inspired accommodated itself only gradually to the surrender of this one of its positions. John Mill's edition of the Greek New Testament (1707) mentioned variants only in the apparatus below the printed received text.[37] Johann Jakob Wettstein was put on trial and released from his parish when it became known that he planned to incorporate variants into the main text itself. He contented himself in his final edition (1751–1752) with marking in the main text indications referring to variants in the apparatus below.[38] The much later editions of Johann Jakob Griesbach (1774–1775) [39] and Karl Lachmann (1831) [40] were the first, in fact, which did not print the received text.

Griesbach's edition appeared almost one hundred years after the pioneering, yet conclusive, investigations of Richard Simon. Simon—who died of shock after being forced to burn his many manuscripts for fear they would fall into the wrong hands—summarized with his usual acute humor his peculiar situation in history: "Unhappy learning, to know what many do not know; much unhappier still, to know that of which all are ignorant." [41]

To us today, this controversy seems odd and not even apposite. But we must realize that the theologians of Simon's time regarded his findings as an attack on the theory of unity. That we no longer so regard them indicates that we have somehow modified our theory of unity.

The disunity of the text of the New Testament was finally accepted; but it was held that this disunity did not affect the real unity of the New Testament: the unity of its content. A new, even more serious challenge to the theory of unity was the discovery that the New Testament writers contradicted each other in their reports of historical events.

Notes

¹ See Heinrich Philipp Konrad Henke, *Allgemeine Geschichte der christlichen Kirche nach der Zeitfolge* 4 (Braunschweig: Verlage der Schulbuchhandlung, 1801), pp. 208 ff. Werner Georg Kümmel, *Das Neue Testament, Geschichte der Erforschung seiner Probleme*, Orbis Academicus, Problemgeschichten der Wissenschaft in Dokumenten und Darstellungen; III, 3 (Freiburg-Munich: Verlag Karl Alber, 1958), pp. 41 ff. Henri Margival, "Richard Simon et la critique biblique au XVII_e_ siècle" in *Revue d'Histoire et de Littérature Religieuse*, Paris: I (1896), pp. 1 *seq.*, 159 *seq.*; II (1897), pp. 17 *seq.*, 223 *seq.*, 525 *seq.*; III (1898), pp. 117 *seq.*, 338 *seq.*, 508 *seq.*; IV (1899), pp. 123 *seq.*, 193 *seq.*, 310 *seq.*, 435 *seq.*, 514 *seq.*

² Margival, *op. cit.*, I, p. 10; II, pp. 528–531. Catholics shared this opinion.

³ *Ibid.*, III, p. 522.

⁴ Kümmel, *op. cit.*, e.g., pp. 41, 51 f.

⁵ Margival, *op. cit.*, III, p. 523.

⁶ *Ibid.*, III, pp. 130 f.

⁷ *Ibid.*, III, p. 130.

⁸ *Ibid.*, II, p. 225.

⁹ *Ibid.*, III, pp. 124 ff.

¹⁰ *Ibid.*, III, pp. 513 ff.

¹¹ *Ibid.*, III, p. 133.

¹² *Ibid.*, I, p. 10; II, p. 528.

¹³ *Ibid.*, III, p. 521. Résumé of Margival.

¹⁴ *Ibid.*, III, p. 522. Words of Margival.

¹⁵ *Ibid.*, II, pp. 37–40; III, pp. 142, 341. Kümmel, *op. cit.*, pp. 42 ff. Henke, *op. cit.*, pp. 209 f.

¹⁶ Margival, *op. cit.*, II, p. 39. The quotes within the quotes mark the words of Simon.

¹⁷ *Ibid.*, III, p. 345.

¹⁸ *Ibid.*, III, p. 525. See also Henke, *op. cit.*, pp. 209 f.

¹⁹ Margival, *op. cit.*, II, pp. 528–531.

²⁰ *Ibid.*, II, pp. 531 ff.

²¹ *Ibid.*, III, p. 138.

²² *Ibid.*, IV, p. 132.

²³ Margival guesses that Bossuet's principal objection was

to the doubts Simon cast on the Mosaic authorship of the Penta-teuch in its entirety (*ibid.*, II, pp. 224, 233), but he states elsewhere that Bossuet was against Simon's method altogether, and certainly such criticisms are abundantly quoted and referred to, one of the most interesting being that Simon reduced "incredulity to a method" and that he wrote in French (*ibid.*, I, pp. 22 f.).

24 Quoted *ibid.*, I, p. 5.

25 Quoted *ibid.*, III, p. 134.

26 *Ibid.*, IV, pp. 315 f.

27 *Ibid.*, IV, p. 314. The quotation marks within the quota-tion marks enclose the words of Bossuet.

28 Henke, *op. cit.*, pp. 213 f.

29 Margival, *op. cit.*, III, p. 526.

30 *Ibid.*, IV, p. 133.

31 Two of his replies on other subjects typify his humorous style of debate. When Arnauld of Port-Royal objected to his use of Mohammedan authors to describe Mohammedanism, instead of using only Catholic theologians, as was the custom, Simon asked him whether a scholar, writing someday the history of Jansenism, should consult only the writings of the Jesuits.

When the theologian Jurieu of Rotterdam claimed that the beast of the Apocalypse was papal Rome because the letters of its name worked out to 666, Simon used all his Talmudic learning to show that, by following exactly the rules of the Cabala, the words "Minister Jurius" and "Rotterdam" also worked out to 666. He concluded solemnly: "It is an admirable result of Providence that the name of Mr. Jurieu contains in the holy language, according to the numerical virtue with which the Hebrews invest their letters, this number 666 . . . Hence it appears manifestly that God willed to make known to the whole earth that there is absolutely no other Beast of the Apocalypse than Mr. Jurieu, lodged amidst the waters of Rotterdam" (*ibid.*, III, p. 529).

32 *Ibid.*, II, pp. 542 f.

33 *Ibid.*, II, pp. 543 f.

34 Richard Simon, *Histoire Critique des principeaux Com-mentateurs du Nouveau Testament depuis le commencement du Christianisme jusques à notre tems: avec une Dissertation Critique sur les principaux Actes Manuscrits qui ont été citez dans les trois Parties de cet Ouvrage* (Rotterdam: Chez Reinier Leers, 1693), p. 707.

35 Kümmel, *op. cit.*, p. 80.

36 *Ibid.*, p. 124.

37 *Ibid.*, pp. 50 f.

38 *Ibid.*, pp. 52 f.

3

The Historical
Disunity
of the
New Testament

Several contradictions in New Testament reports of apparently the same historical events had been recognized for some time. For instance, in Mark 6:8, Jesus allows the disciples to carry staffs on their mission. In Luke 9:3, he expressly forbids them to.

St. Augustine had established the principle that, when such contradictions appeared, the two accounts referred to two very similar, but still different episodes. This solution was accepted; and, in any case, such contradictions were felt to be peripheral, and were not systematically investigated.

The Bible was inspired and true. There could be no contradictions in historical truth. Jesus could not at that time have allowed and disallowed his disciples to carry staffs. Therefore there could be no historical contradictions in the Bible. But this theory also was susceptible to observational verification. Were there in fact historical contradictions in the New Testament?

The English Deist critics of the New Testament had already discovered some and had drawn from the fact a number of important conclusions.[1] But the historical disunity of the New Testament did not become an acute problem for theology as a whole until the publication in 1777 of the *Fragments from Wolfenbüttel,* edited by Gotthold Ephraim Lessing.[2] These fragments were extracts which Lessing had made from a larger work by Hermann Samuel Reimarus, a teacher of Oriental languages at the Hamburg Lycee. Although he had written this critique of the Bible "in order to quiet his conscience," [3] he

[39] *Ibid.*, p. 88.

[40] *Ibid.*, p. 179.

[41] "Infelix eruditio est scire quod multi nesciunt; multo etiam infelicior scire quod omnes ignorant." Quoted in Margival, *op. cit.*, I, p. 172.

feared to have it published under his own name. Since his family, until much later, was too ashamed to acknowledge his authorship of the fragments, their author was referred to until 1813 as "the unnamed one from Wolfenbüttel."

Basing himself on the work of the English Deists, Reimarus decisively established the existence of a number of contradictions between the different gospel reports, not of some peripheral episode, but of the founding event of all Christianity: the Resurrection.

He concentrated on only a few of the more obvious contradictions: [4]

1) In Mark, the women buy spices *after* the feast day to prepare Jesus' body. In Luke, they buy the spices on the evening *before* the feast day. "This is an obvious contradiction," writes Reimarus, "which, next to many others, the men of older days had already noticed and therefore preferred to omit the story of the Resurrection according to Mark."

2) In John, Joseph of Arimathea and Nicodemus bring one hundred pounds of spices and do everything necessary to entomb Jesus immediately according to all the regulations of Jewish law. Therefore, the women need not buy spices, as in other accounts; John therefore has Mary Magdalen come to the tomb alone.

3) In Mark and Luke, the women see from far away that the tomb is already open. In Matthew, an angel appears as they are there and opens the tomb.

4) In Mark and Matthew, there is only one angel; in Luke and John, there are two. In each account, they are given different actions to perform and different speeches to deliver.

5) In each account also, different women do different things and have different reactions. Peter and/or John also act differently according to the various narratives.

6) In Matthew, Jesus appears to Mary Magdalen as she is on her way toward town. In John, he appears to her before the doors of the tomb. At this point, Reimarus remarks that "when it comes to such small peripheral circumstances, human beings always have the cheap excuse that they did not pay such exact

attention to such unimportant things because they wanted to observe the main object; according to this view, their mistake is only that they state that which they do not know exactly and about which they can easily deceive themselves and contradict each other; therefore, the main thing can still be true . . . But we are concerned here with witnesses who cannot excuse themselves by the limitations of human attention or by the common human failing of adding the minor circumstances without exact knowledge; they claim to be and, of course, should be, in all portions, in all passages, directed by the Holy Spirit, who leads them into all truth. How then can such a contradiction arise among them—one that, even humanly, by the most careless observation of the circumstances, would not easily be committed?" 5

7) In Matthew, when the women see Jesus, they approach and touch him. He only says, "Do not be afraid." In John, however, he forbids Mary Magdalen to touch him. "Here no further explanation is necessary," Reimarus says. "To want to be touched, and not to want to be touched, is an obvious contradiction." 6

8) A number of contradictions arise concerning the locations of the appearances of Jesus after his Resurrection. Sometimes these are in Galilee, sometimes in Jerusalem; the Evangelists contradict each other on the number of the appearances, their order, on those to whom Jesus appeared, and so on. "When now the one witness says that the appearance took place in Jerusalem and was not supposed to take place outside of Jerusalem; the other, that it took place in Galilee and was supposed to; when the one reports that their master ordered them not to leave Jerusalem from Easter to Pentecost; the other, that he ordered them to be, within the same time-span, far from there; when the one offers him roast fish in Jerusalem behind closed doors; the other, by the Lake of Galilee: then they themselves, in this way, destroy from both sides the credibility of their witness." 7

Reimarus emphasizes two contradictions within this group. In Matthew, the Galilean appearance is the first; in John, it is preceded by two appearances in Jerusalem. Furthermore, in Matthew, the Galilean appearance has been determined beforehand; the apostles are expecting it, and they recognize Jesus immediately. In John, Jesus appears unexpectedly and is not immediately recognized. Moreover, the speeches of Jesus are different in each report.

Reimarus concludes in a peroration: "Tell me before God, you readers who possess conscience and honor, can you consider unanimous and upright this witness, in so important an affair, that so multifariously and manifestly contradicts itself about persons, time, place, manner, purpose, speeches and events?" [8] As he had written earlier: "Witnesses who, in their statement, varied so much as to the most important circumstances would not be recognized as good and legally valid in any earthly case, even if it only concerned merely a little money of one person; so that the judge could base himself securely on their account and build his judgment on it. How can one then demand that, on the statement of such four varying witnesses, the whole world, the whole human race, at all times and in all places, should base its religion, faith and hope of bliss? Moreover, it is not even a question merely of the difference of their accounts: they contradict each other undeniably in many places and cause much useless torture for the good interpreters who wish to tune this tetrachord to a better harmony." [9]

Reimarus' observation of the historical contradictions in the gospel accounts of the Resurrection was accurate. P. W. Schmiedel emphasizes that these narratives "exhibit contradictions of the most glaring kind. Reimarus . . . enumerated ten contradictions; but in reality, their number is much greater." [10] He lists additional contradictions,[11] admits that some of them might arise as natural discrepancies, but insists: "To this, however there are limits." Many contradictions "are matters with regard to which the eye-witnesses or those who had their information directly from eye-witnesses could not possibly have been in the least uncertainty. Yet, what differences! Differences, too, of which it is impossible to say that they are partly explicable by the fact that one narrator gives one occurrence and

another another without wishing thereby to exclude the rest." [12]
"And as a matter of fact we cannot avoid the conclusion from
the contradictions between the gospels that the writers of them
were far removed from the event they describe. If we possessed
only one gospel, we might perhaps be inclined to accept it; but
how far astray should we be according to the view of Lk., if we
relied, let us say, on Mt. alone, or, according to the view of Jn.,
if we pinned our faith on Lk. In point of fact, not only do the
evangelists each follow different narratives; they also each have
distinct theories of their own as to Galilee or Jerusalem as
being the scene of the appearances, as to whether Jesus ate and
was touched, and so forth." [13]

This position is considered self-evident for New Testament
scholarship and for most Christians today,[14] but, at the time,
the discovery of historical contradictions in the gospel reports,
especially about the Resurrection, caused a tremendous uproar.
Churchmen, scholars, and literati leaped to the attack against
"the unnamed one" and his editor Lessing. The *Fragments* were
condemned and forbidden by both church and state. As Leo-
pold Zscharnack, an editor of Lessing's writings, explains: in
the *Fragments,* "a redemptive fact was attacked that belonged
for Reimarus, as did the other miracles, to the 'tottering facta'
and that he could criticize radically since his religion had long
ago been detached from it; but he had thereby sprung the rock
on which Christianity as the saving religion of redemptive history rested." [15] Newly discovered evidence had disproved an
old theory that had become a doctrine. All of Christianity was
considered to be endangered.

Lessing hoped that the publication of the *Fragments* would
call forth a great champion of religion; he published himself, in
the meantime, a few *Antitheses* to various conclusions of Reimarus in order "to guide the first panic-stricken terror, that
could befall the faint-hearted reader." [16]

Whereas Reimarus had completely rejected the old theory,
and constructed a new one that the apostles had stolen the body
of Jesus; [17] Lessing sought to change the old theory just enough
to allow for the newly discovered evidence.[18] Two kinds of con-

tradictions are possible here, Lessing assured his readers: those between eyewitnesses, and those between writers who later reported what the witnesses had said. There is no evidence of the first sort in the New Testament reports of the Resurrection, although, of course, small discrepancies may naturally have appeared in the memories of those eyewitnesses as time passed. But one can say fairly surely that all the contradictions in the New Testament reports can be attributed to the later writers. But, the objection is made, was not the Holy Spirit with those writers, inspiring them to write the truth? We have seen that Reimarus made one of his most important objections against the whole of the old theory of Biblical truth by attacking this one of its principles. For Lessing, this is the point at which the old theory must yield. "But the Holy Spirit was at work in these reports.—Certainly; namely so, that he directed each one to write, as the thing was known to him according to his best knowledge and conscience." [19] This, however, is quite different from saying that the Holy Spirit had directed them, and led them, to write only what was, in fact, the truth, as the old theory claimed. Lessing seeks to justify his entirely novel teaching on inspiration. "Now when [the object of their reports] was known, and had to be known, by this person in such a way, by another in another way, was the Holy Spirit supposed to prefer, the moment they took up their quills, to make their different representations uniform and, through just this uniformity, suspicious; or should he have granted that the difference would be preserved, which is no longer of any importance whatsoever?" [20] "Suspicious" is good. Lessing continues: "Only a continual miracle could have prevented such degenerations of the oral account of the resurrection from occurring during the 30 to 40 years before the evangelists wrote. But what right have we to assume this miracle? And what forces us to assume it." [21] That "continual miracle" was precisely inspiration according to the old theory. Lessing concluded by inviting those who disagreed with him simply to resolve the contradictions Reimarus had discovered.

Many thought that Lessing had not meant his *Antitheses*

sincerely but had written them rather to give indirect support to the positions of Reimarus. Though this was most probably unjust,[22] Lessing was certainly one of those who would "surrender the Bible to preserve religion." [23] His own Deistic beliefs became increasingly apparent during the continuing debate occasioned by the *Fragments*.[24] One of his adversaries, Johann Melchior Goeze posed the question as to "what sort of religion Lessing understands under the Christian religion, and what sort of a religion he himself confesses." [25] Goeze was certain that it was not "the Christian as that which stands and falls with the Bible." [26] He could not have been very reassured by Lessing's argument against Reimarus: "How do the hypotheses and explanations and proofs of this man concern the Christian? For the Christian, it is, in spite of everything, simply there, Christianity, which he feels so true, and in which he feels himself so blissful." [27]

But those who confessed a Christianity which "stands and falls with the Bible," and who believed that it fell if the old theory did, still had the contradictions of Reimarus to resolve. Many attempts were made, and Lessing could not resist parodying them in his *Eine Duplik* of 1778.

The fourth contradiction of Reimarus read: "According to the evangelists Matthew and Mark, the women see only one angel and only one speaks with them. When more angels had hovered in the thoughts of these evangelists, there was no reason why they should leave the one out of their account, since it would not have cost them more of an effort to write two angels instead of one, and since two angels would make the appearance still more certain or, at least, would magnify the miracle. It is therefore quite settled that Matthew and Mark thought of only one angel that would have appeared. Accordingly, the two other evangelists, Luke and John, contradict them because they say that two angels appeared to the women and two spoke with them. Furthermore, according to Matthew, the women see the one angel travel down from the sky, overturn the stone and set himself down on it, and he speaks with them so in front of the tomb, before they go inside. But, according to Mark, the women find no angel in front of the tomb; rather, they go in and find the angel inside the tomb sitting on the right. According to Luke, the women find also no angel in front of the tomb and do wish to go in; and since they are distressed about where the corpse of Jesus could be, two angels stand, or place themselves next to them . . . According to John, however, Mary Magdalen looks from outside into the grave and sees two angels in white garments sitting, the one at the head, and the other at the foot. Furthermore, in Matthew, Mark and Luke, the angel or the angels says to Mary Magdalen and the others that Jesus has risen and order [28] them to say the same to the disciples and Peter. According to John, however, the angels ask Mariam only: 'Woman, why do you weep?' " [29] And so on.

Lessing discusses possible resolutions of some of these contradictions. For example: "If, then, it were also true that the words of Mark (16:5) ["and going into the tomb, they saw a young man seated on the right"] did not necessarily mean that the angel appeared to them, as they entered, *inside* the tomb at the right; if it were also true that Mark should be rather so understood that the women first caught sight of the angel in front of the tomb *after* their entrance into the tomb, either by looking out or by exiting from the same; does not then the unanswerable question arise why they did not immediately on going into the tomb also see the angel sitting on the left? Of course, he already sat there in front, on top of the stone that he had turned over before the women had yet arrived. Is then an angel, whose form is like lightning, a thing which one so easily overlooks?" [30]

After a number of such solutions and refutations, Lessing has reached the bursting point.

"And why all these improbabilities, all these evasions? In order that one nowhere comes out with more than two angels because the Evangelists mention at the most only two of them? In order that the angel who sits on the stone in front of the tomb can always be counted with the others?

"O poverty of soul to end all poverty of soul!—so *niggardly* to *haggle* over angels on behalf of him for whom they stood in legions to serve.

" 'Yes, we haggle so,' I hear my neighbor say, 'only to maintain the Evangelists in respect and honor.'

"Not the Evangelists, neighbor! but your narrow-hearted, lame, squinting, *Thersitical* harmony of the Evangelists. Thersitical, for it is as shapeless as it is slanderous against each Evangelist in particular. It, it, because it is so completely *your* work, should suffer nothing.

"What? Would it not show more respect toward the Evangelists if I said: cold contradiction-picker! Do you then not see that the Evangelists are not counting the angels? The whole tomb, the whole vast area around the tomb teemed invisibly with angels. There were not merely two angels (like a pair of Grenadiers left in front of the quarters of the decamped general until all his gear has been removed); there were millions of them. It was not always the one and the same that appeared; not always the same two. Now this one appeared, now that one; now at this place, now at another; now alone, now in company; now they said this, now that." [31]

Lessing's parody would be more amusing if so many similar resolutions of these contradictions had not been constructed later, even into this century: with apostles and disciples, male and female, rushing in different combinations around Jerusalem and to Galilee and back in order to attend the next appearance at which they were due, and which never seemed to fail to surprise them. Lessing was right when he declared that all such attempts revealed a deep disrespect of Scripture.

But the clearness of these contradictions and the increasing realization that all attempts at harmonizing them did inexcusable violence to the texts, slowly effected a major revision of the old theory. The principle that *all* truth had been guaranteed by the inspiration of the Holy Spirit was abandoned. True, the New Testament was inspired by the Holy Spirit and could thus contain neither error, nor self-contradiction; but that inspiration restricted itself to the area of *theological* truth. The New Testament was a *theological* unity. In fact, did not the New Testament writers share the ancient conception of historical writing whereby facts could be manipulated and even stories invented in order to make the point which the author wished to communicate? So too, the New Testament authors had fallen into historical contradictions among themselves, but shared a unity of point, of theology.

Christians today who begin to feel impatient with those who twisted and turned to avoid admitting any historical contradictions in the New Testament are usually placing their confidence in the solution offered by the above revision of the old theory. Of course there are historical contradictions in the New Testament! But the *point* is the same! They do not realize that they would find it as hard to admit theological contradictions as eighteenth-century Christians did historical ones.

Bible scholars were soon to learn, however, that those who contradicted each other in reporting historical events could also contradict each other in interpreting them.

Notes

[1] Kümmel, *op. cit.,* pp. 59 ff. The German texts which we will discuss can be found in *Lessings Werke,* ed. J. Petersen, W. von Olshausen, etc. (Berlin: Deutsches Verlagsbuchhaus Bong, Parts 22 and 23, *Theologische Schriften* III and IV, ed. L. Zscharnack, 1925).

[2] Kümmel, *op. cit.,* pp. 105 f. See Lessing, *op. cit.,* Vol. 22, pp. 9–29; Vol. 23, pp. 9–29 (introductions by Zscharnack).

[3] Kümmel, *op. cit.,* p. 105. Lessing, *op. cit.,* Vol. 22, p. 15.

[4] *Ibid.,* pp. 169–184.

[5] *Ibid.,* p. 178.

[6] *Ibid.,* p. 179.

[7] *Ibid.,* p. 181.

[8] *Ibid.,* p. 184.

[9] *Ibid.,* p. 169.

[10] P. W. Schmiedel, "Resurrection- and Ascension-Narratives," in *Encyclopaedia Biblica,* Vol. 4, eds. T. K. Cheyne and J. Sutherland Black (London: Adam and Charles Black, 1903), cols. 4039–4087, col. 4041.

[11] *Ibid.,* cols. 4041–4044.

[12] *Ibid.,* col. 4044. He gives examples in cols. 4044–4045.

[13] *Ibid.*, col. 4045.

[14] See Ernst von Dobschütz, *Ostern und Pfingsten, eine Studie zu 1 Korinther 15* (Leipzig: J. C. Hinrichs'sche Buchhandlung, 1903), p. 31. Martin Dibelius, *Die Formgeschichte des Evangeliums*, ed. G. Bornkamm (Tübingen: J. C. B. Mohr [Paul Siebeck], 1961), pp. 178–218. Rudolf Bultmann, *Die Geschichte der synoptischen Tradition* (FRLANT; 29), (Göttingen: Vandenhoeck & Ruprecht, 1961), pp. 282–316.

[15] Lessing, *op. cit.*, Vol. 22, p. 20.

[16] The words of Lessing. *Ibid.*, p. 27. See also p. 26.

[17] *Ibid.*, pp. 153–169.

[18] *Ibid.*, pp. 203–206.

[19] *Ibid.*, p. 204.

[20] *Ibid.*, p. 205.

[21] *Ibid.*

[22] *Ibid.*, p. 25.

[23] This phrase was actually used by Karl Gotthelf Lessing of Johann Melchior Goeze, whom he mistakenly believed at first to be sympathetic to the position of G. E. Lessing. See Lessing, *op. cit.*, Vol. 23, p. 20.

[24] *Ibid.*, pp. 21 f.

[25] *Ibid.*, p. 22.

[26] *Ibid.*, p. 20.

[27] *Ibid.*, p. 27.

[28] The plural of "order," which clashes with the singular of "says," is in the original German text.

[29] Lessing, *op. cit.*, Vol. 22, pp. 174 f.

[30] Lessing, *op. cit.*, Vol. 23, p. 83. My italics.

[31] *Ibid.*, p. 84. I have added the interior quotation marks. The italics are Lessing's.

4
The Theological
Disunity
of the
New Testament

There had been many indications of the theological disunity of the New Testament long before the beginnings of scientific research. Passages such as I Corinthians 1:12 and II Corinthians 11:4 were sufficient evidence of controversy within early Christianity. Different theological tendencies based themselves on different passages and formed their own groups within or outside of the church. The Antiochene school of exegesis was famous both for the literalness of its interpretations and the heresy of its resulting views. The Alexandrian school preserved its orthodoxy by generously allegorical and symbolical readings of the texts. In fact, the New Testament could so clearly be employed to found unorthodox doctrines that Tertullian was forced to contest the very right of heretical groups to use it. If he had been able to refute their doctrines by himself referring to the New Testament, he certainly would have done so.

Of course, the New Testament's theological disunity played a large role in the Reformation. But, though many conflicting doctrines suddenly arose, all based on Scripture, no one seems to have drawn any conclusions about the New Testament itself. Luther held that Scripture itself was a unity and that all disunity came merely from the various interpretations to which it had been subjected: "all error has come from the fact that one let the clear words go and fabricated peculiar Interpretations through tacked-on conclusions and metaphorical expressions out of one's own brain." [1] Obviously, a grave problem was bound to arise when Luther discovered the contradictions between the theology of Paul and those of the epistle to the Hebrews, the epistle of James, and the Apocalypse. The epistle to the Hebrews contradicted Paul's continual demand for conversion when it denied the possibility of a second penance. The teaching of James on justification could not be harmonized with that of Paul. The Apocalypse seemed to Luther utterly fantastic and to miss the central point of Christianity.[2] "Many sweat a lot," he wrote, "about how they can bring James into accord with Paul—as Philip [Melanchthon] in the *Apology*—however not in earnest. 'Faith justifies' contradicts 'Faith does not justify.' Whoever can make those rhyme together, on him I'll set my jester's cap and let him be scolded as a fool." [3]

Luther was forced to draw the only possible conclusion: these books must not be part of Scripture. He therefore put Hebrews, James, Judas, and Apocalypse at the end of his translation of the New Testament and did not list them in the table of contents.

Luther's discovery of the problem of New Testament disunity was gradually forgotten, but his original solution lived on. Thus a Lutheran theologian writes in 1567: "There is nowhere a true contradiction in the Scriptures . . . ; rather, where it seems to be different, it is to be assumed that it is the fault of our guilt and great ignorance . . ." [4]

In England, a similar problem confronted Thomas Cranmer as he tried to decide on the justice of Henry VIII's divorce. Should he follow Deuteronomy 25:5, which validated Henry's first marriage and prevented the divorce; or should he follow Leviticus 18:16 and 20:21, which invalidated Henry's first marriage and allowed the divorce?

Such problems were not broached at the Council of Trent. It was affirmed that Hebrews, James, Judas, and Apocalypse belonged to the New Testament; the old theory continued undisturbed.

The problem of the theological disunity of the New Testament became acute once more with the rise of scientific Biblical research. In 1718, the English Deist John Toland discovered the distinction between a Christianity composed of former

Jews, which retained the Jewish Law, and a Christianity made up of pagan converts, which rejected it.[5] Thomas Chubb, in 1738, discovered the difference between the eschatological, future-oriented preaching of Jesus and the theologies of Paul and John, which were based on the idea of past redemptive events. Thomas Morgan, in 1737–1740, found a conflict between a Petrine, Jewish Christianity and a Pauline, authentic version. Griesbach published the three Synoptic Gospels in parallel columns—and John's Gospel completely separate—in his 1774–1775 edition of the New Testament in order to demonstrate the impossibility of harmonizing them. Johann Salomo Semler, in his *Abhandlung von freier Untersuchung des Canons*, 1771–1775, again pointed out the differences between a Pauline party of former pagans and a Judaistic party of former Jews. In 1800–1802, Georg Lorenz Bauer published the first survey of New Testament theology that dealt with the various, separate theologies in fully separate sections.

But the theological disunity of the New Testament first became an inescapable problem through the work of the German theologian Ferdinand Christian Baur. Starting in 1845, he showed that the historical differences between the various writers were the result of their remodeling the tradition, which they had received, to express better the points they themselves wished to make. One could only understand a particular book if one recognized the tendency of its author. Baur and his school divided the books of the New Testament into roughly three categories: 1) those that belonged to the Pauline, Gentile Christianity, 2) those that belonged to the Petrine, Jewish Christianity, and 3) those that tried to reconcile the two. For example, a comparison between what the Acts of the Apostles recounts about Paul and what he writes in his own letters reveals irreducible contradictions.[6] Only one of the two accounts could possibly be accurate. Baur showed that the author of Acts had changed the account which he had received in order to minimize the historical differences between Paul and the early community. For instance, Paul emphasizes his independent status to the Galatians by stating that, after his conversion, he did not turn to "flesh and blood," the Christians, but rather retired to the desert alone. Only three years later did he pay a visit to the leaders of the Jerusalem community.[7] The author of Acts, however, has Paul turn immediately to the Christian community in Damascus and leave very quickly for Jerusalem.[8] He wishes to accentuate Paul's close dependence on the community, and models the story according to that tendency. Similarly, where Paul defends fiercely his right to be called an apostle,[9] Acts mentions this title only once in connection with him and then very much in passing.[10] The author thereby sidesteps one of the bitterest conflicts between Paul and his opponents; or, rather, decides it in their favor.

Baur's principle of tendency criticism has been accepted [11] and has proved helpful in linking the divergent reports of events to the divergent theological views of the reporters; or, in other words, in linking historical to theological disunity. The contradictions between the different reports of the Passion and Resurrection are indications of different theological traditions, different interpretations of those same events.[12] The same is true of the different reports of the "words of institution" at the Last Supper. When Matthew has Jesus go up a mountain to deliver the Sermon on the Mount,[13] and Luke has him come down a mountain to a plain to give the same sermon,[14] they are remodeling a story according to their theological ideas. For Matthew, the mountain is the place of God's revelation; it carries a connotation of Sinai, and Jesus speaks from there as Moses did. For Luke, Jesus comes down from that mountain to communicate with men; the horizontality of the plain symbolizes their "conversation," the level on which they meet.

But the division of New Testament tendencies into only three categories was soon recognized as a great simplification. Scholars began to discover theologies that had no connection either with the ideas of Paul or with those of the Jewish-Christian groups who were his opponents; or necessarily, with those of any mediating school. There were not three groups, but many groups in the New Testament; each had its different interests, theologies, and worship. Many of the different groups seem not to have known each other. Some show no influences from any quarter; others show possible influences, but use whatever similar elements can be found among them in such different ways that they are almost unrecognizable.

This disunity has become a principle of New Testament scholarship. One cannot begin to understand the various New Testament writers until one accepts the fact that their theologies cannot be systematized with any others in the New Testament, and often not even within themselves. Even as conservative an exegete as Werner Georg Kümmel states: "there is above all no other methodologically unobjectionable way than the investigation of each writing or level of tradition individually." [15] He speaks also of "two presuppositions, which make a historical study of the New Testament impossible in practice." That is, that "Because Scripture is the sole source of divine revelation and should be able to be explained from itself, it must be understood as a unity, and there cannot be any contradictions in it . . ." [16]

Since the theological disunity of the New Testament has already been so accepted by scholars, the following brief survey is intended to give only an idea of the depth and breadth of that disunity. I confine myself largely to opinions that have been established or at least widely accepted.

Considering the absoluteness with which the theory of the unity of the New Testament has been held and, in certain circles, is still being held, the discovery of even one small divergence between two New Testament theologies would be enough to demand serious modifications of the theory. Is not every word inspired? Are the New Testament writers supposed to be unerring only in their principle opinions on exclusively central problems? But, in fact, disunity is one of the essential characteristics of New Testament theology. When the students of the Roman Catholic professor and exegete Friedrich Wilhelm Maier tentatively suggested that he might have once contradicted himself in a lecture, he is reported to have said: "Any small contradictions you might hear in my lectures are nothing against the wealth of enormous contradictions you will find on every page of the New Testament."

VARIETIES OF CONTRADICTIONS

I have restricted myself to a very few examples,[17] but hope to illustrate through them the broad lines of the more general differences to be found. I will discuss first what I will call "successive" contradictions: that is, those which arise in chronological succession, through changes in situation, interests, thought-worlds, etc. Then I will discuss "contemporary" contradictions, those which are found at roughly the same stage in the history of the early Christians. This is a purely methodological division, and no further conclusions should be drawn from it. I will speak freely of contemporary contradictions while discussing successive ones. Finally, I will discuss the logical status of the contradictions to be found in the New Testament.

Successive Contradictions

JESUS AND AFTER

The first great successive difference arises with the transition from the teaching of Jesus to that of the later community. Jesus had taught a very definite message: the kingdom of God was just about to come. The last few moments left should be used to repent and make oneself ready for entry into the kingdom. This could be done, not through the cult or the hundred thousand little prescriptions of the Law, but rather by turning as a child toward God as our Father and loving one's neighbor as one's self.[18]

Such a teaching distinguishes itself most obviously from later theology in that it provides no central place for Jesus himself. The original teaching of Jesus was purely theocentric. But, quite naturally, the place of Jesus himself was one of the greatest preoccupations of later Christian theology, and various attempts were made to define it. One of the methods of this later theology was to put words into the mouth of Jesus himself; he himself was made to speak about himself, to speculate on his place in redemptive history. No one of the passages in which Jesus is supposed to discuss his theological status—be it that of Messiah, Son of Man, or whatever—can be convincingly shown to be, in fact, from Jesus himself. On the contrary, most modern scholars accept that these passages have been constructed by the later communities as a form of their own theologizing.[19] They speculated by creating stories of *his* speculations. Jesus himself, as far as the evidence goes, never departed from his purely God-centered preaching.

By putting Jesus in the center of their theologies, the early Christian theologians had clearly departed from his own teaching. His immediate and concentrated theocentrism was dissipated. But it is equally clear that this was an almost inevitable step: they had to find a place for Jesus. They also had somehow to explain his Crucifixion and proclaim his Resurrection. These were problems which Jesus himself did not have to solve. A new situation had arisen and had brought new attitudes and difficulties with it. A new theology *was* obviously needed. But it is equally clear that it differed markedly from the teaching which it replaced.

What the historical Jesus had been and had taught was gradually being forgotten, reinterpreted, or misunderstood. Very limited collections of his sayings were made and preserved. But these were progressively rewritten in order to make them more appropriate to the times or simply because the Christians no longer knew what Jesus had been trying to say.

A good example of this process can be observed in the parables.[20] The parable is a very special Semitic literary form that was current, widely practiced, and universally understood at the time of Jesus: a short story is used to make one and only one point. This point is not to be grasped by interpreting the parable allegorically, by finding a particular reference for each

element of the story. Rather, the story as a whole, and not its
individual parts, makes the point. Therefore, the original form
of a parable is relatively easy to reconstruct, because *all* the elements, and *only* the elements, that are necessary to make the
point, can claim to be original. Later additions can be clearly
recognized as encrustations around the main story.

At the beginning of his study,[21] the German exegete
Joachim Jeremias discusses what happened to various parables.
There were changes caused by the translation into Greek, the
substitution of different background material, and by interior
elaborations. Story motifs from the Old Testament and from
Jewish folklore were worked into the texts. Jesus spoke his parables to the crowds, the Scribes and the Pharisees. The parables
were now being told to the Christian community, and their
points were changed so that they would be appropriate for the
new audience. The parables were also taken up by various
preachers and fitted to their different needs. The progressing
situation of the church demanded a continual reinterpretation
of the parables so that they might illuminate the new problems
that arose. Parables began to be interpreted *allegorically* by the
Greek converts, who had no knowledge of Semitic literary
forms. This not only contradicted the form of the parables, but
often their message as well. Several parables would sometimes
be melted together so that their points were lost, and others had
to be created. Finally, the parables were put into various frameworks which interpreted and sometimes perverted their meaning. Jeremias gives many examples of all these processes and
shows clearly how far the interpretations of the community had
developed away from the original points expressed through the
parables by Jesus.

Since so many examples are examined in the books I have
cited, I need develop only two here.

The parable of the Pharisee and the Publican in Luke
18:9–14, shows how the original point of a parable of Jesus
was forgotten and how a very opposite interpretation was put
upon it.[22]

Luke 18:9. He said to those who trusted in themselves that they were just and who despised the others, this parable:
10. Two men went up to the temple to pray, the one a Pharisee, the other a Publican. 11. The Pharisee stood there and prayed the following to himself. 12. O God, I thank you that I am not like other men, robbers, cheats, adulterers, or even like that Publican. I fast twice a week and tithe everything I earn. 13. But the Publican stood far back and did not even want to raise his eyes to heaven, rather he beat his breast saying: O God, forgive me, a sinner.
14. I say to you, the latter went down justified to his house, but not the former,
for everyone who exalts himself shall be humbled, and he who humbles himself shall be exalted.

This parable, like many others, is introduced by a verse that has been added later to arrange the received parable into the whole story. The original piece begins then with verse 10. One must realize also that Jesus spoke this parable to the Jews of his time and place, and they understood it much differently than one would today. For them, startling as it may seem, the Pharisee *was* the good man, and the Publican *was* bad. The religious view of the time, that Jesus is referring to here, was based almost exclusively on the Law. He who followed the hundreds of rules set down by the learned Pharisees could *claim* to be just before God. This Pharisee, as he says, did even more than the Law required, so he was perfectly within his rights to say, and to exult in the fact, that he was a good man. It was also perfectly proper to despise, and even hate, those who did not follow the Law. The Publican, on the other hand, was a genuinely bad man, a toadying servant of a corrupt system, squeezing as much money as possible out of a defenseless people. The sympathies of Jesus' audience were decidedly against him. If he truly repented, he could find written in the

Law the many prescriptions which he would be obliged to fulfill over the years before he could claim once more to be just before God. For Jesus' audience, the parable is, up to this point, quite clear and perfectly natural. Then Jesus springs his point. The Publican, and not the Pharisee, is justified, and on the spot. Jesus overturns the old religious idea and puts an entirely new one in its place: one's attitude to God decides one's relationship to him and not the rote fulfillment of external rules. The audience must have been profoundly shocked. They had come to hear someone religious, and had heard a parable that was radically offensive to their own idea of religion.

This parable is then handed down through the years, leaves Palestine and comes to a land where the people know neither who Pharisees and Publicans are nor what they stand for. They do not know that the Pharisee is supposed to be considered good and that the Publican is known to be bad. The Christian preacher or writer has to find a point for the parable that will have some meaning for his audience. He adds the second half of verse 14, which then becomes its meaning for them and, in fact, for most people today. The Pharisee here does not have a radically false view of man's relation to God. He is just proud. The Publican is not really so bad; he is just "humbling himself." The point of the original parable is lost. Moreover, the new point about the Publican is closely bound to the very attitude which the original parable criticized: external moralism. The point of the parable, which is a fundamental point of Jesus' whole teaching, has, in fact, been turned against itself. Those who held this new view would be as shocked to hear that the Publican was really bad, as the original audience was shocked to hear that Jesus considered him justified.

The parable of the sower in Mark 4:1–9 is too well known to require quoting.[23] Its original purpose was to console the disciples by assuring them that, though many were being lost, the harvest would be great when the kingdom came in the very near future. The principle of a parable having one point to which all its details tend is the key to the correct interpretation here. When the parable reached non-Jewish converts, the original message was no longer very timely, and the various elements of the story, the different fates of the seeds, cried out for the allegorical interpretation to which the Greek mind was addicted. Mark 4:13–20 is, therefore, a good example of a typical, early Christian allegorical interpretation, put into the mouth of Jesus.

Moreover, in verses 33–34, one can see the early Christian mind at work, trying to solve a problem that faced it. For these Christians, the parables were incomprehensible. Why had Jesus spoken this way? Mark gives the answer: the parables were riddles.[24] They were not meant to reveal, but to conceal, from the crowds the true message of Jesus. A more complete reversal of the function of parables could not be imagined. One of Jesus' most effective means of communication had been transformed into a block to understanding. This entailed also a very distinct theology of Jesus' mission: he had been sent, not to proclaim and communicate his message, but to hide it. This was of course very different from Jesus' own view.

There are many other differences between the teaching of Jesus and that of the early Christians. Very often, as in the last two examples, the positions of Jesus are much more interesting than their later "reinterpretations." This is certainly true of the two following examples.

Matthew 18:22 undoubtedly contains a genuine saying of Jesus. Peter has asked Jesus how often he should forgive his brother—until seven times? "Jesus said to him: 'I don't say to you till seven times, but till seventy-seven times,' " that is, always. Contrast this with the words that are put into Jesus' mouth in Matthew 18:15–17: "If your brother sins [against you], go discuss it between you and him alone. If he listens to you, you have won your brother. If he does not listen to you, take with you one or two others, so that 'on the word of two or three witnesses, every dispute will be settled.' [Deuteronomy 19:15] If he will not listen to them, tell it to the *ecclesia*. But if he will also not hear the *ecclesia,* let him be to you like the Gentiles and Publicans."

In the place of the free, inexhaustible generosity advocated by Jesus has been set a very elaborated and scripturally supported code of law. No one could deny that it was more practical and was probably even necessary. But it was also a direct contradiction of the spirit and even the letter of Jesus' teaching.

Mark 2:27 preserves a most important saying of Jesus. When his disciples were criticized for plucking a few ears of corn on the Sabbath, Jesus replied by alluding to David's opening the temple grain stores on the Sabbath to feed his starving people. Jesus then laid down the principle: "the Sabbath was made for man, and not man for the Sabbath, 28. for man is lord even of the Sabbath." Jesus hereby overthrows the cultic emphasis of the religion of his time. Man should not be ground beneath the heavy burden of ritual regulations, which were originally created as a help and not a hindrance. Man is the sacred, and not the cult. A more startling remark for his hearers can hardly be imagined. But emphasis on cult is a strong instinct in all religions, and this tendency reasserted itself among the early Christians. They could not accept the freedom Jesus wished to give them, but rather re-created the cultic system for themselves and used Jesus as its founding authority. Thus Luke 6:5, and Matthew 12:8, change the last verse in a most interesting way. For "man," Mark has used a literal Greek translation of the Aramaic *bar-nasha,* "son of man," which was just another way of saying "man." By leaving out the beginning of Mark's argument in verse 27, and placing the literal translation "son of man" in a very emphatic position, Matthew and Luke imply by the phrase, not just "man," which was the original meaning, but rather the theological *title* "Son of Man" which was applied to Jesus much later. In other words, they are saying: Christ is the Lord of the Sabbath! They are twisting Jesus' whole argument to mean exactly the opposite: instead of abolishing the cultic emphasis, they are emphasizing the cult by the authority of Christ himself! [25]

Similarly, the original saying of Jesus in Mark 7:15, which also expressed a rejection of this particular religious view, is moralized by both Mark and Matthew. Luke does not even include it in his gospel! [26]

However, some of the corrections which the later Christians imposed on their tradition of Jesus would win our approval. For instance, Jesus himself categorically forbade divorce,[27] but Matthew allows it in the case of "unchastity." [28]

In Mark 7:27, Jesus says to a pagan woman who implores him to drive a demon from her daughter: "It is not good to take the bread of the children and throw it to the dogs." Now many have interpreted this verse as if Jesus were testing the woman. The word for dogs, it is asserted, really stands for "little dogs," a more tender term. In fact, this remark of Jesus' is perfectly natural and representative of the attitude of the convinced Jews of the time toward the Gentiles. Jesus shared the view of his contemporaries that the kingdom of God was to come very much primarily, if not even exclusively, for the Jews.[29] Thus, in the later community, the legitimacy of its Gentile mission was a most difficult and much debated question. Paul had to fight continually even to be allowed to preach to non-Jews. Through many efforts of many people, but mostly through the destruction of the conservative Jerusalem community, which was trying to preserve intact the tradition of Jesus himself, the Gentile mission was finally accepted. A command was then put into the mouth of the risen Christ to "Go forth and teach all nations." [30] Most people today would certainly agree.

In view of these changed circumstances, Mark, in 7:24–30, and Matthew, in 15:21–28, are naturally desirous to reinterpret the story of Jesus and the pagan woman so as to suppress, as much as possible, the contradiction between the opinion of Jesus and the practice of the later community. First, Mark offers, in verse 24, the excuse that Jesus wanted to remain unrecognized. In Matthew, instead of Jesus replying immediately as brusquely as he did, Matthew has him remain silent. Then all the apostles implore Jesus to aid her, as she continues to follow them (in Mark, Jesus is in a house; in Matthew, he is on the road). Jesus says that he was sent only "to the lost sheep of

Israel." Therefore, when Jesus refuses to help the pagan woman, he is merely restricting himself to his own personal (and tender) mission. Thus no larger consequences should be drawn about the place of the pagans in God's plan. But the woman continues to implore him, and now the brusque rejection of Jesus is quoted. The preceding verses have, however, removed some of its sharpness of tone, just as Matthew intended. Mark adds to the quote: "Let the children eat first," thereby implying that Jesus' rejection is not based on principle, but on timing! Then the woman gives a very clever reply. Jesus, as most Semites of his and, indeed, of all times, dearly enjoyed cleverness of words. In Mark 7:29, Jesus congratulates the woman on her cleverness, grants her request, and sends her away, again rather brusquely. But in Matthew 15:28, he marvels at her *great faith* and says, "Let it happen to you as you will." Matthew thus pays the Gentiles a fine compliment. Clearly, each writer, in his own way, has twisted a received story in order either to conform its point to the new practice on which the community had decided; or, at least, to lessen the obviousness of its contradiction of that practice.

But the most important changing of Jesus' original teaching was forced upon the later Christians. Jesus had believed that the kingdom of God was to arrive literally at any moment. He and his contemporaries were living in the last, brief period of world history. A few last-minute intentions were all one had time for. The delay of that cosmic ending caused the most far-reaching changes in all of Christian theology.

THE DELAY OF THE PAROUSIA:
CONSEQUENT PROBLEMS AND SOLUTIONS

Jesus expected the coming of God's kingdom in his day, and the earliest Christians expected that kingdom, or Christ's coming, in theirs. (This coming of the kingdom, or of Christ, is referred to as "the Parousia.") That their hopes remained unfulfilled posed a serious problem for the theologians of the New Testament.

Did this error of Jesus and the earliest Christians not, in

fact, give the lie to all of Christianity? This conclusion has been, in fact, drawn by at least one of the first discoverers of this event. Matthew Tindal argued in 1730 that, if the apostles had made such an enormous mistake on this point, they could obviously be in error on others.[31] This problem is no less thorny and important for Christian thinkers today, yet dogmatic theologians are being slow to turn their attention to it.[32]

Jesus had taught the coming of God and his kingdom. Needless to say, later Christians often transformed this teaching into one about the coming of Jesus and *his* kingdom. In fact, these two thought complexes were never fully synthesized. The kingdom, in different New Testament theologies, can be either of God, of Jesus, or of both; and it can be brought either by God or Jesus or by both. There was no really necessary and central role for Jesus in the old scheme and various possible alternate schemes were employed. Should Jesus be called the Messiah and be imagined as establishing the kingdom on the earth by means of a great military victory? Or should he simply appear, as the Son of Man, and bring the kingdom from heaven? Each of these ideas, the one Jewish, and the other originally from various apocalyptic sources, had its advantages and disadvantages, which I will discuss later.

In any case, however the early Christians pictured it, their expectation of the imminent coming of the Parousia was a determining factor in their lives: for example, it was their ethical motive [33] and the basis of such decisions as whether to marry or not.[34] Paul had to urge his converts not to give up their jobs and their normal lives because of their expectation, but rather to go on as before. They interpreted the events around them as signs of the imminent coming: their very opponents were mere indications of the end that would be a destruction for them, but a salvation for the Christians.[35] Their services were built around their eschatological convictions, as such expressions as "The Lord is near," and "Lord, come" or "The Lord is coming," show. So strong was this expectation, and so deeply did it impress itself upon Christian theology that, even later, when alternatives to this future hope had been perforce devised,

expressions of the older view often rise to the surface like fragments from another age.[36]

The problem of the delay of the Parousia became acute as
the first generation of Christians began to die. In I Thessalonians 4:13 ff., Paul has to resolve the conflict between his earlier
preaching, that they would all live until the Parousia, with the
fact that several from the Thessalonian community had just
died. He does this by once again affirming that they would live
to see the Parousia and by assuring them that their dead would
not come into the kingdom after them, the living, but rather
would precede them. Jesus would first revive the dead, then the
living would be reunited with them and they would all be carried up on clouds to meet the Lord in the air.[37]

But such hopes and solutions could not be sustained as the
years passed and most of the first generation died. A new situation had arisen, new evidence, that demanded changes in theology that reached as far into early Christianity as the hope
of the early coming of the Parousia had permeated: the whole
foundation of every single Christian belief had to be reexam-
ined. That disappointed hope had *been* Christianity; it had been
more even than their theology: it had been the basis of their
theology and of every aspect of their lives. Christian theologians had now, on the one side, a very definite theological tradition and, on the other, an irreconcilable situation. For these
new problems, new solutions were required, and each theologian was forced to search for his own. As might be expected,
very different solutions were found.[38] I will discuss only a few
of them here.

The possibility of the most direct solution lay in a reinterpretation of the Parousia itself, the most famous example of
which is the second chapter of what is called Paul's Second
Epistle to the Thessalonians. This letter is, in fact, a direct refutation of Paul's first and genuine letter to the Thessalonians.
The writer of II Thessalonians begins by casting doubts on the
authenticity of I Thessalonians. The Thessalonians should not
be fooled by any word "nor by any letter as from us." [39] The
"as" implies that there is in fact no such letter. He then creates

within the old eschatological scheme the need for a long space of time before the actual Parousia. He does this by introducing a whole set of apocalyptic themes that did not originally belong to the Christian view of eschatology: first the apostasy must come, and the adversary, the impious one. There will be a conflict between him and the Lord, who will win easily. Instead of living in the last moment, the Christians are *approaching* the last age. The attitude they should have is not one of near expectation, but, rather, of humble perseverance.[40] The writer has contradicted the view of I Thessalonians. We can see from this example that the mere addition of further elements to a theology can essentially change it.

Käsemann has shown that the pseudonymous Second Epistle of Peter is, in fact, an attempt to explain away the early near expectation.[41] He shows how the author substitutes, for the old-time scheme, a new one that allows more than enough room for a long wait until the Parousia. The "last time" becomes the period in church history posterior to the time of Jesus and of the first Christians. All the old eschatological terms are now given psychological and anthropological meanings. The Parousia itself becomes the individual's participation in the divine *physis,* or nature. By transposing the old theology into a new frame of reference, the author has managed to twist it against itself.

Again, let me emphasize that the necessity of creating a new theology had then become obvious. But just as the new situation discredited the old hopes, so did the new theologies contradict the old ones.[42]

I will look very briefly at a few solutions of some of the problems which were raised by the new situation. One of the first problems was to establish some sort of continuity with the old theologies, even if violence had to be done to them. The main method used to harmonize the teaching of Jesus with the new conclusions was to reinterpret his parables. A parable that originally warned the Palestinian audience of the sudden coming of the kingdom was allegorized or expanded to urge the later, disappointed Christians to persevere: they could not be sure when the kingdom would come. What had been originally a mark of the frightening nearness and soonness of the coming of the kingdom became an encouragement to the faithful that it might still come after all.[43]

I have already mentioned that one of the preoccupations of II Thessalonians and II Peter was to provide a new interpretation of the time in which the Christians were living. They could no longer hold the view that it was the very last time, a short, breathless pause between the first act of the coming, the Resurrection of Jesus, and the final coming of the whole kingdom. These two events were originally considered to make up really only one, and the actual time span between them was not an object of reflection. As that time span extended, however, the Christians began to feel that they had to explain it in some way.[44] The first attempts were occupied simply with justifying it; then positive aspects were discovered. Luke created an entirely new time scheme consisting of three periods: the time before Christ, the time of Christ, and the time after Christ. Christ stood at the turning point of history, and that a third, later period existed only placed Christ in a more honorable position. This last period was to be a time for spreading the proclamation about Christ to the far corners of the earth. But, however magnificent such a scheme might be, it is clearly a contradiction of the old view that Christ was the *end* of history and that after him there would be the kingdom alone. John's Gospel shows even another view: Jesus has brought a new age which somehow already *is* the kingdom. Traces of the older futuristic eschatologies are still to be found in John, but they are definitely ill at ease in his new conception. Prior to John, there had been certain other attempts to show that the Christian community, at least, was already living in the kingdom, and we will discuss aspects of these views later. But it is so far obvious that these new interpretations were essentially different from the old view and not to be reconciled even with each other. They were all very different solutions to the same problem.

I have noted earlier that the ethic of the earliest community was based on its near expectation of the kingdom. The early

Christians believed that they were saved and were entering into the kingdom. As time replaced the old enthusiasm with the need for continual perseverance, the question arose: how can we already be saved, and yet still be in danger of falling? Since no provision had been made for the *time* to fall, no thought had been given either to its possibility or to the problems it would create. Soon there arose, on the one hand, some who held that since they *were already* saved, they *could not* fall and that therefore everything was allowed. On the other hand, others, possessed of more anxious and scrupulous consciences, turned to pagan types of puritanism or to the old, Jewish morality of the Law in order to try to *earn* their salvation. Paul had to provide an answer that would correct the exaggerations of both these groups. He did this simply by affirming both ends of the dilemma: yes, Christians *were* saved already, and, yes, they had to persevere in their ethic.[45] This was not a very satisfactory solution; in fact, it could be reduced to a particularly eloquent statement of the problem. But it was all that was possible, as- suming that both points had to be preserved. But for particular questions of conduct, the Christian teachers were increasingly dependent for their decisions, not on the eschatological hope, but on vague ideas of natural law, Jewish and Gentile customs, prejudices, and superstitions. Christians began to base their conduct not so much on the coming kingdom as on the present world.

New problems arose and led to controversy. Should a Christian who had fallen be allowed to repent and return to the fold? The author of Hebrews forbade this and the author of the first letter of John allowed it.[46] The new problems had elicited directly contradictory solutions, and on a question of utmost theological importance for the early communities. Their very conception of themselves was at stake and not a mere question of arbitrary discipline.

Just as the early Christians had not speculated about the time between the Resurrection and the Parousia, so also they had not attempted to establish a position or role for Jesus *dur- ing* that period. He had been raised, and he would come again very soon. They did not ask themselves where he was or what he was doing in between, because that short time was not important. However, as that period became a problem in itself, the Christian theologians had to place Jesus in some meaningful way within it. To do this, they used the various theological frameworks and schemes employed in other religions of the time. Some, originally Oriental religions, honored mythical figures: a being had lived in heaven from the beginning; he was sent down to earth, accomplished a task and then returned to his heavenly place of origin. Other religions spoke of an especially good man being *exalted* to a special relationship with God. Others spoke of him being *adopted* as a very special son. Some Hellenistic religions even spoke of certain men as being the natural sons of a god. Several such men were known to the Hellenistic world and were worshiped by particular cults.[47]

Accordingly, one of the earliest solutions to the problem of Jesus' present position was the theology of the exaltation. The Resurrection was not just the raising of Jesus from the dead as a sign of the coming kingdom or in order to allow him to come with it. Rather, Jesus was given a new status; he was exalted to the Father.[48] The advantage of such a view over the old one is that it gives Jesus a position that does not depend entirely on his past or future role. Formerly *eschatological* titles were now applied to Jesus in his *state* of exaltation. They thus lost their future reference and applied to the present situation; they were deeschatologized.[49]

Another theology stated that Jesus had been adopted by God and received his status from that act.[50]

Another used the aforementioned scheme of some non-Jewish Oriental religions: Jesus had lived in heaven with the Father, had then come down to earth, worked and died, and then *returned* to his Father.[51] He was always his Son. I will discuss later the use of the scheme of divine sonship.

One is struck by the differences between these different solutions. Jesus could not have been exalted above his natural state when he really was the Son. He could not have been adopted if he was already the Son. To be exalted is not the same as to be made a son or to be already a son. In the exaltation and adoption schemes, the life of Jesus began with his birth; in the third scheme, Jesus had preexisted with God from all eternity. These solutions show irreconcilable differences and cannot be harmonized without losing just that which makes each one the solution that it is.[52] To add two of the solutions together is to destroy them both, just as is the case when two schemes of the eschatological events are joined.

Some of the most important attempts to solve the problem of Jesus' role during the in between time posited various activities that he performed within the actual Christian community. The place of Jesus was increasingly emphasized in worship. The title "Lord" emphasized his present role as leader of the earthly community. Most interestingly, a theological position arose that held that it was Jesus who was sending down the spirit to the community.[53]

The various theological notions of the spirit contradict each other so manifestly that I may simply refer to the literature here.[54] I shall examine here only three large categories: the broad original idea of the spirit, the spirit as the spirit of God and as the spirit of Christ.

The first idea of the spirit was based on phenomena observable inside the community. Members began to "speak in tongues," to prophesy, to speak with extraordinary eloquence, to read the hearts of others, etc. These phenomena were not unknown to the ancient world, and the Christians quite naturally adopted the terminology used by their contemporaries: the cause of these phenomena was a thing called "the spirit." Of course, this term acquired peculiarly Christian connotations: the spirit was considered to be a sign of the new age, one of the first symptoms of the coming of the kingdom. The spirit was in the community, and the individual received it through baptism and especially through the laying on of hands. But it remained largely a term for the phenomena: the spirit was thought of as a force, an energy, which charged those with whom it came in contact. It was not thought of as personal, and no attempt was made to connect it immediately with Jesus or with God; the spirit was thought of rather in connection with the situation, as a result, a sign, a creative force all at the same time. Many contradictions and problems arose quite naturally at this stage between various conceptions of the spirit and its workings.[55]

A very different stage is marked by theological statements referring to the spirit as *God*'s spirit. The people of the time could speak of the spirit of a person just as we can, and the word was characterized by many of the same ambiguities: it could mean intelligence, the thinking faculty, *esprit,* character, tendency, personality, etc. It is never very clear just what is meant by "the spirit of God," and even a suggestion, such as that it refers to "the personality of God as a separable active force," though it offers useful links to aspects of the earliest notion, can cover only a limited number of texts. The main impulse to use the phrase thus seems to have been the desire to connect this one term, in some way, to God. But, by proceeding in this vague way, the theologians of the New Testament could not put the two into a consistent system.

Similarly, the phrase "the spirit of Christ" and its like seem to have originated in a desire to make connections between the different elements of New Testament thinking. The resulting ambiguity is even greater in this case.

The writers of the time had, in fact, tried to reduce a very complex notion to another very different one. If the spirit was the spirit of God, then it must be somehow personal; but this was very different from the original impersonal idea. And how could it be the "spirit" of God and of Jesus at the same time? This was a very different idea of spirit than the one used when one spoke of the spirit *only* of God or *only* of Jesus. I need hardly point out that not one of these variations could possibly be interpreted as a *third* person. On the contrary, the idea of "God's spirit" excludes just such a possibility, because "spirit" is his uniquely individual, let us say, personality. Similarly, a "spirit" that would be shared between God and Jesus could not be personal. The Paraclete of John's Gospel is the only possible basis in the New Testament for a doctrine of a third divine person.

I can now turn to the peculiar idea of spirit involved when it is said that God gives Jesus the spirit to send down to the community. Clearly this is neither the "spirit of God," nor "the spirit of Christ"; nor of both. It shares important aspects with the most primitive notion: it is impersonal; it causes the observable extraordinary phenomena. But an important distinction remains: the primitive view was that spirit was simply in and of the situation created by God (or Christ or both of them together). One could almost say that it was the force of the situation. In any case, the spirit was not expressly regarded as immediately dependent on Christ. In the later theology, Jesus directly hands down the spirit. Now this could appear as a sort of shorthand for the earlier view: instead of God or Jesus creating a situation in which there is spirit, the spirit is given directly. But this is a very different view of spirit, of its origin and of the situation as well. The creative influence of the spirit on the situation is observed as in the earlier view; but not the fact that, according to that view, the situation and the spirit are somehow inseparable. In other words, to say that the situation and the spirit were there together characterizes the situation as itself extraordinary; to say that the spirit was given to the situation, says just the opposite: that the situation was ordinary until the spirit was sent to it. The later theologians, one sees again, had lost the sense of the urgent peculiarity of the time between the Resurrection and the Parousia. For them, that time now *needed to be filled* with significance; it was not the significance of the situation that filled them.

The change in the entire eschatological hope of the early community brought with it, naturally enough, several changes in the ways the early Christians pictured the end to themselves. I have already noted how II Thessalonians reinterpreted I Thessalonians by adding new pictures, new episodes, to the drama of the final coming as portrayed by Paul. But Paul himself changed his opinion several times about how the end would take place. His first view—while he still reckoned that the kingdom would come when at least most of the first Christians would still be alive—was that Christians at the Parousia would all put on their new bodies *together,* as one would put on a new set of clothes, and that these new, heavenly bodies would destroy the old mortal ones.[56] However, in II Corinthians 5: 1–5, Paul develops an opposite view. By then, Christians had been dying for quite some time, and the question naturally arose: where were they between their death and the Parousia? How could they exist once they had lost their earthly bodies, but had not yet received their new, heavenly ones? Paul changes his conception to solve this problem. They receive their new bodies immediately after death, a flat contradiction of his former position. But then the problem arose, what was to happen at the Parousia? Was that not, in fact, exactly the moment when all were to receive their new heavenly bodies? Was there even a need, then, for the Parousia? Paul was apparently impressed by these difficulties and therefore, in Romans 8:23, returned to his first position.

Another attempt was made to solve the problem of where the Christians are after their deaths, but before the Parousia, in Philippians 1:23.[57] Here Paul claims that he will be reunited with Christ immediately after his death. This is very different from both the other views, which demanded that the dead Christian wait, with or without body, until all would be reunited with Christ together at the Parousia.

These are only a few, clear examples of the many contradictions between the different early Christian conceptions of the last episodes of history. A similar inconsistency reigned in their ways of imagining the Last Judgment. Jesus was either judge, prosecutor, or advocate for the defense. Or God was judge, or there was no forensic judgment. Especially debated were the signs that were to precede the end; the reactions of the people involved; the roles of the Jews and the Gentiles, etc., etc. The fertile imaginations of the early Christians created a wide range of possibilities, and each author syncretized the elements he desired or was attracted by into unbalanced and inconsistent complexes. Paul was just one good example of this.[58]

Thus the new situation created by the delay of the Parousia contradicted the old hopes and views that had been based on the expectation of its imminent coming. The whole of Christian thought had to be restructured and solutions found to the many new problems that arose. These new views and solutions contradicted those that had been accepted before the delay of the Parousia became acute. They also contradicted each other.

FROM PALESTINE TO HELLENISM

A brief survey of the different situations of early Christianity in Palestine and in the Hellenistic world will show how different problems, ideas, and tendencies led to different theological positions.

Indeed, an important contributing factor of this process of divergence was the fragmentation of the ancient world. Christian communities often evolved in virtual isolation, knowing little or nothing of other Christian groups, much less of their theological views. Paul had to fight continually to try to establish in his far-flung missions some sense of common brotherhood. The great collection for the poor of Jerusalem was a means of bringing the different groups into some sort of concerted action. These efforts were, however, largely unsuccessful, and many of the books of the New Testament and of the apostolic fathers display an ignorance of all or at least most of the preserved Christian literature. Startling differences in doctrine and practice between the large centers of Christianity were preserved as traditions until very late. Regional and local traditions lasted even longer. Unity, as most idealize it, did not exist in the early church.[59]

The Christians of Palestine had many problems that the Gentile converts of the Hellenistic world did not share. Should they pay the Temple tax? To what extent should they continue to follow the precepts of the Law? Should converts be circumcised? Should they fast and abstain according to Jewish regulations? Every Jewish practice and belief demanded a decision from these Christians.

The Christians of Palestine were also in competition with a number of sects that were less known in the Hellenistic world. One of their most important rivals was a community of the followers of John the Baptist. These Johannists had an important argument against the Christians' claim that Jesus was more important than John: did not the fact that Jesus had allowed himself to be baptized by John show that he had accepted him as his superior? The various remodelings of the account of Jesus' baptism were designed to answer this objection. Another method of subordinating John to Jesus was by placing him in a lower position in a scheme of redemptive history. The Synoptic Gospels repeatedly claim that John is Elias, who was to appear before the Messiah in order to proclaim him. But John the Evangelist directly contradicts this theology by having John the Baptist deny categorically that he is Elias (John 1:21).

Similarly, the New Testament shows signs of negative and positive attitudes toward the Proto-Ebionites, who claimed that riches were bad and poverty was good per se.

Among the decisions that fell to the Palestinian community but not to the Gentiles was whether to allow or forbid the Gentile mission itself. I have argued that the authorities in Jerusalem remained faithful to the original, exclusivist teaching of Jesus; their hesitation to abandon the opinions of their master and founder and accept the new views is perfectly understandable.

On the other hand, Christianity in the Hellenistic world faced problems that were unknown in Palestine. The fact that Christianity was based on a history was difficult to reconcile with the Hellenistic view that reality and truth were to be found in the static world order. What was the relation of temporal events to nontemporal truths? Should theology base itself on history or on nature? One possible solution was to consider historical happenings as allegories of eternal truths. Another was to say that events at one point in time created lasting *states*. The conflict between these two thought worlds will always pose a problem for sensitive exponents of the one or the other. Similarly, what was the relation of revelation to the knowledge that one acquired of God from nature?

New decisions of practice had to be made and justified. Why should converts from paganism refrain from eating the meat of animals that had been sacrificed in pagan rites? Those gods did not exist; what possible harm could they do?

The Hellenistic world had its own enthusiasms, and there is evidence that some of the early converts quite naturally continued their usual orgiastic style of life. They were already saved, were they not? Others rushed into dangerous experiments with their newly acquired purity; such as married and unmarried couples living together as brother and sister.

Not only did the Palestinian and the Hellenistic converts have different problems; they also had different means of forming solutions: different categories of thought, different terms, different positive and negative reactions. James Barr has properly deflated a number of exaggerated and nonscientific arguments about these differences,[60] but he himself admits that for certain special linguistic areas, such as kinship terms, different terminologies might indeed indicate different ways of dividing and ordering experience. The technical theological terms of different languages and their use might be similarly indicative; though, of course, great caution must be used in deciding what are, in fact, technical terms. Since there was a good deal of mutual influence between different cultures in the ancient world, the difficulties of deciding in individual cases whether a word or term is being used in a "Hebrew" or a "Greek" sense are often insuperable. The whole question needs the detailed and positive attention of a scholar with a background such as Barr's.

Ian T. Ramsey, however, would find legitimate indications of differences in thinking in that two peoples "possess different dominant models in terms of which their whole thinking is characterized . . . there are characteristic differences between the dominant models of Hebrew and Greek discourse, and in this sense we may speak of the Hebrews and the Greeks 'thinking differently.' " [61]

I will discuss later this whole question at greater length. Nevertheless, certain general observations can be made here. First, the earliest, Semitic forms of Christian preaching were in themselves hardly ideal. The earliest theologians expressed their beliefs in various Jewish terms that were appropriate only up to a certain point. For instance, when they called Jesus the Messiah, this had the advantage of linking him with an older Jewish tradition and of expressing the view that he would be instrumental in establishing God's kingdom (I will discuss later variations within the thought complex associated with the term "Messiah"). Unfortunately, the title was inappropriate in that it always had a military connotation and said nothing about the events that were regarded as the most important and particular of Jesus' life: his death and Resurrection.[62] All other titles of Jewish origin, such as "rabbi," "teacher," "prophet," etc. are equally inadequate. Moreover, the early Christian preachers who were converts from Judaism adopted the *schemata,* the sermon outlines, of the Jewish missioners among the Gentiles. These frameworks of teaching were exclusively theocentric: there was no natural, necessary, and inevitable place for Jesus within them. Specifically Christian theology seems to have begun, to a certain extent, as an insertion into Jewish missionary sermons.[63] The inappropriateness of these frameworks led to a number of ambiguities, false accents, and even contradictions.[64] To suppose then that "Hebrew categories" or "the Semitic mind" are more congruous than any other to Christianity is a mistake.

I have already mentioned the difficulties created among the Hellenistic converts by the Christian emphasis on history. We have also seen earlier that the new converts had little or no understanding of Semitic literary forms, such as parables. They tended to turn what they had received into new and completely different forms, such as allegory. This often resulted in a changing of the sense.

The Hellenistic Christians introduced many different terms, complexes of ideas, and world views into New Testament theology. I have already mentioned the notion of a preexistent being who is sent down to earth, accomplishes a task and later returns to his heavenly place of origin. The theology of the exaltation of Jesus also shows Hellenistic elements. The ideas and terminologies of the Greek mystery religions played a large role in various theologies of the worship of the community,[65] especially in Paul and I Peter. Expressions originally from Hellenistic mysticism found their way into Christian theologies: Paul is referring to a mystical theme that is well known from Hellenistic sources, when he says, in II Corinthians 3:18, that we are transformed into the image we contemplate. Such terms and themes and those from other sources were gradually mixed into Christian language and theology. Often they suppressed the original meaning of the theologies into which they were introduced.[66] Often they were simply not understood. More often still, they were simply set beside the earlier elements without regard to the incongruous effect produced when such widely varying thought complexes and terms were joined.[67]

The most important novelty for Christianity was the Hellenistic idea of God. For the Jews, "God" referred to a unique person, known through the history of Israel and revealed in the Bible as God (the tautology is intended). For the Hellenistic man in the street, there were many gods, and "the divine" had become, as it were, a category to which someone or something belonged. Since many persons were called divine, there must be, it was reasoned, some common element. Once this element was thought of as distinct—in a way it was never able to be in Judaism—it could be applied to this or that person or object. Was Hercules divine, it was debated, or just a hero? The predicate "divine" had, of course, the character of a universal which could be individuated in a number of particulars.

In deep contradiction to the Jews, the Hellenistic world also spoke, as we have seen, of the real and actual earthly children of the gods. Far from being a very esoteric idea, this had become quite natural and everyday in popular religious thought.

To be acquainted with these ideas and terminologies was, in itself, a temptation to use them. Jesus was honored in the cult. Not to call him "divine," when all rival sects called their founders so, placed the Christians at a distinct disadvantage. I will discuss later the influence which this new idea of God, and the new language that went with it, had on Christology. Nevertheless, from this one example alone, one can already see what a profound effect the introduction of Hellenistic terms and thought patterns had on Christian theology.

TOWARD EARLY CATHOLICISM

I have already discussed the fact that several of the earlier, more extreme, and more original elements of the teaching of Jesus and of the early Christians were later attenuated or suppressed: instead of forgiving their brother seventy-seven times as Jesus had directed,[68] the later Christians followed an elaborate set of rules either to bring their brother to order or to exclude him from their community.[69] As time went on, similar adjustments of earlier teachings or practices were made until the Christian community became very different from what it had been before. This new Christianity has been given the name of "Early Catholicism" by many New Testament scholars, and I shall use the epithet here, although other labels, such as Scott's "Western Christianity," have equal if not identical advantages and disadvantages.[70]

One of Paul's main tasks was to bring order into the practice of the community, which was originally ruled by "the spirit." The spirit moved this or that person to speak in tongues, to prophesy, to preach, to minister, to lead, to do this or that good work, etc. Needless to say, the result was often chaos. Someone would be speaking in tongues as another person would be trying to prophesy. Paul urged his communities to establish some sort of order, even if they had to wait their turn to let the spirit move them. In making his rules, Paul used as his model the synagogue regulations as well as those of the mystery cults. On the other hand, Paul was very careful to respect the spirit, in no way wanted to hinder its work, and recognized that it was the ultimate structuring force and authority in the community.[71]

As time passed, however, the phenomena attributed to the spirit began to disappear. When they were rediscovered in schismatic sects of enthusiasts, the "workings of the spirit" became suspect in the eyes of those who had assumed responsibility. Preachers, ministers, missionaries, and all the other workers for the community began to be chosen, not by the spirit, but rather by those who were already in charge. A new theology of *office* replaced the old one of *charism*. Charism was given with the office; the officeholder had the charism. Authority was considered by this theology to be grounded in the apostles and transmitted from one officeholder to the next. Here, the spirit was not literally moving the community and the individual; rather, the hierarchy was perpetuating itself. A theology and a practice had arisen that were very different from what had formerly prevailed.[72]

Similar attempts were made to restrict the variety of teaching that had characterized Christianity from the beginning. Of course, the Judaists from the Jerusalem community had tried to suppress Paul, and he had tried to suppress his opponents. The Second Epistle to the Thessalonians had tried to suppress the first. The author of Acts had tried to suppress the evidence of discord in the early community. But fortunately, most of these divergent teachings found their way into the inspired canon of the New Testament and were preserved, however completely their authors along with their separate schools and communities disappeared.

But in all these conflicts, there was no ultimate court of appeal, no juridically constituted body that could decide in each case according to some criterion. All of these mechanisms had to be created and accepted. Paul and others began, then, to appeal to a tradition, though Paul felt free to add to or subtract from it, and used it more as a point of departure for his own thoughts. He did not regard the tradition which he had received as sacrosanct, and felt free to disregard, or even contradict it in a roundabout way. But it was convenient as an *ad hoc* authority for use in arguments. Similarly, if the "council of Jerusalem" ever took place, its origin and structure is not to be found in some early Christian canon law book. The establishment and procedure of such a meeting had to be envisioned, had to be invented as a new solution to a new problem. The Christians had no need of such councils while they still expected the kingdom to come soon. Only when decisions became inevitable was an apparatus constructed for making them.

But these early traditions and decisions had in no sense the authority which we attribute to ours today. Individual Christian teachers demanded the right to proclaim "their gospel," and continued to do so well into the Christian era, despite all the efforts of the authorities to stop them. When a Christian felt moved by the spirit to teach, when he felt he had been given a charism to proclaim a certain message, he considered it his duty to obey God and not men. If the authorities were to be successful in suppressing such individuals, a new theology had to be constructed to show that obedience to the orthodox teaching and to the official teaching authority was, in fact, the only authentic obedience to the spirit.

The most important elements of this new theology are found in certain very late books of the New Testament, especially in the Pastoral Epistles. First, the claim was made that, at the beginning of Christianity, the teaching of the church had been a unity. This body of doctrine had been preserved by the proper authorities and handed down by them. They continued to teach it and preserve it from all error. The Christians were exhorted to "hold to the old teaching." Now the most that Paul, who *was* an apostle, could claim was: no matter what the other apostles and teachers in the community said, he *also* had a right to teach, to proclaim "his gospel." He would like to claim that it is *"the* gospel," and is happy to point out the few points on which he and the others are in agreement (for instance, in I Corinthians 15:11, he is gratified to report that they are all of one mind in the conviction that Jesus had been crucified, buried, and raised from the dead).[73] But his continual conflicts, not only with new rivals, but with old, established authorities, show that his was not *the* gospel, but one hotly contested one among many.

The Early Catholic view of the original unity of Christian doctrine was, in fact, a myth; the very theology on which this view was based and which it served was a contradiction of early Christian practice and conviction. Moreover, very different theologies were to be constructed long after the Pastoral Epistles and included in the canon of the New Testament. The theology of the Pastorals takes its place among the many, very diverse theologies of the New Testament, although it claims more systematically than many of the others to be the only true one.

A similar evolution is observable in the theologies and practices of the Christian worship services. The earliest Christian community in Jerusalem seems to have baptized and held more or less regular assemblies, one of which was a meal. That community still, quite naturally, took part also in the cult of the Temple; the private assemblies that they held among themselves were thus visibly distinct from the cult. A difficulty was bound to arise when the question was posed as to which of these was, in fact, more important. Naturally enough, the first to pose it were those who stood nearest to those who were not allowed to participate in the cult and yet were part of a Christian community that did: that is, the Hellenists of the Jerusalem community. Inevitably, the objection to the practice assumed the absoluteness of a principle: the center of a Christian's life was the Christian assembly and not the cult. The Christian was to be able to turn personally to God and to find him in every corner of the earth, and not just in the Temple of Jerusalem. God was everywhere, and Jesus had taught the Christians to reach God, not through external actions and ritual, but rather through the conversion of their hearts. The conservative, Judaizing Christians fought against the innovating Gentile converts, as is seen from the epistles of Paul. There seemed to be no way of deciding the conflict, until it was settled by history: the Temple of Jerusalem was destroyed by the Romans and the first community dispersed.

There was never any question in this whole controversy of considering the Christian services a cult. They were lay services without priests, altars, sacrifices, special vestments, or even a set order. Everyone agreed on this.[74] The only question was whether Christians should attend the cult as well. History decided this negatively. But in the controversy, the question of the nature and importance of the Christian services had been posed and became a theme of theological reflection. The first attempts were made to connect the services somehow with other religious convictions. Very original and independent theologies were devised, as can be seen in the contradictory traditions of the "words of institution" and in Paul's speculative departures from the received teaching.[75] Certain cultic terms, as well as analogies, from Judaism and the Hellenistic mystery religions were used as an aid to articulation, but there is no reason to believe that the fundamental distinction between the Christian services and the cult had been blurred. One finds even in the apologists of the next century unambiguous denials that the Christians had founded a new cult.

But, as the various spontaneous functions within the community began to harden into offices, the first step was taken toward turning the services into cult: [76] one man was appointed leader of the services. When, where, and how this happened, or what his functions were, is impossible to say. But by the time of the Pastoral Epistles, there was, at least in that one community from which those epistles originated, the beginnings of a hierarchy that regulated order and worship. But the conviction that the Christian services were essentially different from the cult was too deep to disappear easily, and this aspect of the evolution of Early Catholicism reaches into the next centuries.

I need not add the example of the evolution of Christian asceticism [77] to make clear how different Early Catholicism was from the Christianities that had preceded it. As all new movements, it had arisen to meet a new situation, new needs, and new problems. If it proposed solutions and constructed theologies that were irreconcilable with earlier ones, it was not the first to do so. In Early Catholicism, we meet just another example of a process that has characterized Christianity from its inception. Such radical change cannot therefore be condemned as such. The theological result of any such inevitable revolution has undeniable functional worth and must be respected for it. On the other hand, the contradictions between these valuable theologies cannot be denied, nor the problems ignored which are raised by the fact of those contradictions.

ATTITUDES TOWARD THE STATE

One of the most striking contradictions in the New Testament is that between the attitudes of Paul and the writer of the Apocalypse toward the state. In Romans 13:1–7,[78] we see that Paul is speaking of the actual Roman state because he refers in verses 6 and 7 to the taxes which the Christians pay to it. This state, he says, comes from God. But Paul is also speaking of every state at every time, because, in verse 1, he says that there is no authority which does not come from God. Every state per se is divinely ordered and part of God's authority, an expression of *his* ordinance for the world. To go against this state or any state is to rebel against God himself. There is no way to circumvent the clear meaning of this passage, naïve as it must appear to us. Indeed Paul's attitude toward the courts here is very different from that of I Corinthians, 6:1–11.[79]

Infinitely more important is the absolute contradiction between Romans 13:1–7, and the Apocalypse which insists continuously and with great vehemence that the Roman state and all its works is the greatest enemy of God and his community.

The change in theology is, of course, a reflection of the changed situation. In Paul's time, the state was hesitating as to what stance it should assume toward the new communities. By the time the Apocalypse was written, the state had become their ruthless persecutor.

Of course, these circumstances do not in any way resolve the contradiction. Paul establishes as a principle that *all* authority, *all* government *as such* is from God. Nor, obviously, can it be a question here merely of different aspects of the state. Paul and the writer of the Apocalypse are speaking absolutely.

Significantly, this text in Romans was used by the German churchmen who were for the Nazi regime before and during World War II; and the Apocalypse was used by those who were against it.

Contemporary Contradictions

I have already discussed the discovery of the existence of many different parties within early Christianity. Of course, these parties need not have succeeded each other; many were contemporary. I have already noted many contemporary contradictions: for instance, the opposing judgments on the possibility of a second penance; the various solutions to the problem of Jesus' position after his death and before the Parousia, and to that of the state of dead Christians before the Parousia. Before I discuss more such contradictions, let us look briefly at the backgrounds and origins of the various groups that made up early Christianity and left their impressions on the New Testament. The diversity of these groups will indicate, to some extent, the possible variety of theologies.

GROUPS IN EARLY CHRISTIANITY

The following is a mere list, and an inadequate one at that. The different groups within early Christianity are classed only according to their origins.

First, there were the converts who had been Jews, but of these there were many types. They could be from Palestine or from either the western or eastern Hellenistic worlds. They could be of the strict or lax observance. They were or were not influenced by Hellenistic thought. There were many groups or even sects within the Judaism of the time. The converts could have belonged to or sympathized with the Sadducees, the Pharisees, the "Proto-Ebionite groups," the Essenes, the Zealots, the people, etc. Each of these categories had its own more or less fixed problems, solutions, sets of ideas, attitudes, hopes, and theologies.

Similarly, the Gentile converts could be from Palestine or from the Hellenistic world. Some of them could have already been converted to Judaism, which could either have been strictly observant or not. Some had not been Jewish converts but had been interested in Judaism. Some had gone so far as to begin attending synagogue services, but had not undergone circumcision. Others were not at all interested in Judaism, or were even ignorant of or hostile to it. Some of these Gentile converts could have once joined or been influenced by any of the many state, mystery, or private religions that were current then. Some may have been interested in one or more of the various popular philosophies that were attracting attention here and there. Others may have had puritan, libertarian, spiritualist or orgiastic tendencies. Some may possibly have had proto-gnostic or even gnostic thoughts.

Whether the Christian *communities* were homogeneous or not could have had a bearing on the evolution of their theologies.

Add to all these categories the differences of social class that were so grave at the time and so dangerous for the Christian sense of community; add the differences of multiple local and regional influences, irresistible when the tiny Christian communities were spread over the whole of the known earth: then the variety of the New Testament becomes not only natural, but inevitable.

CONTRADICTIONS BETWEEN AND WITHIN SCHOOLS,
FORMS, AND INDIVIDUAL THEOLOGIES

The most obvious school in the New Testament is formed by the three Synoptic Gospels on which so much scholarly research has been expended over the last centuries. The results of source- and form-criticism are well-known: Mark was written first and was used by both Matthew and Luke. They expanded the outline of Jesus' life, that Mark had created, by inserting new material which came mainly from one other source, called Q, and also from other individual sources, labeled collectively M, for Matthew, and L, for Luke. But Mark, Q, and the other sources are not themselves homogeneous; they were constructed of many different, isolated stories and sayings which had gone through a long process of formation. Many "primitive" peoples, including the Palestinian classes in which these stories were told, construct their folk literature according to very definite rules; the stories assume special *forms,* which can be recognized and studied. These formed stories can then be used in very definite ways. I have shown, in the example of the parable of the Pharisee and the Publican, how a definite form is imbedded by an introductory verse into the larger context and is reinterpreted by a concluding sentence or clause. There are, of course, other forms and other uses made of them.

The individual formed units are often not homogeneous in themselves. Certain sayings of Jesus, for instance, were handed down without being imbedded in a story, which would provide context and thus help clarify the phrase. So contexts were sometimes provided later, either by creating a story for the saying or by attaching the saying to an already existing story or saying.

There are thus many levels in the gospels: first, the elements of the various formed units; then those units themselves, which are *used,* added to, subtracted from, elaborated, changed, misunderstood etc., etc. The first connections between stories are made, sometimes running them into each other, or mixing them together. Then the first short collections of stories or sayings are made. Next, a long one, such as Q, the form of which changes from place to place and time to time, as new stories are added, or old ones are dropped or changed. Then the first gospel is written by artificially constructing a story- or plot-framework into which the various independent forms are introduced. Other writers then compose other gospels by using that general, invented framework and inserting other materials from further sources into it. Sometimes those finished gospels or parts of them were revised by later redactors, or else handed down in different versions with more or less serious variations.

Clearly, at any one of these points of discontinuity, differences and contradictions can arise, and, in fact, do. Luke, or a writer before him, misinterpreted the parable of the Pharisee and the Publican; Matthew and Luke attempted to change the point of Mark 2:27.[80]

In Matthew 5:22, the word for judge is mistakenly thought to refer to the Sanhedrin. Matthew 28:2 f. has been inserted into the story of the women at Jesus' grave to increase the importance of the witnesses. But it contradicts the whole representation of Jesus emerging from an open grave. The point of Luke 2:11, that the childhood stories of Jesus are really about the Messiah, contradicts his larger view that Jesus received his designation as Messiah at his baptism.[81] Large, irreconcilable thought complexes are found throughout all three gospels: for instance, Jesus' scheme of the coming of God's kingdom cannot be harmonized with those employed by later theologians to give Jesus a central place in that coming. In the one, God was simply to establish his kingdom himself and immediately; in the others, Jesus was to play a large variety of more or less essential roles. Also the time of the coming of the kingdom was postponed to the distant future. These thought complexes formed definite patterns and they cannot be reconciled with each other in some larger system.[82]

The writers of the gospels as wholes had their own theologies and tried, with varying degrees of success, to impose them on their material. Matthew belonged more to the Jewish world, emphasized the nearness of Jesus to the Law, and pictured Jesus as the bringer of the Messianic Torah. Luke, from the Hellenistic party, tried to find in Jesus some justification for the Gentile mission and put words into Jesus' mouth to provide one. They all interpreted the great events of Jesus' life, such as the Resurrection, in very different ways.

The Synoptic Gospels display irreducible contradictions both between each other and within themselves.

The Johannine school—the Gospel of John, the three epistles, and the Apocalypse or Revelation—forms, with the exception of the Apocalypse, a much more unified group. But we have already mentioned that John's theology of the already established and present kingdom jars with the remaining indications of the older faith in its *future* coming. A redactor may have tried many years later to harmonize the Gospel of John with the Synoptic Gospels, leaving traces of a different theology in the text of John. The Apocalypse, as is well known, is a confusing welter of different and conflicting apocalyptic themes and outlines.

I need hardly emphasize again the differences between the Johannine writings and the rest of the New Testament. The author of the gospel has constructed the most extreme Christology in the whole New Testament: as far as we know, he is the first, and in the New Testament certainly the only, writer to call Jesus God. And he projects this whole new theology into the earthly life of Jesus. I shall discuss later the different idea he must have had of God to be able to form such a theology. Let us now recall only that the French historian Ernest Renan felt compelled to reject his faith on the grounds of the incompatibility of the Johannine and the Synoptic Christologies. Cardinal Mercier once stated that Renan was the only man he had ever known who had left the faith for genuinely intellectual reasons.

I need not repeat what I have already said about the Pastoral Epistles, the third major school; nor need I discuss in any detail the miscellaneous letters of the New Testament. What I have said before about other individual writers applies equally well to the writers of these letters. Letters, such as Hebrews and James, are the last survivors of what must have been extensive schools of writing representative of very distinct groups. They display an independence and even an ignorance of the other writings of the New Testament. Of course, these letters are neither completely homogeneous nor consistent. The point of II Peter 3:9, that God's patience is intended to give the godless time to repent, contradicts one of his main themes: that the godless are destined to ruin.[83]

Paul falls into many direct contradictions in his writings, and the impossibility of turning his thought into some consistent system has often been remarked. Paul sometimes even notices himself that he has been carried away by his argument and hastens to correct himself by qualifying his former statement,[84] or by contradicting it.[85] Sometimes Paul seems simply to lose track.[86] Sometimes the contradiction arises from his desire to make a polemical point; as when he argues (Galatians 3:19) against the advocates of the Law, that the Law was given to man through the mediation of angels and not directly from God, as is his usual view (Romans 7:12, 14).[87] These two positions, I should add, marked two very distinct attitudes toward the Law and were considered contradictory.

Paul can also contradict himself on important theological points. In Romans 5:12 ff., he uses the theme that the human situation came from the fall of Adam into sin. But in I Corinthians 15:24 and 44–49, he holds the position that this situation arose simply from the lowness of Adam's human nature as such, without the event of the fall.[88] There is, of course, an essential difference between these two positions.

Paul also contradicts at times his deepest thoughts, the most profound insights of his entire theology. One of Paul's great themes is that the Jewish Law, with its regulations and demand for cultic purity, brought sin into the world. The Christians have been freed by Christ from the Law and need no longer live under it. However, in Romans 6:19, Paul characterizes the evil world before Christ as being "without the Law" and "impure"![89] He has spoken against himself.

Similarly, Paul usually insists that salvation is a pure, unearned gift from God. However, he contradicts this view several times by returning to Jewish doctrines of good works that *earn* salvation, notably in I Corinthians 4:5. These two views cannot be synthesized.[90]

I will discuss later the disunity of the so-called "credal formulas" in the New Testament. I must now broach the large problem of the contradictions in and between the various Christologies of the New Testament.

NEW TESTAMENT CHRISTOLOGIES

The field of New Testament Christology is vast, complicated, and crucially important for the Christian religion.[91] Even more perhaps than the other questions discussed, it is marked by deep tensions, unresolved problems, and contradictory solutions. These are so obvious that they can be discovered without any special training, and are fast becoming a problem for all thinking Christians. The following question appeared in *Question Box,* the syndicated column of Monsignor J. D. Conway:

Q. Can you answer this one for me? Easter Sunday con-gregations had to listen to the new Gospel text, the new and watered down version, which says of the Resurrection: "He has been raised . . ." "Has been" is a passive verb that refers back to the subject "Raised by whom?"

The old version always read, "He has risen," or "He has risen even as he said . . ." (Matt.)

Don't tell me he was raised by God the Father, for Christ Himself said, "Destroy this temple, and in three days I will raise it up." (John 2, 19.) His personal raising is proof of His divine mission and the most important mir-acle of our Holy Faith.

Please give me one good reason for this new weak-ened text.

A. One good reason is that the new reading is a more exact translation of the original Greek text—the text in-spired by the Holy Spirit. Matthew, Mark and Luke—all three—use the same verb in exactly the same form to report the words of the angel (angels) announcing at the tomb the resurrection of our Savior. My memory of Greek is badly faded, and the stem of this verb is irregular, but the ending can't be anything but a passive aorist. The Acts of the Apostles has the same verb in the active aorist in 3, 15: St. Peter is preaching and reminding his hearers that Jesus, whom they had killed, "God raised up."

Peter uses the same verb (according to some Greek texts) when he told the lame beggar at the temple gate: "arise and walk." (Acts 3, 6.)

Surely you would not accuse St. Peter of watering down his statements regarding Jesus' resurrection, but he distinctly states three times in his first two sermons that God raised Jesus from the dead. (Acts 2, 24; 2, 32; 3, 15.)

Monsignor Conway then goes on to solve this problem ac-cording to later Christian theology: Jesus is, of course, man *and* God, and, as God, he raised his human nature. His questioner might, in all innocence, object that the text fails to make the distinction and that when one refers to a person by name, one refers in fact to a person and not to one or more of his natures. In this way, one could discredit the offered solution even if one did not know that in the gospels the word "God" always referred to a certain *person* (later to be designated as "God *the Father*") and that these different ways of speaking of one event were symptomatic of profound uncertainties and contradictions in the interpretations made by the early Christians of the history that was the foundation of their religion.

In Judaism, redemptive history was wholly the work of God. That work was described in a large number of created outlines of history and of its final consummation. The last time, the coming of the kingdom, the great battle between the forces of good and evil, the Last Judgment; each of these representations was pictured in dramatic terms. They were large categories, one could say, with many internal variations. But none of these different outlines could be fully reduced to each other.

Throughout most of the New Testament, the problem of who Jesus was was the new problem of his own role in that history; and the means used to solve that problem, the descriptions or titles that were applied to Jesus, were those that had been used in one or other of the many different theocentric eschatological outlines that were current at the time to describe redemptive history and its end.

The Early Christians were thus trying to understand Jesus, his life, death, Resurrection, and their future hopes, all within frameworks and patterns that had been devised long before Jesus had even been born. They had also been devised for a very different purpose: to show that redemptive history was the work of God. There was no natural or necessary place for Jesus in these schemes. That a deep uncertainty should result as to the relative roles of God and Jesus and as to Jesus' place in redemptive history was inevitable. These schemes included, however, a number of figures in roles which offered some possibilities of providing a means of positioning Jesus within redemptive history and of placing him in some relation to God. Of course, those figures with their roles were only partially appropriate to Jesus, and thus only partially helpful in providing some means of understanding him.

Let us look at a few of these roles, each within its distinct, created eschatological framework, and see how they did or did not apply to Jesus and his history.

Of course, in his own lifetime and after, Jesus had been called rabbi and teacher. Both of these terms were felt to be inadequate. Though he did have a school of followers, like the rabbis, his teaching and his manner were hardly identical to theirs. The term "teacher" admitted of more expansion,[92] but never gave enough satisfaction to come into general use.

The first great model used in Christology was that of the eschatological prophet. As prophecy began to die out in Israel, the idea arose that the next great prophet would be the last. He would prophesy the imminent coming of God's kingdom, which would arrive immediately after his mission had been accomplished. He would call the Jewish people to repentance so that they might enter that kingdom. In the Jewish apocalyptic writings, much speculation was devoted to this figure. He was thought of as *the* prophet who had been reborn successively in all the prophets of Israel. He was thought to be Elias, Henoch, Moses, or other prophets or even combinations of prophets. He was imagined as accomplishing a wide variety of tasks and figured in many stories.

In its simplest form, the figure of the eschatological prophet was useful in explaining Jesus' life and work. Jesus also had prophesied the coming of the kingdom and had called Israel to repentance. Nevertheless, this title also was felt to be inadequate. A prophet is not resurrected. The kingdom did not come immediately. Moreover, a prophet merely indicates an event; he is not instrumental in bringing it about. Jesus, it was felt, should have an even more important role. That of the eschatological prophet finally fell in Christian theology to John the Baptist.

Jesus was proclaimed as the Messiah. The Jews pictured the Messiah in a great number of different ways. In the Old

Testament, he was anyone selected by God, and thus "anointed," to perform a special task. These simple beginnings were elaborated in the Jewish apocalyptic literature. The Messiah was to be of the tribe of David. He was, in fact, to be himself another David. God would appoint him to establish his kingdom on earth, which he was almost always supposed to do by military means. There he would rule politically over the Jewish people and with them over the whole world. Sometimes this kingdom was thought of as the last, sometimes as preliminary to the one God himself would establish and rule alone.

Now this pattern had the advantage of giving Jesus a central and instrumental role, but it had the great disadvantages of being concerned with a kingdom that was earthly, military, political, nationalistic, and usually temporary.

Another, more arcane model was that of "the Son of Man." Its origins are appropriately dark. In Daniel 7:13, the Son of Man appears, arriving on the clouds to accept the authority of the kingdom from God after the four successive kingdoms of the world, represented by animal figures, have gone to their destruction. In Daniel, this figure would seem to be a symbol for the people of Israel. In the apocalyptic literature, however, he soon became an individual about whom multiple speculations clustered. Two large types were formed. In the one, as seen in the Book of Henoch, the Son of Man was created at the beginning of time and kept hidden until the end, when he would appear. He was definitely a preexistent heavenly being, but the main accent of this view lay still on his eschatological role. In the second type, the Son of Man, originally the *last* man, as it were, was identified with the *first*. Interest was clearly transferred from the last, the eschatological, elements, to the first, the origins.

Just what the early Christians first found in this model or how they wanted to use it is not clear. In any case, the Son of Man seems not to have been identified with Jesus immediately, but rather used to justify him: when the Son of Man comes, Jesus will be justified. But, as the coming of Jesus himself was much discussed, he was soon identified as the Son of Man, and what was originally predicated of that figure was now predicated of Jesus. The oldest statements, then, of Jesus as the Son of Man are all concerned with his future work. Only later was the title applied to Jesus in his activity on earth, still later to his suffering, and finally to his Resurrection. The title was most useful, however, when applied to someone with a mission more like that of the Son of Man in Daniel as used by the apocalyptic literature: to appear at the end of time to accept the kingdom. That was its one strong point and its limitation. It did not answer any of the many other questions about the role of Jesus in redemptive history.

The title "the Son of God" originally referred to a role also. The title as used in the Old Testament referred to any particularly close or faithful servant of God. However, this title was bound to be misunderstood by Hellenistic converts who interpreted such a title much more literally. Moreover, the title Hellenistically understood refers not so much to a role as to a nature; instead of to something active, it refers to something static. In fact, a great turning point had been reached in Christian theology, and such titles and expressions were to be given interpretations radically different from those which the earlier Christians had given them. For instance, to say that someone was "foreordained" to accomplish a certain task meant for the Jews that God had intended it from the beginning. For the Hellenistic converts, it implied that the *person* foreordained to fulfill the mission must have existed from the beginning. An intention had been turned into a being.

An interesting example of a title which is almost completely ontological, but preserves elements of *role,* is that of the Johannine "Logos." The Logos means not so much a word, as an expression; in this case, *the* expression of God. Through this expression, the world is created, which therefore is *formed* by this expression. The Logos, one might say, is the equation according to which the universe, in one unique act, is simultaneously created and rationally structured. The Logos is a thing, but it is also a role.

The fully ontological title was to be applied to Jesus when

he was called "God." I will discuss this later but now remark only how even the Logos title has itself a very different function and point from those of the earlier titles discussed.

The large schemes or patterns of exaltation, adoption, and the coming and return of a heavenly being were used in different ways in conjunction with these titles. For example, the appointment of Jesus to the office of Messiah was joined to the theme of his adoption. Very complex patterns could be created in this way. Often a title or scheme lost thereby its distinctive content. "Christ," which means "the Anointed" and refers to the Messiah, evolved into a mere second name for Jesus. But more than enough deep differences remained to make New Testament Christology as uneven and in fact as contradictory as it is.

I adumbrated the most important of those contradictions when I began to discuss New Testament Christology by mentioning the difference between the statements "Jesus was raised from the dead" and "He rose from the dead." At the beginnings of Christian theology, as I have constantly repeated, the sole active force was considered to be the person God. The earliest theologies imagine that history as being the unfolding of God's will. Jesus is the servant of that will; he obeys it; he is in fact *subordinate* to that will. Up till the Gospel of John, all New Testament Christology is frankly and insistently subordinationist. As time went on, Jesus was allowed to be instrumental up to a certain point; he was allowed a certain amount of initiative. He was given increasingly honorable positions. He was brought as near to God as possible. But he was always, in the end, essentially subordinate to God. When Paul says that Jesus is God's "image," he is trying to bring him as near as possible to God, and yet preserve a final distance, an ultimate subordination. The various titles already discussed clearly mark Jesus as subordinate to God: the Messiah is the servant of God, appointed by and responsible to him. The Son of Man *receives* the authority of the kingdom from God. The Son of God in the Jewish sense is merely a particularly faithful servant of God. Even the Hellenistic understanding of Son of God as some sort of divine being expressed a subordination in that that being was a *son* of God. The schemes we have discussed also show a subordination. If Jesus is exalted or adopted, he is clearly subordinate; and if he is a preexistent heavenly being, he is not God, but one of the *many* heavenly beings subordinate to God, albeit possibly the most important.

In those late, but pre-Johannine, texts where every effort is made to raise Jesus to the very highest possible position, great care is taken to preserve his subordination to God. Paul writes (I Corinthians 15:23–28) that everything has its rank. All is in an order. Jesus is at the head. Jesus will destroy all his enemies, the principalities and powers; but, at the end, he will *give back* his kingly power to "God and Father." Paul then quotes the Old Testament to the effect that Jesus will place all under his feet, will subordinate everything to himself. But, argues Paul, this of course does not include him who subordinated everything to Jesus. *God* is the one who has subordinated all under Jesus. *God* is the power. Paul then makes the subordination of Jesus to God absolutely clear: "When all has been subordinated to him [Jesus], then also he himself, the son, will be subordinated to him [God] who has subordinated all to him [Jesus], so that God will be all in all."

God is here clearly distinct from Jesus. Jesus is not God. In the order of all things, Jesus is at the head. But just as the order is subordinate to God, so is Jesus. Jesus is clearly *subordinate to God*.

Needless to say, there is not the slightest hint in this text that Paul is referring only to the human nature of Jesus. He is referring to Jesus as a person, to Jesus *entirely*. The person or individual Jesus in his entirety is subordinate to God. This is the common teaching of extra-Johannine, New Testament theology.

In the first two chapters of the Epistle to the Hebrews, the author is emphasizing the superiority of Jesus to the angels and every created being, even to the point of applying to him predicates which, in the Old Testament, were applied only to God.

But the author clearly calls Jesus "the son whom *God estab-lished* as heir of all things." *God* was the author of creation, even if through Jesus. Jesus sits *at the right hand* of God, in the position of highest honor, but not equality.[93]

For most people today, to say that Jesus preexisted his birth and was instrumental in the creation is almost equivalent to saying that he is God. But one must recall that for the people of antiquity there were many possible heavenly beings, each with his own rank. The usual view was that there was an almost infinite series of ranks of angels, reaching from those nearest to men all the way to those closest to God. The author of the Epistle to the Hebrews is claiming that Jesus is above these ranks of angels; he is closer to God. Of course, he is not him-self God.

Similarly, the author of the Epistle to the Colossians says of Jesus: "He is the image of God invisible, the first-born of all creatures, for in him were all things created . . . All was cre-ated by him and for him. He was before all things and all sub-sists in him." [94] But the reason is indicated in verse 19: "be-cause it pleased God . . ." The word "pleased" here is—as other words and expressions, such as "it had to be," "foreor-dained," etc.—a term of the ultimately theocentric theology that saw God as the principal actor in the redemptive history and Jesus as essentially subordinate to him.

Up to the Johannine literature, the Christology of the New Testament is therefore subordinationist.[95] I need hardly add that these theologies cannot be transformed into nonsubor-dinationist ones by claiming that they are only referring to Jesus' *human nature* and not his divine nature, as is the Johan-nine literature. These theologies know of no such distinction and cannot be supposed to employ it. They are referring to Jesus as a *person,* to him in his normal or ultimate unity. No later orthodox theologian has ever claimed that there were two persons or individuals in Christ. There is no way that the sub-ordinationism of these theologies can be "counterbalanced" or "compensated for." To add to them a whole new theology of

Jesus as God would be to contradict one of the main points they make: however near Jesus is to God, he is not God himself.

When the Gospel of John claims, then, that Jesus is "God," a radically new theology is introduced: ". . . and the word was God" (John 1:1). The other claims made for the Word in this passage are very like some that were elsewhere made for Jesus: he was from the beginning with God; through him all things were made; he spoke through the prophets, etc. But the claim that the Word or Jesus *is God* is something quite new. Similarly, in John 20:28, when Thomas confesses "My Lord and my God," the old liturgical creed "Jesus is Lord" has been expanded to express a very new theology.

This Christology clearly contradicts the others discussed: in it, Jesus is not subordinate to God, he is equal to him. Just *how* John conceives of this equality is debated. However, no reasonable interpretation can be given of it which does not contradict the subordinationist Christologies of the other New Testament writers. His idea of God must also be somehow different.

Thus on the two most fundamental questions of Christian theology—who is God? and who is Jesus?—irreconcilable differences are observable in the New Testament. Disunity, not unity, is the characteristic mark of New Testament theology.

THE LOGICAL STATUS OF THE CONTRADICTIONS IN NEW TESTAMENT THEOLOGY

Attempts have been made to deny that logical contradictions exist in the New Testament. Differences may be admitted, it is held, but no direct contradictions. An example given is the conflict between the teaching of John's Gospel that Jesus is God and that of the other New Testament writers that Jesus is subordinate to God. These two views cannot be in contradiction, it is argued, because two different meanings of "God" are involved: for John, "God" is a level, a nature, a predicate that can be applied to different individuals; for the other New Tes-

tament writers, "God" refers to one unique person. Thus, these
are different, but not contradictory, theologies.[96]

First, this example holds, if at all, only for a very limited
number of the very many examples of contradiction in the New
Testament; it cannot apply to the contradiction between the
near and distant expectations of the Parousia (different "meanings" for the Parousia were constructed precisely to resolve the
contradiction of its delay). It cannot apply to the contradiction
between the allowance or refusal of a second penance, or between the view that all human government, including the
Roman state, is established by God and should thus be obeyed
religiously and the view that the Roman state is against God.
More examples could be given.

But can a direct contradiction be avoided even in the proposed case of John's Gospel vs. the other writers of the New
Testament? Let us put into logical terms the argument of those
who would deny a logical contradiction here. All would certainly admit that two theories or systems contradict each other if
one theory entails some statement "P," and the other entails
"not-P," its direct contradiction. But, in this case, those who
would deny that "Jesus $=$ God" contradicts "Jesus $\neq$ God" would
claim that "God" is ambiguous, having a different meaning in
each statement. This particular conflict follows rather the rule
that when the statement "P" is deducible from one theory, but
not from another, then they are irreducibly different, but not
contradictory. A theory is irreducible to another when one or
each has an essential element (not excluding a set of elements)
which has no counterpart in the other, and which cannot be de-
duced by ordinary logical procedures.

The most obvious objection to this argument is that, even
if the conflicting Christological views of these two theories are
not in direct contradiction, their views of "God" are. Here a direct contradiction emerges as a matter of fact, since both theories claim to be discussing the same reference, God, and are
applying contradictory descriptions to that reference: the one
describes "God" as a unique person; the other, as something
that can be predicated of at least two persons. One might wish

to argue that the word "God" is used in two senses in John's Gospel itself—in one, when applied to God ("the Father"), and in another, when applied to Jesus. A contradiction with the other writers of the New Testament would thus be avoided. But, in point of fact, this argument has merely established the same contradiction within John's Gospel itself rather than between it and the other theologies of the New Testament.

If two theories are referring to one and only one thing, then the attributes which each theory applies to that same thing can be tested for contradiction or noncontradiction. Thus we can say that if certain things follow about Christ and God from one view and their denial follows from the other, then a logical contradiction between the two theories exists. We may thus speak properly of logical contradictions in the New Testament.

However, the existence even of irreducible theories or theologies in the New Testament would be sufficient to disconfirm the theory of the unity of the New Testament, because the different theologies of the New Testament would be impossible to reduce to each other or to synthesize. The New Testament would still be a collection of different, and *irreducibly different,* theologies, and would therefore not be a theological unity.

Thus, the attempt to salvage the theory of the unity of the New Testament by admitting differences but not contradictions was doomed from the start. What has been admitted is enough to disconfirm the theory whose salvage is being attempted.

No matter what areas of unity are discoverable in the New Testament, they do not nullify the differences and contradictions that are to be found there. In any case, those contradictions pervade at least the two most important areas of Christian teaching: Christology and Theology.

Notes

[1] Kümmel, *op. cit.*, p. 16. See also pp. 14 ff.

[2] *Ibid.*, p. 17.

[3] *Ibid.*, p. 20.

[4] *Ibid.*, p. 25.

[5] Kümmel, *op. cit.*, p. 59. For the following see pp. 60, 62 f., 79 f., 88 f., 124.

[6] See Heinrich Schlier, *Der Brief an die Galater* (Meyer; 7) (Göttingen: Vandenhoeck & Ruprecht, 1962), pp. 105–117.

[7] Gal. 1:16 ff. See also Schlier, *op. cit.*, pp. 113 f.

[8] Acts 9:19 ff.

[9] Gal. 1:11–2:21.

[10] Acts 14:14.

[11] E.g., Dibelius, *op. cit.*, p. 205.

[12] *Ibid.*, pp. 184–200.

[13] Matt. 5:1.

[14] Luke 6:12, 17.

[15] Kümmel, *op. cit.*, p. 519. Also pp. 88, 161 f., 168. See also Ernst Käsemann, "Begründet der neutestamentliche Kanon die Einheit der Kirche?" in his *Exegetische Versuche und Besinnungen,* Vol. 1 (Göttingen: Vandenhoeck & Ruprecht, 1960), pp. 214–223, p. 217.

[16] Kümmel, *op. cit.*, pp. 24 f.

[17] All general surveys of New Testament theology are divided into sections which deal individually with the various theologies. See, for example, Rudolf Bultmann, *Theologie des Neuen Testaments,* Neue Theologische Grundrisse (Tübingen: J. C. B. Mohr [Paul Siebeck], 1961). He offers good bibliographies for the various schools, individual writers, and particular problems. See the pioneering work of Ernest F. Scott, *The Varieties of New Testament Religion* (New York: Charles Scribner's Sons, 1943); and the important article by Käsemann which we have mentioned: *op. cit.* (Begründet). The page numbers of the most relevant remarks in Kümmel, *op. cit.*, can be found under "Inspiration" in the Index, p. 592.

[18] For a survey, see James M. Robinson, *A New Quest of the Historical Jesus,* Studies in Biblical Theology; 25 (London: SCM Press, 1966). Günther Bornkamm, *Jesus of Nazareth* (New

York: Harper, 1960). Heinrich Kahlefeld, *Der Jünger, Eine Aus-legung der Rede Lk. 6, 20–49* (Frankfurt: Verlag Josef Knecht, 1962).

[19] See, for instance, Ernest Käsemann, "Das Problem des historischen Jesus" in his *op. cit.* (*Exegetische* 1), pp. 187–214, p. 211. Philipp Vielhauer, "Gottesreich und Menschensohn in der Verkündigung Jesu," now in his *Aufsätze zum Neuen Testament,* Theologische Bücherei, Neudrucke und Berichte aus dem 20. Jahrhundert, Neues Testament; 31 (Munich: Chr. Kaiser Verlag, 1965), pp. 55–91. Also his "Jesus und der Menschensohn, Zur Diskussion mit Heinz Eduard Tödt und Eduard Schweizer" in his *op. cit.* (*Aufsätze*), pp. 92–140. See J. M. Robinson, *op. cit.,* for method of research and bibliography.

[20] See C. H. Dodd, *The Parables of the Kingdom* (Digswell Place, Welwyn, Herts: James Nisbett, 1961), esp. pp. 1 ff. Joachim Jeremias, *Die Gleichnisse Jesu* (Göttingen: Vandenhoeck & Ruprecht, 1962). Heinrich Kahlefeld, *Gleichnisse und Lehrstücke im Evangelium* (Frankfurt: Josef Knecht, 1963). Two volumes.

[21] Jeremias, *op. cit.,* Section II.

[22] See especially Kahlefeld, *op. cit.* (*Gleichnisse*), Vol. 2, pp. 55–64.

[23] See Kahlefeld, *op. cit.* (*Gleichnisse*), Vol. 1, pp. 28–38. Dodd, *op. cit.,* pp. 145 ff.

[24] See Kahlefeld, *op. cit.* (*Gleichnisse*), Vol. 1, pp. 35 ff.

[25] See Käsemann, *op. cit.* (Problem), p. 207 and *op. cit.* (Begründet), p. 219.

[26] Käsemann, *op. cit.* (Begründet), p. 219.

[27] Matt. 19:6; Luke 17:18.

[28] Matt. 19:9.

[29] See Matt. 10:5 f., 23.

[30] Matt. 28:19 f.; see also Luke 24:47.

[31] Kümmel, *op. cit.,* pp. 59 ff. See also pp. 32 f., 256.

[32] See James M. Johnson, *Letter from Rome,* "Behind the theological ferment," in NCR, August 11, 1965:

" 'I really don't think there's any doubt about it now,' the scripture scholar remarked . . .

" 'From the scriptural evidence, Christ expected the end of the world, *the parousia,* in the lifetime of His Apostles. He thought He would return to them before their deaths. He did not know that the *parousia* would not occur for at least 2,000 years after His crucifixion and death.'

"Some Protestant Biblical scholars had reached the same conclusion even years before. But while they were free to state their opinions publicly, the Catholic scholar had to operate under the close watch of the Pontifical Biblical commission . . .

"Catholic Biblical scholars soon learned what they could and could not say . . .

"As a result, Catholic Biblical scholarship generally lagged behind Protestant work . . .

"The theologian must depend to some extent on the labors of the biblical scholar. Weakness in biblical research, therefore, produced a corresponding weakness, sometimes in the very premises, in theology.

"The Bible scholar interviewed in Rome was approached one day by a leading theologian at the Gregorian university in Rome. The theologian wanted some information on recent biblical research into the New Testament. When informed of Christ and the *parousia,* he demanded:

" 'Now what am I supposed to make of that?'

" 'That's your problem,' responded the biblical scholar. 'You're the theologian. I can only give you opinions based on research. It's up to you to make something systematic out of them.'

"The theologian, reported the biblical scholar, went away muttering to himself."

Needless to say, it is about time that systematic theologians stopped walking away.

[33] See, as just one example, Rom. 13:11, and the various commentaries on the text.

[34] See I Cor. 7:26.

[35] See Phil. 2:8.

[36] See, for instance, Rom. 13:11, which expresses a pure eschatology very different from the diluted form found in most of the rest of the letter.

[37] See the commentaries on the text, esp. Martin Dibelius, *An die Thessalonicher I, II, An die Philliper,* HNT; 11 (Tübingen: J. C. B. Mohr [Paul Siebeck] , 1937).

[38] See Otto Kuss, "Enthusiasmus and Realismus bei Paulus" in his *Auslegung und Verkündigung,* Vol. 1, *Aufsätze zur Exegese des Neuen Testamentes* (Regensburg: Verlag Friedrich Pustet, 1963), pp. 261–270, esp. pp. 269 f.

[39] II Thess. 2:2.

[40] II Thess. 2:17. See Dibelius, *op. cit. (Thessalonicher),* on this text.

[41] Ernst Käsemann, "Eine Apologie der urchristlichen Eschatologie" in his *op. cit. (Exegetische* 1), pp. 135–157.

⁴² Many further examples could be given: e.g., see Ferdinand Hahn, *Christologische Hoheitstitel, Ihre Geschichte im frühen Christentum* (FRLANT; 83) (Göttingen: Vandenhoeck & Ruprecht, 1963), pp. 340 ff. and esp. pp. 342 f., on Mark 1:10 f.

⁴³ See Otto Kuss, *Der Römerbrief* (Regensburg: Verlag Friedrich Pustet, 1957, 1959), pp. 396–430.

⁴⁴ See Jeremias, *op. cit.*, pp. 45–60. Hahn, *op. cit.*, pp. 98 ff.

⁴⁵ This is called the problem of the Indicative and the Imperative. See, e.g. Kuss, *op. cit.* (*Römer*), pp. 396–432.

⁴⁶ Heb. 6:4 ff. and I John 1:7, 9. See Bultmann, *op. cit.* (*Theologie*), pp. 105 f., 122.

⁴⁷ Bultmann, *op. cit.* (*Theologie*), pp. 132 ff.

⁴⁸ See Hahn, *op. cit.*, pp. 184 f. on Acts 3:20. See also pp. 41 f., 107. Bultmann, *op. cit.* (*Theologie*), p. 84.

⁴⁹ Bultmann, *op. cit.* (*Theologie*), pp. 254 f. on Rom. 1:4.

⁵⁰ Hahn, *op. cit.*, pp. 252, 254 f., 257 f.

⁵¹ This is behind the hymn in Phil. 2:6–11.

⁵² Hahn, *op. cit.*, p. 258, n. 1. Bultmann, *op. cit.* (*Theologie*), pp. 133 f.

⁵³ Hahn, *op. cit.*, p. 107.

⁵⁴ See Bultmann, *op. cit.* (*Theologie*), pp. 155–166, who discusses many contradictions which we do not discuss here. Kuss, *op. cit.* (*Römer*), pp. 540–595. Also Ernst Käsemann, "Anliegen und Eigenart der paulinischen Abendmahlslehre" in his *op. cit.* (*Exegetische* 1), pp. 11–34, pp. 17 f.

⁵⁵ See Bultmann, *op. cit.* (*Theologie*), pp. 158 ff. Kuss, *op. cit.* (*Römer*), pp. 544 ff.

⁵⁶ See esp. I Cor. 15:53 f. See for this and the following points, Hans Lietzmann, *An die Korinther I · II*, notes by W. G. Kümmel, HNT; 9 (Tübingen: J. C. B. Mohr [Paul Siebeck], 1949), pp. 117–120.

⁵⁷ See Dibelius, *op. cit.* (*Thessalonicher*), on Phil. 1:26, essay. He points out that this view is a contradiction of I Cor. 13:12.

⁵⁸ See Lietzmann, *op. cit.*, on II Cor. 5:6 ff., and Dibelius, *op. cit.* (*Thessalonicher*), at Phil. 3:10 f.

⁵⁹ See already Newman, *op. cit.* (*Development*), pp. 9–29.

⁶⁰ James Barr, *The Semantics of Biblical Language* (London: Oxford University Press, 1961).

⁶¹ Ian T. Ramsey, *Christian Discourse, Some Logical Explorations* (London: Oxford University Press, 1965), p. 20. See also

Stephen Ullmann, *Semantics, An Introduction to the Science of Meaning* (Oxford: Basil Blackwell, 1964), pp. 252 f.

[62] There are great objections against the theory of the existence of a Jewish tradition of a suffering Messiah.

[63] See Bultmann, *op. cit.* (*Theologie*), pp. 69 ff., 81 f. Also Kuss, *op. cit.* (*Römer*), pp. 29 ff. Also Paul Billerbeck, *Kommentar zum Neuen Testament aus Talmud und Midrasch*, Vol. 3, *Die Briefe des Neuen Testaments und die Offenbarung Johannes* (Munich: C. H. Beck'sche Verlagsbuchhandlung, 1926), esp. pp. 31 ff.

[64] See, e.g. Bultmann, *op. cit.* (*Theologie*), p. 78.

[65] *Ibid.*, pp. 150 f.

[66] See, e.g. Hahn, *op. cit.*, pp. 335 f., on Mark 9:2–8.

[67] See, for instance, Dibelius, *op. cit.* (*Thessalonicher*), on I Thess. 2:12, 15 f.; and on Phil. 3:10 f. Also Lietzmann, *op. cit.*, on II Cor. 12:3 f.

[68] Matt. 18:22. See my chap. 4, p. 39.

[69] Matt. 18:15 ff.

[70] "Early Catholicism" is polemic, and "Western Christianity" excludes a similar evolution in the east. On the following, see Scott, *op. cit.*, chap. VIII. Ernst Käsemann, "Paulus und der Frühkatholizismus" in his *Exegetische Versuche und Besinnungen*, Vol. 2 (Göttingen: Vandenhoeck & Ruprecht, 1964), pp. 239–252, esp. p. 239, n. 1. Martin Dibelius, *Die Pastoralbriefe*, notes by H. Conzelmann, HNT; 13 (Tübingen: J. C. B. Mohr [Paul Siebeck], 1955). Heinrich Schlier, "Die Ordnung der Kirche nach den Pastoralbriefen" in his *Die Zeit der Kirche, Exegetische Aufsätze und Vorträge* (Freiburg: Herder, 1962), pp. 129–147. Luke-Acts, the Pastoral Epistles, and Hebrews are considered to contain the most prominent examples of Early Catholic views, though elements are found elsewhere as well.

[71] See Kuss, *op. cit.* (Enthusiasmus), pp. 260–270.

[72] See Ernst Käsemann, "Amt und Gemeinde im Neuen Testament" in his *op. cit.* (*Exegetische* 1), pp. 109–134. For qualifications, see Otto Kuss, "Kirchliches Amt und Freie Geistliche Vollmacht" in his *op. cit.* (*Auslegung*), pp. 271–280.

[73] I will show later how little these few points of agreement can be used to establish a case for a general, "contemporary" theological unity in the New Testament.

[74] Bultmann, *op. cit.* (*Theologie*), pp. 117 f., 124 f., 461.

[75] *Ibid.*, pp. 137–146, for baptism; and pp. 146–153, for the central meal. For Paul, see esp. Otto Kuss, "Zur vorpaulinischen Tauflehre im Neuen Testament" in his *op. cit.* (*Auslegung*),

pp. 98–120; "Zur paulinischen und nachpaulinischen Tauflehre im Neuen Testament," *ibid.*, pp. 121–150; and his "Zur Frage einer vorpaulinischen Todestaufe," *ibid.*, pp. 162–182.

[76] Bultmann, *op. cit. (Theologie)*, pp. 125 f. Hans Frhr. von Campenhausen, "Die Anfänge des Priesterbegriffs in der alten Kirche" in his *Tradition und Leben, Kräfte der Kirchengeschichte, Aufsätze und Vorträge* (Tübingen: J. C. B. Mohr [Paul Siebeck], 1960), pp. 272–289.

[77] See Hans Frhr. von Campenhausen, "Die Askese im Urchristentum" in his *op. cit. (Tradition)*, pp. 114–156.

[78] See esp. Otto Kuss, "Paulus über die Staatliche Gewalt" in his *op. cit. (Auslegung)*, pp. 246–259.

[79] See C. H. Dodd, "The Mind of Paul: II" in his *New Testament Studies* (Manchester: Manchester University Press, 1954), pp. 83–128, p. 114.

[80] See Käsemann, *op. cit.* (Begründet), pp. 214–221.

[81] Hahn, *op. cit.*, pp. 271 f.

[82] See, e.g., Vielhauer, *op. cit.* (Jesus), p. 148.

[83] Käsemann, *op. cit.* (Apologie), pp. 156 f.

[84] E.g., I Thess. 1:6 ff. See Dibelius, *op. cit. (Thessalonicher)*, on these verses. Also II Cor. 1:23 f. Lietzmann, *op. cit.*, on these.

[85] See Kuss, *op. cit. (Römer)*, p. 209.

[86] In Rom. 15:20, he contradicts Rom. 1:13 ff. See Hans Lietzmann, *Einführung in die Textgeschichte der Paulusbriefe An die Römer*, HNT; 3 (Tübingen: J. C. B. Mohr [Paul Siebeck], 1919), on Rom. 15:20.

[87] See Bultmann, *op. cit. (Theologie)*, p. 178.

[88] *Ibid.*, p. 177.

[89] See Kuss, *op. cit. (Römer)*, pp. 391 f.

[90] Ernst Käsemann, "Eine paulinische Variation des 'amor fati' " in his *op. cit. (Exegetische 2)*, pp. 223–239, pp. 226 ff. and esp. p. 231. Also Rudolf Bultmann, "Karl Barth, 'Die Auferstehung der Toten' " in his *Glauben und Verstehen*, Vol. 1 (Tübingen: J. C. B. Mohr [Paul Siebeck], 1961), pp. 38–64, pp. 60 f., 64.

[91] Oscar Cullmann, *The Christology of the New Testament* (Philadelphia: Westminster Press, 1959). H. E. Tödt, *The Son of Man in the Synoptic Tradition* (Philadelphia: Westminster Press, 1965).

[92] Hahn, *op. cit.*, pp. 77–81.

[93] Heb. 1:2 f.

[94] Col. 1:15 ff.

[95] For another example, see Hahn, *op. cit.*, pp. 326 f. on

Mark 11:27. The only possible reference to Jesus as God outside the Johannine Christology is in the Hellenistic theology of II Pet. 1:1; but such an interpretation of the verse is very uncertain.

96 For the principle involved, see Ogden-Richards, *op. cit.*, pp. 111, 123, 130 ff.

II
ATTEMPTED
SOLUTIONS

*"No one
has power over
the issues
of his principles;
we cannot
manage our argument,
and have
as much of it
as we please and
no more."*

JOHN HENRY NEWMAN

5
The Search
for a
Unifying Creed
in the
New Testament

The analysis of the New Testament into ever smaller units naturally awakened an interest in the broader, unifying elements of the New Testament. As is well known, the New Testament writers used a number of older forms and schemes. Once these were recognized, several passages that had baffled scholars were seen to follow definite patterns. A case in point was the discovery that Paul's argument in the first chapters of Romans followed an outline employed by Jewish missionaries working among the Hellenistic Gentiles. Nor were Jewish frameworks the only ones used; the form of the stoic diatribe as well as that of gnostic sermons have also left traces in the New Testament. Similarly, fragments of different catechisms were found there; recurring phrases and sequences of material indicated outlines that could have been used to instruct converts or encourage, exhort, or sermonize the Christians themselves. The liturgy was also seen to have given form to certain passages. The gospels, we have already noticed, were very extended attempts to unify various strands of tradition.

But naturally, no one has ever dreamed of claiming that these elements could have possibly provided a framework for *all* of the different theologies of the New Testament, much less that they could in any way resolve the many contradictions that appear there. Each one provides a very loose framework within its own limited area. The various forms can be at odds with the different propositions which they attempt to unify. There can also, of course, be differences between the various units that have been inserted into the same framework. Furthermore, there is clearly not *one* catechism, one liturgy, one ethical perspective, any more than there is only one gospel. Just as the different theologies expressed by the gospels as wholes can be at odds, so can the various theologies expressed by these other different forms. Each individual theologian might equally well *use* those outlines and the material they unify in very different ways. What can be said then of the theological disunity of the gospels can be said of any one of these forms. These frameworks do not, therefore, unify theologies; and, accordingly no attempt has been made to claim that they do.

Such a claim has been made, however, for another literary form in the New Testament: a form which can be found in such passages as, for example, I Corinthians 15:3–5; Romans 1:3–4, and, it is claimed, the general outline of the speeches in Acts. These are stereotyped sentences or phrases, which are usually introduced by some phrase such as "we proclaim that," or "we believe that." They usually contain statements about important objects of belief and were very probably used in situations where some sort of confession of faith was needed, such as at baptism, before judges, or in preaching. The conclusion has been drawn that they form some sort of creeds. Great caution, however, is exercised in using the word "creed" for these formulas, because it so easily evokes circumstances that first developed many decades and even centuries after the appearance of these forms. We may have, in the New Testament, a creed-form—that is, a stereotyped formulation of a certain belief —and not necessarily have the "creed-thing": a formulation which possesses the kind of authority with which only a certain sort of hierarchy can invest it.[1] Therefore, expressions such as "formulas of faith" or "summaries of belief" would be less anachronistic.

Nevertheless, one may legitimately speculate whether these formulas or summaries could possibly provide some sort of theological unity for the New Testament and thereby solve from within the problem of its disunity.

These summaries could not of course provide some framework within which all the contradictory theologies of the New Testament could be united. The contradictions between the various inserted elements would remain.

The only possibility would be 1) to regard these formulas of faith or summaries of belief as essentially more authoritative than the other theological statements of the New Testament and 2) to prove that there was, in fact, only one such fundamental creed.

Two major attempts have been made to formulate a theory along these lines by Alfred Seeberg [2] and C. H. Dodd.[3] The latter's theory has enjoyed immense prestige. When one talks of the *kerygma* of the New Testament, one is almost always dependent on his theory.

Seeberg and Dodd proceeded in the same way and often used the same arguments. They began by trying to establish what could be called a dogma-opinion distinction within the New Testament. Seeberg argued that the stereotyped formulas of the New Testament were more authoritative than the usual theology. He did this mainly by a complicated interpretation of the word "word" in I Corinthians 15:2: "word," he argued, should be translated as "norm." [4] This interpretation has, with only one notable exception, been rejected by scholars. He then argued that what Paul said about the formula in I Corinthians 15:3 ff., applied to all formulas. This of course is not at all clear. He further argued that all formulas must in fact belong to one larger and complete formula; scholars have rejected his arguments. He attempted then to describe that formula by investigating the word *kerygma:* it should be a definite message independent of its bearer.

Dodd argued from a distinction between the terms *kerygma* and *didaché* which he characterized respectively as proclamation and teaching.[5] As Seeberg, he felt he could define the thing by defining the word. This is a mistake in method. However, no clear distinction can in fact be drawn in the New Testament between the two terms. Similarly, it cannot be demonstrated that there were two distinct things to which Dodd can apply the terms. Dodd himself must sometimes describe the one in the terms of the other.

Neither Seeberg nor Dodd was successful then at imposing their distinction on the New Testament. Both of them more or less assumed what they had to prove: that there was a unified theology in the New Testament. They did this by assuming that, when Paul and other writers speak of the *kerygma*, they must be speaking of the same very definite thing.

Even more apparent difficulties arose for their theories when they attempted to formulate the unifying creed they had posited. Seeberg felt he could include all the observable formulas in his one creed.[6] These, however, were not sufficient for him. He assumed that the fundamental creed must be complete; therefore, if a teaching was of primary importance, it must have been included in the creed. He argued that Paul followed the creed as exactly throughout his letters as he followed the formula in I Corinthians 15:3 ff. in that chapter. Thus Paul's writings could be used as an index to the creed.

Dodd used all of the above methods with two main differences.[7] First, he placed greater emphasis on the speeches of Acts. Second, he was much vaguer about the relationship of the creed he was reconstructing to the observable New Testament formulas. He never made it clear, as Seeberg did, whether he considered them to be literal parts of the creed.

The reason for Dodd's hesitation is clear: the most important objection against the theory of one unifying New Testament formula is that the New Testament formulas themselves do not constitute a theological unity. One New Testament formula contradicts another.[8] Moreover, there are contradictions even within the speeches of Acts: Stephen's speech cannot be reconciled with the others.[9]

The reconstructed creeds of Seeberg and Dodd are then just what one would expect them to be: merely artificial constructions, which attempt to include the irreconcilable. They are bundles of fragments from very different formulas and theologies.[10] Dodd tried to be vague about the relation of formulas to the creed, but clearly based his reconstruction on them. His vagueness merely accentuates the fact that at no level of New Testament theology, in no set of writings or in no form can one find theological unity. This unity certainly cannot be *assumed*. There are in fact no good grounds even to speculate that it might hover behind what one can observe in the New Testament. For those texts which should be closest to unity—the stereotyped formulas of faith—are themselves in theological contradiction.

The theory of Seeberg has been unanimously rejected by Bible scholars. Many theologians still hold to the theory of Dodd. His theory is, however, merely a less explicit version of Seeberg's. One must conclude that the existence of a unifying creed cannot be convincingly demonstrated in the New Testament. The existence of such a creed is in fact highly unlikely in view of the disunity even of the creedlike New Testament formulas.

These theories are, in fact, less interesting as New Testament scholarship than as attempts to save the dogmatic theory of unity in the face of Biblical evidence. Seeberg and Dodd are in fact proposing solutions. They would seek to preserve the theory of the unity of the New Testament by further restricting the field of that unity. Not total unity; not total unity minus textual unity; not total unity minus textual and historical unity; but also not quite total unity minus textual, historical and *all* theological unity. They would argue that the New Testament *does* possess theological unity, but only on *one level* of New Testament theology: the level of the community formulas of the faith. The method of saving the old theory by restricting its area of application has been used for another step in the gradual retreat from the original lines. Even that maneuver has, however, proved ineffective. The level of community formulas displays only theological disunity. The vague recourse to a creed behind these formulas is not convincing: one has no reason to suspect such a hidden creed.

Could there possibly be still one further step in retreat: to make the traditional claim, not for every formula of faith or summary of belief, but only for *one?* But the key demand of the old theory was for a certain *unity,* and one thing is of course not united, but rather identified, with itself. The problem of choosing one New Testament formula, teaching, writer, or level as *normative* is totally different from the problem of finding a New Testament unity.

The old theory has, therefore, made its last stand with this attempt to find a unity in and between the formulas in the New Testament. The solutions I will discuss next will somehow or other presuppose the theological disunity of the New Testament.

Notes

[1] Arnold Ehrhardt, "Christianity before the Apostles' Creed" in his *The Framework of the New Testament Stories* (Manchester: Manchester University Press, 1964), pp. 151–199, p. 153.

[2] Alfred Seeberg, *Der Katechismus der Unchristenheit* (Leipzig: A. Deichert'sche Verlagsbuchhandlung Nachf. [Georg Böhme], 1903).

[3] C. H. Dodd, *The Apostolic Preaching and Its Developments, Three Lectures, with an Appendix on Eschatology and History* (London: Hodder & Stoughton, 1936).

[4] Seeberg, *op. cit.,* pp. 49–58 for this and the following.

[5] Dodd, *op. cit.* (*Apostolic*), pp. 7 f.

[6] For this and the following, see Seeberg, *op. cit.,* pp. 58–85.

[7] For this and the following, see Dodd, *op. cit.* (*Apostolic*), pp. 8–35.

[8] See Hahn, *op. cit.,* p. 258, n. 1. Ehrhardt, *op. cit.,* pp. 154 f. Ulrich Wilckens, *Die Missionsreden der Apostelgeschichte, Form-und Traditionsgeschichtliche Untersuchungen,* Wissentschaftliche Monographien zum Alten and Neuen Testament; [5] (Neukirchen: Neukirchener Verlag, 1961), p. 192.

[9] Hans Conzelmann, *Die Apostelgeschichte,* HNT: 7

(Tübingen: J. C. B. Mohr [Paul Siebeck], 1963), p. 8. See also pp. 50 f.

[10] Werner Kramer, *Christos Kyrios Gottessohn, Untersuchungen zu Gebrauch und Bedeutung der christologischen Bezeichnungen bei Paulus und den vorpaulinischen Gemeinden*, Abhandlungen zur Theologie des Alten and des Neuen Testamentes; 44 (Zurich: Zwingli, Verlag, 1963), p. 33, n. 74.

6

Attempts
to Formulate a
Central Teaching
for the
New Testament

Obviously, the claim cannot be made that there is a central teaching in the New Testament, which provides a common basis or outline for the individual teachings. This supposed central teaching, basic body of doctrine, or general outline, is nowhere to be found. One meets contradictions at every step and on every question. Thus, attempts at unifying the New Testament theologies from within the New Testament itself were bound either to be arbitrary in simply choosing some New Testament element as authoritative, or were bound to be unhistorical by artificially reconstructing some "basic teaching" supposedly common to all the writers of the New Testament.

But lately, frank attempts have been made to fabricate *ad hoc* an outline, however abstract and generalized, into which all the New Testament theologies could be fitted. One might take the example: "God did something through Jesus." This, it is claimed, is the basic structure of all New Testament theologies. They differ only in their interpretations of the various elements, "God," "something," and "Jesus." Unity and variety are thus provided for.[1]

The most obvious objection to this outline—aside from the one that it cannot be found in the New Testament and that any Moslem could subscribe to it—is that it does not touch a number of problems that were of some importance to the early Christians: their life in the community, the Christian services, and, most important, the Parousia: what God *will do*. The artificiality of this attempt at providing unity is revealed when so many varied, contradictory, but, for some, crucial teachings must be subsumed under "something."

This sentence can even claim to summarize such differing theologies only because it is so abstract and nondescriptive. Words can be used both to refer to something and/or to describe it. The sentence in question is careful to use the words "God," "something," and "Jesus" only to refer and not to describe. Different contradictory theologies are, according to this theory, the different, contradictory descriptions which can be applied to the "things" to which the words refer; in this way, it is held, this unity of reference provides the solution for the disunity of description. But this is clearly no solution at all. The unity provided here is clearly not one between the various theologies. When pressed, the theory admits that there is no theological unity, and wishes rather to provide a point of unity *outside* of theology itself. I will discuss such attempts later. At this point, I need only say that this solution is not what it would claim to be: it does not provide a possibility of unity on the level of theology.

But the sentence not only refers to God, something, and Jesus; it places them in a certain ordered relationship to each other. This, one could claim, is the real point of the theory: that despite contradictions in the theological descriptions of God, something, and Jesus, all New Testament writers would agree that "God did something through Jesus."

But this ordering of the different elements, this outline, is itself descriptive. It is therefore a theology and contradicts, for example, a theology which would allow for a certain initiative on the part of Jesus. The pure theocentrism expressed by the proposed unifying sentence is only one among many theologies of redemptive history and of the relationship of the roles of God and Jesus in that history.

Moreover, this theology cannot remain unchanged as contradictory descriptions are applied to its various elements. The sense in which "did" and "through" are used will change according to the descriptions applied. There may, in fact, be languages which do not contain as conveniently ambiguous a word as "through." "Through Jesus" can mean "by him" (Jesus = cause, agent, though this contradicts the tenor of the sentence), "through him" (Jesus = Mediator), "on the occasion of his being there" (Jesus as, say, announcer of the coming kingdom), etc. The unity which this sentence provides depends ultimately on an ambiguous use of terms. It is therefore purely verbal and cannot supply a genuine theological unity.

As all attempts to provide even the most generalized formulation of "the New Testament teaching," this one fails by excluding some important elements of New Testament theology and by contradicting others. No unity is to be found in the New Testament on the level of theology.

Of course, the less general and abstract these attempted summarizing sentences are, the less effective they can be at unifying *all* of the New Testament theologies. For to propose "Through Jesus, God has given men salvation," with the accent on salvation, provides a sentence which has the advantage of being clearly un-Mohammedan. But the very specificity of this sentence sets it against more New Testament theologies than the more abstract one: for instance, "salvation" is, of course, the term of one very particular theology ("Through Jesus" is, naturally, capable of the ambiguity necessary for this sort of attempt). Moreover, this sentence presupposes that men *are* saved; the theology of salvation expressed contradicts, therefore, the view of the earliest Christians that they *would be* saved *when the kingdom came.* The very specificity of the point of this sentence eases the task of discovering which New Testament theologies it contradicts.

Even a unity based on a single point is bound to find its contradiction somewhere. For instance, even as generalized a proposition as that Jesus is the crucial decision point can be contradicted by texts which accord that position to the spirit (Mark 3:28 f.; Luke 12:10; and Matthew 12:32).[2] I need not discuss such attempted unifying propositions as: "God is the completely other." I have already shown what very different opinions about God are held in the New Testament.

Such attempts at solving the problem are, at their most effective, purely verbal. No theological position, let me repeat, is common to all writers and levels of tradition in the New Testament.

Notes

¹ Comp. Ian T. Ramsey, *Religious Language, An Empirical Placing of Theological Phrases* (New York: Macmillan, 1957), pp. 200 ff.
² In the text, I have presumed that "the Son of Man" is to be identified with Jesus in these passages. There are, however, good arguments against this presumption. In any case, if this identification should not be made, my point is still valid and even reinforced. For Jesus is still not considered in these passages to be the crucial decision point; and "the Son of Man" becomes even another alternative for that position.

7
Development

Can the disunity of New Testament theology be understood according to the theory of development? Or, in other words, are the various conflicting theologies of the New Testament really just stages in the process of some sort of development? The classic theory of development, that of Newman, attempted to explain the difference between the theology of his day and that of the earliest fathers as a development through the ages of the original "idea" of Christianity. But how was this development to be distinguished from a mere corruption? Newman gave seven tentative rules of thumb, prominent among which was logical consistency. The new stage of development was not supposed to contradict the previous stage. Development in theology was analogous to the gradual clarification of an originally vague idea, or to the drawing of logical conclusions from first principles. The end was already contained in the beginning. Newman considered development to be the gradually perfected realization of the original "idea." [1] Such a development had to occur, according to Newman, when the minds contemplating Christianity were not inspired.[2] Newman's theory is thus not so far removed from the older theory that there was a revelation of a body of truths, or an "idea," in the New Testament and that this body has been taught and safeguarded since then by the proper authorities. Newman saw a difficulty for this theory—namely, that certain differences seem to have appeared since the beginning—and solved this difficulty by his theory that these apparent differences were due to a development as described above.

I need not criticize this theory any more than to say that it cannot apply to the contradictions of the New Testament; for instance, to those caused by the delay of the Parousia. Here, a radically new situation had arisen which called forth theologies which contradicted older ones. Similarly, no one of the other different theological movements called forth by the changes in the situation of the early Christians could possibly be thought of as a development, either in itself or in relation to what preceded or followed it. Paul's contradicting his first theory about the fate of the Christian after death and then later returning to it and contradicting his second theory, cannot be considered a development. Furthermore, many contradictions in the New Testament are contemporary; there is no time for a development between them, even if a development could possibly produce a contradiction. Some New Testament theologies were simply forgotten; others, as seen in the example of the parables, were reinterpreted in radically different ways. Other, once living theologies or theological positions stiffened and were institutionalized, or became mere rote. None of these processes could be considered development; on the contrary, they contradict each other and several of Newman's proposed marks of a true development: for instance, chronic vigor, logical consistency, power of absorption.

Moreover, if the New Testament theologies were an example of development, one would be able to notice in them a certain common teaching or, at least, direction; they would at least tend toward, and not exclude, a certain synthesis. Contradictions cannot be synthesized.

The theory of development cannot solve the problem of the theological disunity of the New Testament simply because the very phenomenon to be explained disconfirms the theory which seeks to explain it; the theory fails the moment the existence of contradiction is established. But only by resolving this contradiction could the theory of development solve the problem of the theological disunity of the New Testament. The attempt is revealed as self-contradictory.

What then do various exegetes and theologians *mean* when they say that the theological disunity of the New Testament is "development." Some stick to their guns; such as Barnabas Lindars, who asserts: there is "a *logical sequence* in the development of dogmatic expression." [3]

Others, such as Otto Kuss, seek to minimize the differences: concluding that the spirit is nowhere considered a person in the New Testament, Kuss notes that one now considers it to be the Third Person of the Blessed Trinity and speaks of "recognizing this development then as still legitimate and willed by God, when perhaps many elements and motifs developed with particular energy, so that the total picture changed to a definite, if also for the most part very limited, degree." [4] But the change from a conception of "the spirit" as nonpersonal to one of "the spirit" as a third divine person is not to be minimized!

Most theologians and exegetes who desire to solve this problem with the theory of development simply label any change or contradiction a "development" and leave it at that. Dodd, noting clearly a contradiction between I Corinthians and Ephesians (which Dodd considers Pauline), writes: "It is clearly impossible at the same time to follow the two maxims . . . This radical contradiction has been taken as one reason for denying the Pauline authorship of this epistle. But it lies on the line of development which we have traced." [5] The whole new attitude and theology caused by the final realization of the delay of the Parousia is, according to Dodd, "a real development." [6]

"Development" has obviously become a meaningless label or, at best, has come to mean a contradiction which has somehow been mysteriously defused. Since all possible criteria for distinguishing between a development and a corruption have been ignored, "development" has become a blanket excuse for any possible change in the history of theology. No wonder that George Tyrrell was once moved to comment that all speak of "development" but avoid religiously any mention of "evolution." That Tyrrell was not exaggerating can be seen from many examples: for instance, Leonard A. Bushinsky comments on the many differences in the theologies of the Old Testament: "It is what we would call a development, not an evolution, in the strict sense of the word." [7]

A problem is obviously not solved by labeling it, and the genuine theory of development, in its only meaningful form, cannot solve the problem of the theological disunity of the New Testament.

No matter how sophisticated a theory of development one constructs, it could never fit the situation or process of New Testament theology. To continue, therefore, to apply the label "development" to the many contradictions in the New Testament is to evade the problem which they pose.

Notes

[1] For Newman's "Perfectionism," see, for example, Newman, *op. cit. (Letters)*, pp. 373 f., 496 f.

[2] Newman, *op. cit. (Development)*, p. 30.

[3] Barnabas Lindars, *New Testament Apologetic, The Doctrinal Significance of the Old Testament Quotations* (London: SCM Press, 1961), p. 29. Italics his.

[4] Kuss, *op. cit. (Römer)*, pp. 591 f.

[5] Dodd, *op. cit.* (Mind), p. 117.

[6] *Ibid.*, p. 113. See also pp. 127 f. See also Bultmann, *op. cit. (Theologie)*, pp. 464 ff., 469 f.

[7] Leonard A. Bushinsky, in a review of H. H. Rowley: *The Unity of the Bible*, in *The Catholic Biblical Quarterly*, Washington, 1956, p. 178.

8
Criteria

Another very different attempt to solve the problem of the theological disunity of the New Testament is that of establishing some criterion by which the different theologies can be judged. The greatest disadvantage of this method is that it depends on an arbitrary choice. No principle or argument arising from the texts themselves can be offered to support the choice of the criterion itself. One simply chooses to use one criterion rather than another.

Other difficulties arise. The application of the criterion to the different theologies of the New Testament can also be arbitrary. The New Testament theologies might not lend themselves to picking and choosing. Finally, the criterion itself may prove unworkable.

I will examine a few of the criteria which have been suggested in the recent history of theology. I will divide them roughly into criteria which are directions for value judgments; criteria based on a certain level of tradition or on a certain teacher in the New Testament; and criteria based on a certain teaching.

CRITERIA FOR VALUE JUDGMENTS

A paradigm of this sort of criterion is the one which Johann Philipp Gabler proposed in 1787: one should distinguish what in the New Testament was only of temporary value and what is of permanent worth.[1] This solution, let it be mentioned, arose to meet the problem felt by the first discoverers of the radical distinction between the faiths of the New Testament writers and our own. Many resisted these discoveries because they ran counter to the theory that Scripture should be understandable and useful for every man.[2]

Certainly, all the writings of the New Testament are very much bound to the time and situation in which they were composed. But several important objections could be made against using this insight to form a criterion. Firstly, there is no principle by which one can establish definitely that a certain teaching is permanent or only temporary: one must choose arbitrarily between the many possibilities at hand. Few would argue, for instance, on behalf of the sexual interpretation of Genesis— that Eve was seduced by the snake; [3] or on behalf of the view that man was created directly by God and that woman originated only later and as a poor copy.[4] But certain practices are revealed by historical scholarship which are more significant theologically, such as that the children of Christian parents were considered saved even before they were baptized; [5] or that the dead ancestors of Christians were baptized by proxy.[6] Also, baptism seems to have been reserved for adults. On what principle can these practices be rejected?

Moreover, certain differences may raise difficulties for certain people and not for others. Some black people have apparently rejected Christianity because Paul condoned slavery. The fact that he adopted this position cannot be wished away simply by saying that Christians no longer hold the same view today. Some principle is needed whereby Paul's position can be rejected.

Secondly, one can question the validity of the method of separating various elements of one theology and calling some temporary and others permanent. The "temporary elements" may be essential to the "permanent" ones. The original writer sometimes obviously conceived of them as building a whole: Jesus' "permanent" teaching is inseparable from his "temporary" expectation of the imminent coming of the kingdom. Paul's hope in the resurrection of the dead is not easily separable from his speculations on the nature of the resurrected body. Surely one changes each of these teachings essentially when one begins to separate their elements. Both teachings are rather to be considered more or less as wholes.

The same criticisms apply to H. J. Holtzmann's attempt to

divide the theological propositions of the New Testament into "the central and the peripheral." [7] Here again, the question of how each theological point should be classified must be answered more or less arbitrarily. Moreover, what may be central for a theology of the New Testament can be peripheral today: for example, the imminence of the coming of the kingdom. In the end, such a criterion merely allows one to accept those teachings of the New Testament which are identical with, or conform to, whatever one has already decided is "permanent" or "central." Such a criterion, just because it permits the arbitrary, is, in fact, no criterion at all.

A similar problem arises in regard to the canon: why should certain books belong to the New Testament and not others? Semler proposed the criterion of "their moral, commonly useful worth"; [8] "the inner conviction through truths"; [9] "the witness of the holy spirit," etc. F. C. Baur objected that "In one word, everything hereby becomes relative the moment one determines the concept of canonicity only according to the moral content of the writing." [10] Feelings such as "inner conviction" are notoriously problematical guides.

Obviously, some more definite criterion must be used if its application is not to be as arbitrary as its choice.

CRITERIA BASED ON A CERTAIN LEVEL OF TRADITION OR ON A CERTAIN TEACHER

This solution would take a writer or level of tradition in the New Testament and use him or it as a criterion. This has the advantage of giving one a consistent principle which can be applied. Everything that conforms to the teaching at this level or of this teacher is accepted and what contradicts it is rejected. Moreover, one is taking as one's standard a position or set of positions that are truly in the New Testament. One's choice is not completely arbitrary, because one is choosing everything in the teaching at that one level or of that one teacher; and the application is not at all arbitrary because one is accepting all that agrees with, and rejecting all that contradicts, the criterion.

J. G. Eichhorn proposed, in 1827, that the New Testament writings be divided between those that were written by eyewitnesses and those that were written by their followers. The writings of the eyewitnesses would be accorded a greater worth and would be the norms of the other writings.[11] Unfortunately, later scholarship established that no New Testament writers were eyewitnesses of Jesus' earthly life. The earliest writer in the New Testament is Paul. But this criterion could not have been effective in any case; no one writing or set of writings in the New Testament is absolutely free from contradiction.

Seeberg himself is ultimately trying to establish some positive and definite criterion for the varieties of New Testament theology: he tried to use the formulas in the New Testament as his final criterion.[12] To do this, he had to prove, of course, that these formulas were noncontradictory; that is, that his criterion was consistent. This, as we have seen, he could not do.

Bultmann and his early school have made a well-known attempt to use "the *kerygma*" as a criterion of the New Testament. Not the historical Jesus and what he taught is the object of our faith, but rather he as preached by the community, as the kerygmatic Christ. The interpretation which the *kerygma* makes of Jesus and redemptive history is the authoritative statement of the New Testament. Certainly it is true that the Christian believes one of many possible interpretations of Jesus, but the fatal objection to Bultmann's theory, just as to that of Seeberg, is that there was not just one *kerygma,* not just one New Testament community interpretation of Jesus and of the redemptive history. There are many. One still needs a criterion to choose among them.

Moreover, for Bultmann, Jesus and his teaching have become a mere "presupposition" of the *kerygma;* [13] such a position is so vulnerable that Käsemann had later only to state it for most scholars to consider it refuted.[14] This theory is interesting because it reduces the successive disunity of the New Testament by excluding one stage of New Testament history: the time and teaching of the earthly Jesus. But this theory must still face all the contemporary disunity in the New Testament and also all the successive disunity which arose after the time of Jesus.

By far the most popular choice as a criterion has, in fact, been Jesus himself. In 1783, Thomas Chubb isolated the message of Jesus from the rest of the New Testament: Jesus' message was not about the events of his life; therefore any speculations that have used these events as a point of departure— such as those about "the Redemption"—are mere private opinion. The message of Jesus is no private opinion of an evangelist or apostle; nor a conclusion drawn from one of these opinions. That Jesus was the Word, God, preexistent, creator of all things etc.; none of these points are in the message of Jesus itself and are therefore mere private opinion.[15] Chubb sees a definite dividing line between the teaching of Jesus and that of the other teachers in the New Testament and opts for that of Jesus as the only norm.

Of course, this choice in itself is arbitrary. No adequate arguments can be given why the teaching of Jesus is chosen as a criterion rather than some other. Chubb himself must have recourse to later interpretations when he supports his choice by saying that it is enough that the Christian believe that the word of God was in Jesus.

The main objections to such a choice would be 1) that one chooses Jesus, in fact, because one has already believed some later interpretation of his importance, and 2) that one cannot accept everything that Jesus taught: for instance, that the kingdom of God would come very soon; or that the kingdom and Jesus' message were reserved for the Jews. On these points, one is forced rather to follow the later New Testament writers against Jesus. The teaching of Jesus cannot be, therefore, an absolute criterion.

But most theologians who have tried to establish Jesus as a criterion have sought to emphasize the continuity of the later writers of the New Testament with him. A brief examination of two such attempts would be instructive.

E. F. Scott goes so far as to claim that all later New Testament theology is simply an unfolding of Jesus' original message: "Every theology has suggested some new interpretation, and the strange thing is that every interpretation is right. Jesus was thinking of all those aspects of the higher life with which his message has been identified . . . To understand the later history of Christianity we must allow for this comprehensive quality in Jesus's own teaching. It was not confined to some rudimentary idea . . . It was itself far larger and deeper than anything which has proceeded from it. The later teachers did not expand and enrich it but sought only to unfold some portion of what Jesus had given." [16] Such an extreme position cannot be maintained. We have seen how obviously the later New Testament writers could misunderstand and/or contradict Jesus. Scott is driven to special pleading to salvage his case: "The disciples felt rightly that they must put him at the centre if they would preserve the meaning of his message." [17] As long as one can resort to so pliable a phrase as "the meaning of his message," [18] a continuity can be established between Jesus and anyone! Scott retreats one more step: "But with Jesus the personality was everything." Thus all interpretations of who and what Jesus was can be considered continuous with him. And further, "What he gave was not a creed or a philosophy or an ethic but a new life, which had its source in himself." [19] Here Scott has abandoned the attempt to use Jesus' message as the source of all New Testament theology. He has added to it, or even substituted for it, quantities which are not to be found in Jesus' message itself and are much less subject to historical investigation: "personality" and "life." He has also left the realm of historical scholarship and entered that of speculative theology. This is not surprising, as the arbitrary choice of a criterion is necessarily based, not on observation, but on individual belief. However, the attempt to support the choice of a criterion within the New Testament by proving that the criterion chosen was in fact the historical norm of the New Testament is doomed to failure. The New Testament, as we have seen, did not have a norm; to set up, in spite of this fact, some part of the New Testament as a norm is not the act of a historical scholar, but of a willful believer.

The latest serious attempt to use Jesus as a criterion has been that of Joachim Jeremias. We will list, however briefly, some of Käsemann's [20] criticisms of his position. The question is not, Käsemann affirms, what role we ourselves would give to Jesus, but "rather what weight is given within the New Testament proclamation to the historical account of Jesus." [21] In the letters "astonishingly little" [22] material about the historical Jesus is to be found. What accounts there are of Jesus in the New Testament are all embedded in the later *kerygma*. If the New Testament writers had laid as much emphasis on the historical Jesus as Jeremias does, they would have certainly written more historical accounts.[23] Furthermore, Jeremias' knowledge of the historical Jesus rests on historical scholarship. He thus makes the object of his faith depend on the scholarly theories of the moment.[24] (Indeed, much of what was previously considered to be the teaching of Jesus has now been revealed as the theology of the later Christians. To construct all of theology on the teaching of Jesus would be much harder today than it was some years ago.) Moreover, for Jeremias, the later *kerygma* is simply an unfolding of the original revelation, which was exclusively in Jesus.[25] But this presupposes that the *kerygma* itself was uniform. Jeremias is in exactly the same predicament as Scott: by attempting to support his criterion from within the New Testament, he has forced himself to establish a continuity between Jesus and the later Christians, a continuity which ultimately demands a unity in New Testament theology. As Käsemann says: "Out of this results an exciting show"; [26] one we have unfortunately seen before.

No one, as far as I know, has ever attempted explicitly to establish Paul as a criterion. He is so much an individual and can so easily be contrasted to Jesus (and if one were to choose one New Testament teacher as normative, one could not very well justify preferring anyone to Jesus!). Nonetheless, Paul has enjoyed a notorious emphasis among certain theologians, who have even gone so far as to attempt to explain away some important teachings of his which conflict with their own "Pauline theologies." Karl Barth in his commentary on I Corinthians [27]

sought to mitigate Paul's old-fashioned emphasis on the historical facts of the death, burial and Resurrection of Jesus and on
the details of the drama of the end of time. All this was meant
exclusively theologically, argued Barth; the historical facts were
not important as such; only the theological interpretation mat-
tered. The apocalyptic drama was also employed only in order
to be theologically interpreted. Bultmann, in a famous criticism
of Barth's book,[28] affirmed that scientific exegesis had established that Paul did, in fact, intend to discuss quite literally the
facts of the death, burial, etc., of Jesus and the various episodes
of the final drama. But this intention of Paul's, Bultmann
agreed, must itself be theologically criticized. "It seems to me
now equally certain that Paul in 1 Cor. 15 speaks of such a
final history as that he, in truth, cannot, and does not wish to,
speak of it. In other words, one cannot manage with 1 Cor. 15
without a constant . . . criticism based on the subject
matter." [29] Bultmann is frank about the results of such a
method: "This means emphatically to interpret Paul critically;
this means, to understand him better than he understood
himself." [30]

Such efforts to reinterpret Paul indicate the nearly normative position he is accorded among certain exegetes and theologians. That such a reinterpretation is necessary, however, shows
once again that no level of tradition or individual teacher in the
New Testament can be used simply as a criterion. At every
level and with every teacher, one is forced to reject some
points, while accepting others. This conclusion leads to the
third type of attempted criterion: those based on a certain
teaching.

CRITERIA BASED ON A CERTAIN TEACHING

The advantage of this sort of criterion is that it enables
one to accept only those teachings which one desires to accept
and to take them from any level of tradition or from any
teacher. One point can be taken from Paul, another from
James, a third from the Apocalypse.

There are, of course, two very obvious objections which could be made to this procedure. Firstly, the choice of the criterion is simply arbitrary. Secondly, points are taken from their original contexts, a process which often basically transforms them. Almost any theology or antitheology can be constructed in this manner. The use of this criterion is finally no different from the medieval use of Scripture as a quarry for proof texts.

The efforts of Barth and Bultmann to reinterpret Paul are a clear example of the use of this sort of criterion: Paul is reinterpreted in such a way—or else his "real intention" is held to be such—that his teaching conforms as closely as possible to that of Barth and Bultmann. We will have more to say later about the method of positing a "real intention" behind—and often contrary to—what a writer actually states.

Similarly, Bultmann seeks to establish a criterion based on a certain teaching for the "development" of a hierarchy in the New Testament: "The development to be described in the following stands therefore under the decisive question whether and to what extent the growing ordinances were and remained appropriate to the essence of the ecclesia as an eschatological community constituted by the word of the proclamation." [31] By using as his criterion a definite, articulated position rather than, say, some earlier stage of the community, Bultmann has a solid working basis. This basis is safe from such possible objections as that, for instance, the earlier stage were not historically as he might have described it. On the other hand, one could object that his criterion cannot be found in all its purity in the New Testament and that Bultmann is imposing it from without onto the New Testament itself. But then, a degree of arbitrariness is inevitable in any use of a criterion.[32]

The very same criticisms apply to the attempt to establish the later tradition as a criterion: only those points of the New Testament theologies would be accepted which were incorporated into the later ecclesiastical tradition. A further, and even more important argument against this attempt is that that tradition itself claims to be *the* interpretation of *the* New Testament theology; one alters that tradition essentially when one claims for it the function of a criterion by which to pick and choose among the various New Testament theologies. It is contrary to the very theoretical basis of that tradition that it be used to *reject* some New Testament theologies. One has changed the tradition simply by desiring to use it as a criterion, because that new use is an attempt to solve a problem whose very existence disconfirms the theory on which the tradition is based. To change so completely a supposedly unchangeable tradition would raise an insurmountable problem of credibility.

Notes

[1] Kümmel, *op. cit.*, pp. 116 ff.

[2] *Ibid.*, p. 291. See also pp. 78 ff., 294, 302 f., 305, 386.

[3] II Cor. 11:3 and I Tim. 2:14. See Lietzmann, *op. cit.* (*Korinther*), p. 145. See also the notes of Kümmel on this interpretation.

[4] I Cor. 11:8a.

[5] I Cor. 7:14.

[6] I Cor. 15:29.

[7] Kümmel, *op. cit.*, p. 241. See also pp. 240 ff.

[8] *Ibid.*, p. 75.

[9] *Ibid.*, p. 76.

[10] *Ibid.*, p. 81.

[11] *Ibid.*, p. 104.

[12] Seeberg, *op. cit.*, p. III.

[13] Bultmann, *op. cit.* (*Theologie*), p. 2.

[14] Käsemann, *op. cit.* (Problem), p. 188.

[15] Kümmel, *op. cit.*, pp. 60 ff. See also pp. 18 ff., 368 f.

[16] Scott, *op. cit.*, p. 11. See also pp. 10–13, 15.

[17] *Ibid.*, p. 13.

[18] *Ibid.*

[19] *Ibid.*

[20] Ernst Käsemann, "Sackgassen im Streit um den historischen Jesus" in his *op. cit.* (*Exegetische* 2), pp. 31–68, pp. 32–41.

[21] *Ibid.*, p. 33.

[22] *Ibid.*, p. 34.

[23] *Ibid.*, p. 35.

[24] *Ibid.,* pp. 35 ff.

[25] *Ibid.,* pp. 37—41.

[26] *Ibid.,* p. 41. Despite his criticisms, Käsemann was convinced by Jeremias that the Bultmannian choice of the *kerygma* as a criterion was one-sided (*ibid.,* p. 21); since then, Käsemann himself has been casting about for a solution, and has actually tried several, which we need not investigate here. But see his "Neutestamentliche Fragen von Heute" in his *op. cit.* (*Exegetische* 2), pp. 11—31, pp. 21 f.; and his *op. cit.* (Sackgassen), pp. 53—68. George Tyrrel, *Christianity at the Crossroads* (London: Longmans, Green, 1910), pp. 35 ff., 93—104, 213 f., is very interesting: the teaching of Jesus provided symbols which are reinterpreted into different symbols for each generation. In criticism, one could say that much of what Tyrrell considered to be the teaching of Jesus originated, in fact, from the later community. Tyrrell's book is, however, in many ways prophetic and important.

[27] Karl Barth, *Die Auferstehung der Toten, Eine Akademische Vorlesung über 1 Kor. 15* (Munich: Chr. Kaiser Verlag, 1935), 3rd ed.

[28] Bultmann, *op. cit.* (Karl Barth).

[29] *Ibid.,* p. 52.

[30] *Ibid.,* p. 63.

[31] Bultmann, *op. cit.* (*Theologie*), p. 452.

[32] Similarly, some scholars have tried to use the contents of a particular writing as the criterion of its canonicity. See Kümmel, *op. cit.,* pp. 100—104.

9
Attempted
Solutions from a
Description of the
Process of
New Testament
Theologizing

To study theology is to study what men have written or spoken; all theology therefore is bound to language. The most efficient methods for the study of language have been intensively investigated by classical and Biblical philologists. Their purpose was to find principles for the scientific understanding of a historical text: the rules by which one could scientifically establish the intended sense of a certain writing. These rules have been accepted as axioms of exegetical method, because they are useful in practice. By following them Biblical scholars have been able to revolutionize understanding of the Old and New Testaments.

An even more systematic study of language is taking place in linguistics and primarily, but not exclusively, in the recent philosophical movement called linguistic analysis. Of course, linguistic study divides into many different kinds of problems. For a few examples:

1) problems of linguistic semantics: the study of meaning and meaning change, lexical and syntactical;

2) problems of philosophical semantics: the study of the relationship between signs and the things they signify;

3) the study of nondescriptive uses of words;

4) the study of subjective influences on communication and so on.

I will be more concerned with the problems of 2), 3), and 4).

These problems have called forth a number of very different solutions. There are many individual and school opinions within this, as within every, philosophical movement. Nevertheless, the parallel investigations of language—philology, linguistics, and linguistic philosophy—have reached in important cases identical conclusions. To name just two examples, Austin's work on performative utterances [1] is parallelled by that on the "Koinzidenzfall" in Hebrew.[2] Both philologists and linguistic analysts adhere to the axiom that each writing should be understood individually without being reduced to some other view or set of views.[3]

In the following sections, I will demonstrate briefly several parallels between Biblical and linguistic philosophical research and discuss whether, through a description of the process of New Testament theologizing, some solution can be found for the theological disunity of the New Testament. I will first investigate whether the New Testament theologies can be unified in the speaker; then in the object spoken about; and then whether they can be united through a description of the general means of human thought and communication.

THE SPEAKER

Attempts have been made to provide a unity for the New Testament theologies in the factors which New Testament writers are supposed to have shared.[4]

The Situation of the New Testament Theologians

The speakers and writers of theology do not exist except in historical situations. Since Baur's pioneering research (1853 ff.), exegetes have recognized the elucidation of the situation of the individual New Testament writers as the basis for the interpretation of their individual writings.[5] In form-criticism, the form of a particular story, sermon, admonishment, etc., comes from the use made of it in a particular and concrete "setting in life," which Dibelius defines as "the historico-social situation, in which exactly such literary forms were developed." [6] Analogously, in linguistic philosophy, Austin, in his discussion of performative utterances, states: "In conclusion, we see that in order to explain what can go wrong with statements we cannot just concentrate on the proposition involved (whatever that is) as has been done traditionally. We must consider the total situation in which the utterance is issued—the total speech act— . . ." [7] Similarly, Ludwig Wittgenstein has said: "An expression has meaning only in the stream of life." [8]

On the most practical level, a certain situation can influence the choice of words: if words have a bad or inappropriate connotation in a certain situation, they will be avoided. The early Christians avoided such words as "priest" and "altar." On the other hand, if certain words have a very good connotation, the temptation will be strong to use them.

Granted then that the study of the situation of the New Testament writers is necessary in order to understand their writings; does this study allow us somehow to unify their theologies? An affirmative answer would depend on two presuppositions: that the situation of the New Testament writers was uniform and that writers in the same situation necessarily agree.

But I have shown that the situation of the New Testament teachers was in no way uniform. There were great changes in situation: before and after the death of Jesus, the resignation to the delay of the Parousia, the disappearance of the phenomena of the spirit, and the structuralization of the community. Each one of these changes in situation naturally demanded a great change in theology.

At every stage in the history of tradition, there were great differences in the backgrounds of the different converts and thus in the influences on them. I have listed some of the different groups noticeable in the New Testament, each of which constructed theologies that differed significantly.

Moreover, no individual is in exactly the same situation or has exactly the same background as another.

The situation of the writers of the New Testament cannot be regarded, then, as uniform. Starting from one stage of the history of the New Testament, after the death of Jesus, after the resignation to the delay of the Parousia, after most of the phenomena of the spirit had disappeared and the organization of the community had considerably progressed, one can speak of a certain general situation of the community. But even then, the local differences persisted in exercising such a strong influence that to speak thus would be a great generalization. In any case, nothing justifies one's ignoring the previous, very different situations in the history of the early communities. One must conclude then that the influence of situation on theology must have tended to disunite rather than to unite theology, because the different situations in which the New Testament theologies were written were themselves so different.

The second presupposition of those who would use the influence of situation to unite theology—that writers in a similar situation will agree—is equally untenable. One need hardly observe that two writers in the same situation may very well construct different theologies, just as different philosophers can construct different philosophies though they are as much as possible in the same situation. Different people obviously react differently to the same situation. When the phenomena of the spirit began to disappear, some reacted by institutionalizing the church; others by looking for the spirit among the enthusiastic sects. This theory cannot, therefore, provide a unity on the level of theology.

In fact, the most it ever could provide would be a point *outside* of theology itself which would be common to a very few of the many New Testament theologies. The theologies of the New Testament *are* different. A supposed common situation would not unite those theologies, but only provide a common *extratheological* point of reference for them. This solution in fact recognizes the disunity of theology and seeks unity elsewhere, *outside* of theology.

On the other hand, the observation that all theologizing occurs in a definite historical situation is essential to any description of the process of theologizing within and after the New Testament.

The Experience of the New Testament Theologians

The experience which a writer undergoes is obviously as important as his situation. Can this experience provide a unity for theology? My objections would be the same as those which I offered against the theory that a common situation could unite those theologies: the experience of the early Christians was neither uniform nor uniformly interpreted. Moreover, experience is not itself theology, but is *extratheological*.

The experience of the early Christians was obviously dependent on their situation. Did they experience Jesus in person during his life? Were they waiting for the Parousia? Were the phenomena of the spirit still to be experienced in the community? Moreover, experience is even more personal and individual than situation. So the factor of experience would tend to influence the writers of the New Testament toward disunity rather than unity.

Experience, even more perhaps than situation, can itself be formulated and interpreted in different ways. Ogden and Richards, discussing different esthetic theories, state: "Whenever we have any experience which might be called 'aesthetic', that is whenever we are enjoying, contemplating, admiring or appreciating an object, there are plainly different parts of the situation on which emphasis can be laid. As we select one or the other of these so we shall develop one or other of the main aesthetic doctrines." [9]

Similarly, Käsemann quotes the German exegete H. Braun in order to criticize him: " 'The constant is the believer's understanding of himself; Christology is the variable.' I consider this statement simply false . . . historically as well as materially . . . But if one speaks now even of constancy, it is simply incomprehensible in what way the self-understanding of a Christendom determined by apocalypticism should be the same as that of the fourth Gospel, of the Epistle of James, of Luke or of the hellenistic enthusiasts. The breadth of variation in Christology could be hardly greater, but would rather correspond exactly to that of the anthropology." [10]

Experience almost demands, one could say, different interpretations. This does not minimize, however, the differences between those interpretations, and it is historically wrong to say that these differences are "not felt to be, so far as the living apprehension of God in worship is concerned, any problem at all." [11] Those interpretations *are* theology; the experience is not theology. One finds one's point of unity, not in the theologies, but outside of them. This, however, does not unite the theologies among themselves, and many would still die rather than deny one and accept the other.

Moreover, a difficulty peculiar to experience is that it varies often according to the interpretation or theology which one accepts. Feelings and experience are so vague that one depends to an extraordinary degree on available verbal interpretations as guides to understanding them; these interpretations can thus, in turn, influence experience practically without check.[12] Ferré elucidates Farmer: "Again, we meet a personality which is both warm and stern . . . and we recognize in this encounter the 'Son', who requires absolute discipleship but who gave himself on a cross for all men. In contrast—but as an integral part of the same encounter-experience—we are aware of an element which penetrates beneath the level of discrete personality (as in the 'Father' and 'Son') to unite with our own subpersonal depths. This we call the 'Holy Spirit'." [13] Such an experience is, of course, by no means impossible, but one suspects the formative preinfluence of certain theological formulations. Certain persons have been convinced that they "feel grace" exactly as Thomas Aquinas has described it. Similarly, Charles Schultz, in *Peanuts,* has Lucy draw for Linus a large human heart, each side of which is colored differently. She explains: "This, Linus, is a picture of the human heart. One side is filled with hate and the other side is filled with love . . . These are the two forces which are constantly at war with each other . . ." Linus clutches his hands to his chest and says: "I think I know just what you mean . . . I can feel them fighting." [14]

Experience, then, cannot unify the theologies of the New Testament. The experience of the writers of the New Testament was not uniform, nor, even if it had been, could it have necessarily given rise to uniform interpretations or formulations. Rather, the experiences of the writers of the New Testament must have tended to influence them toward disunity. Moreover, experience could only provide an *extratheological* point of unity.

The Worship of the New Testament Theologians

Christians, it is also claimed, had a common worship; this could be a unifying factor in theology. We have seen that certain liturgical formulas or forms have left their traces on some of the writings of the New Testament. But no one, naturally, could claim that they in any way unite all of New Testament theology. On the contrary, there were a number of very different theologies constructed to explain that worship. Nor does Christian worship seem to have been everywhere uniform. The variations of "the words of institution" are only one indication of wide divergences in Christian worship and services— divergences which lasted into much later times. Just as situations differed and changed, so did worship and the theologies of worship. Even if "worship" is taken to refer to a very general attitude of reverence toward God, it must have varied with the different conceptions which people had of him, as well as with the situation, experience, and untold personal factors.

Worship, in the strict or loose sense, was not uniform in New Testament times, nor, even if it had been, need it have given rise to unified theologies. This solution again tries not so much to unite New Testament theologies among themselves as to provide for them some common *extratheological* reference point. This objection applies also to any attempted solution from a supposed, contentless act of faith.[15]

*The Motives, Interests, and Emotive Responses of
the New Testament Theologians*

The motive, intention, or purpose of a writer can influence his expression. Ogden and Richards show that "what is said is only in part determined by the things to which the speaker is referring. Often without clear consciousness of the fact, people have pre-occupations which determine their use of words . . . purposes and intentions . . ." [16] This is certainly often true of the New Testament writers: in Romans 6:1–11, for instance, the form and even the theology of Paul's argument is determined by his sermonizing purpose.[17] We have seen that tendency-criticism in New Testament scholarship based its method of investigation on the importance of this factor of purpose.

F. C. Grant attempts to use this principle to unite the different New Testament theologies: "What is everlastingly important is not the fact that these terms were once used, but the *motive* that led to their use—for that motive is still alive at the heart of all christian faith and endeavor." [18]

The same objections can be made against this position as against the previous ones which we have criticized: there is no reason to think that the motives of the early writers were uniform, or that, even if they were, they would necessarily have given rise to uniform theologies. Grant recognizes this somewhat guardedly when he says that this unity comes ". . . not from the language or the ideas commonly used to set forth its convictions, inferences, and beliefs." [19] What kind of a unity is this then? Certainly not one that could provide any sort of unity on the level of theology itself—as the evidence of the New Testament itself shows us.

Similarly, although a man's *interests* can influence him, one cannot say that the New Testament writers all shared the same interests or that, if they had, they would necessarily have agreed in their theologies.

These theories attempt to provide a common point for the New Testament theologies which is also outside theology itself.

In doing so, they, in fact, presuppose the theological disunity of the New Testament, which is the problem.

Finally, all would admit that most words are charged with a certain positive or negative force, which is not necessarily tied to the meaning of the word and cannot be translated. A writer will use a word which is emotively positive, even if it is not otherwise useful. But the same words were not emotively positive or negative to all Christians at all times. The early Christians avoided applying the title "Messiah" to Jesus because they were embarrassed by the fact that he had been executed after being convicted of claiming to be the Messiah. Only much later did the title lose its bad connotation and become current.

No one of these factors provides, then, a solution to the problem of the theological disunity of the New Testament.

The Common Language of the New Testament Theologians

I have already mentioned the view that the Semites "thought differently" from the Greeks, and the fact that James Barr has raised objections to many of the arguments used to prove this view. Ian T. Ramsey held, however, that one could say that Semites had different "dominant models" and that they thus indeed "thought differently." [20] This interchange is symptomatic of the general debate about the differences among languages.

Each language has its own logical structure and characteristics.[21] Each language has its own informal but definite system of distinctions.[22] Each has words which are untranslatable and concepts which are not duplicated in other languages.[23] Each offers its own difficulties and occasions for false conclusions and misinterpretations.[24] All these peculiar linguistic features of a language exercise a definite influence on thinking. Certain systems of philosophy, certain ways of thinking will tend to arise and be perpetuated because of the peculiarities of a certain language. One can even ask whether or to what extent those differences express different total views of the world.

The answers to this question have, of course, varied considerably.[25] I shall discuss briefly here the debate about "semantic fields." [26] Certain fields of observation and experience are divided up by the vocabulary used of that field. There are significant differences between the ways different languages divide up those fields. Some distinctions are found in one language which may not be found in another: for instance, one language may name fewer colors than another; "violet," for the speakers of this language, would be "blue." In English, the husband of my cousin-in-law is "not related" to me. Some languages may have different lists of virtues, or invest the same virtues with very different connotations. One could say that a "semantic field" indeed expresses a way of looking at things: "In each field, the raw material of experience is analysed and elaborated in a unique way, differing from one language to another and often from one period to another in the history of the same idiom. In this way, the structure of semantic fields embodies a specific philosophy and a scale of values." [27]

Several criticisms can be made of the theory of semantic fields: [28] the fields are not so constant and systematic as many would think; the emotive and esthetic functions of language are not sufficiently considered; most important, the theory of semantic fields only applies to certain very limited areas of language, such as colors, kinship, and intellectual or abstract ideas. "The importance of language as the organizer of experience can best be seen in the realm of *abstract* ideas . . . In such spheres everything will depend on the number and nature of the concepts we have, on how we delimit them and how we classify them." [29] An important task for New Testament scholarship is to investigate scientifically the extent to which this theory can be applied to the language of the New Testament. Ullmann remarks that "the comparison of different languages" has been "pursued only too often with uncertain and dilettantish methods." [30] These methods were the object of James Barr's celebrated attack; however, the question itself is by no means closed.

In any case, whatever one's conclusions about the applicability of the particular theory of semantic fields to New Testament language, "The moulding influence of the linguistic on our 'conceptual' analysis of the world, and the linguistic nature of our 'concepts' themselves, are beyond dispute." [31] Even if a language cannot be understood as a gigantic semantic field, and even if it does not, in every aspect, express a total world view, nevertheless, the peculiar features of a language always offer different opportunities and pitfalls for those who use it. At the simplest level, a language is always limited; no language contains a special word for each possible thing, event, attitude, etc. Some words therefore must do double and even multiple duty. This often results in different sets of ambiguities and confusions.

Most scholars would, in any case, agree that many words and expressions are often found in more informal "semantic fields"; looser, less fixed and durable, but still somewhat determined and recurring contexts, which to a certain extent determine the use of the word or expression.

Most scholars would also consider language to be *one of several* essential factors in the formation and transmission of a culture. A language is *an expression of a total culture* just as it can only be understood within that culture.[32]

Language, therefore, influences thought and expression by helping to transmit to the individual certain cultural views and attitudes and by limiting and hampering individual expression and thought.

Can this fact unite the different theologies of the New Testament? There have been, indeed, some theologians who have claimed that the Bible was united by a certain "Semitic mentality." But fatal objections can be raised against such a theory. Firstly, such theories are usually based on unscientific methods, mainly, an extreme generalization of the theory of semantic fields.[33] Secondly, two people who share the same culture and language can obviously disagree; for instance, Plato and Aristotle. Thirdly, there are, in any case, two different language-culture groups in the New Testament: Semitic and Hellenistic. We have seen already that their differences were one of the many influences toward the disunity of the theologies of the New Testament.

Language and culture cannot, therefore, provide a theological unity for the New Testament.[34] Rather, they are occasions of disunity. One language cannot be completely translated into another. Different languages tend, therefore, to produce theologies which differ.

Moreover, no language is ever completely united. Ullmann states: "Recent studies in linguistic geography have revealed the full magnitude of these discrepancies . . . even the apparent uniformity of written Latin is deceptive as it conceals the social and regional differences which eventually disrupted the unity of the Romania . . . Whether we refer to 3000 B.C. or 1950 A.D., a completely uniform language is a fallacy." [35]

Language is discontinuous also in that it must be taught to each generation. Sometimes mistakes in learning can lead to changes in meaning.[36] At the very least, this necessity of learning a language results in the fact that, as Willard Van Orman Quine says, "The uniformity that unites us in communication and belief is a uniformity of resultant patterns overlying a chaotic subjective diversity of connections between words and experience." [37]

Language is discontinuous also in that it is spoken by different people. "It has been proved by experimental data," affirms Ullmann, "that there is a definite connection between language and personality." [38] Thus, in a very real sense, one can say that "Language serves a man not only to express something but also to express himself." [39] Each person at every stage of his life speaks what has been labeled an "idiolect": "the totality of the speech-habits of a single person at a given time." [40] The number of idiolects within a given language is the number of the speakers of that language.

The context in which a word or expression is used very definitely qualifies it. S. I. Hayakawa states that *"no word ever has exactly the same meaning twice."* [41] Similarly, Ogden and Richards hold that "we never use the same word twice with the same value; there are never two absolutely identical linguistic facts." [42] A word and even a statement receives its meaning from the whole body of words or statements of which it forms a part. [43]

Therefore, language, by its very nature and use, is an occasion of disunity. Different people will express themselves differently. It is even impossible for one person to use the words of another in exactly the same way. The context will always change the meaning. Moreover, a language changes with time. Words mean one thing at one stage of their history and another at another. The people of one age cannot use identically the words of another.

Far from providing unity, man's use of language is characterized by natural and necessary elements of disunity. This is certainly true of the New Testament.

THE OBJECT

Most language at least is about some object, thing, person, or event, and attempts have been made to provide a unity for the theologies of the New Testament in these factors. The interpretations may differ, it is held, but the facts are the same. [44]

Certainly, no one would deny that many New Testament theologians are attempting for the most part to explain and interpret certain historical things, persons, and events, and also to a certain extent their own experiences. The New Testament theologies are answers to the questions, or solutions to the problems, raised by the factors we have just mentioned.

But how exactly could one use this insight to solve the problem of the New Testament disunity? The theologians who attempt this solution are at least claiming to refer to things, people, and events which all men, in the proper circumstances, could have observed. For instance, Scott says: "These things were matters of history, and men only needed to be made aware of them." [45] The whole point, in this case, of an appeal to "the facts" is that one is seeking a level which is prior to interpretation, on which all can agree before their interpretations differ. Only thus can one provide a point of unity. An appeal to some basic, common teaching is, as we have seen, impossible.

This attempt at establishing a unity for New Testament theology fails precisely because it does not unite different theologies; just as the solution by situation or experience, it seeks merely to give them a common point of reference *outside* the field of theology itself. In fact, this attempt presupposes theological disunity. The different interpretations of "the facts" *are* theology, and their disagreement constitutes the problem: the theological disunity of the New Testament.

Thus, one can notice in theologians who advocate this view a tendency to salvage their solution by including a good mixture of theology in their statement of "the facts": they say, for example, that Jesus was "sent by God," "was raised from the dead," was "the Messiah," etc. Dodd's statement of the "fact" of the Resurrection is already interpretative,[46] since the opinion that Jesus had been raised from the dead is already an interpretation of the fact that the apostles claimed that they had had some experience of him after his death. Other possible interpretations would be that the apostles were lying, were overexcited, were having hallucinations, or that they had a not unusual vision of the separated soul of Jesus, etc. Similar criticisms can be made of the formulations of Scott and most other theologians. What happened, prior to interpretation, must be that on which all men, regardless of their particular, different interpretations, would agree: that Jesus lived, taught, and was crucified; that his followers claimed to have had some experience of him after his death; and that various psychic manifestations were current in the community of his followers for a certain time after his death.

There is also a tendency in those who propose this solution to put those "facts" on the level of theology by speaking of them as "the message" or "the *kerygma*";[47] then the theologian can say that the New Testament theologians interpreted "the message" rather than "the facts," which is quite a different proposition. A message is already formulated, a set of words. An interpretation of a formulation remains on the same level as that which it wishes to interpret; words are given for words. Although this process itself is problematical, it is in this case a simplification: all the problems of expressing and interpreting things, persons, and events, which are not formulations or words, are evaded.

Moreover, one cannot say even that the New Testament theologians were always seeking to explain the same "facts." The theologians of one time and situation had to explain different "facts" than the theologians of other times and situations. For one generation, the delay of the Parousia was crucial; for others, the disappearance of the observable manifestations of the spirit; for another, the problem of order in the community. New situations brought new "facts" and saw old ones disappear.

However, one can say that this attempted solution is more successful than one which bases itself on, say, experience: not in uniting theologies, but in providing a common point outside of theology in the person, life, death, and "appearances" of Jesus. This point, however, is obviously not common to all the levels of tradition in the New Testament: most notably, not to that of the teaching of Jesus himself. Also, the earliest Christians did not seek so much to explain anything. Rather they anxiously awaited the coming of the kingdom. One *could* say, however, that a certain explanation or interpretation was implied by their expectation. Also, Paul, as most early New Testament theologians, is not very interested in the life of Jesus or even in his "person," as we would be. But he is certainly interested in interpreting the death and appearances of Jesus. One could not say, however, that the death and appearances of Jesus receive the strongest accents in all New Testament theologies, as they do in most later theologies. This is obviously true again for the teaching of Jesus himself and of those Christians who built their faith around either the expectation of the kingdom or the phenomena of the spirit. But whereas the factor of experience was bound to change at every stage of Christianity, the death and appearances of Jesus remained constant objects of reflection after a certain stage in Christian history had been reached. Clearly, however, the death and appearances of Jesus do not unite the reflections which they have occasioned, nor do they give them even a similar structure of accents or emphases.

Things, persons, and events are, in fact, not only the occasions of, but often also one of the influences toward disunity of interpretation. Things, persons, and their interactions are not "simple objects," which are easily verbalized. On the most banal level, things are vague. This leads to vagueness of words, different systems of semantic fields, different ways of dividing up reality. It also explains the facts that witnesses of the same event can disagree. Things and events are just not very clear.

This vagueness is especially evident in "abstract phenomena," such as language and concept systems. Thus the endless debates about the right meaning of a word, the boundaries of a distinction, etc.

On a more exalted level, Ogden and Richards state: ". . . certain of these concrete, immediate, unintellectualized phases of life have in their own right a complexity and richness which no intellectual activities can equal." [48] No thing, person, or event can ever be completely described, much less completely explained. Nothing can be completely put into words; even if hundreds of people talked for centuries in all possible languages, there would still be something to be said.

This richness can occasion *partial* explanations. Things have many different "aspects" or "levels." Seemingly different explanations may therefore all be *partially* true. The sign that these explanations are partial and not irreconcilable is of course that, insofar as they are correct, they do not contradict each other: that the different explanations add up to one, more complete explanation. Thus New Testament theologies cannot be analyzed as such partial explanations.

Austin adds another dimension: "the fact that we can give different descriptions of what we perceive is certainly not the whole story. When something is seen, there may not only be different ways of *saying* what is seen; it may also be seen *in different ways,* seen *differently.*" [49] He gives the examples of a picture drawn so that it can be seen as either a duck or a rabbit, or as either concave or convex. A soldier will see a drill differently; a painter will see a landscape differently. "Thus different ways of saying what is seen will quite often be due, not just to differences in knowledge, in fineness of discrimination, . . . *or in interest in this aspect or that of the total situation;* they may be due to the fact that what is seen is seen differently, seen in a different way, seen *as* this rather than that. And there will be sometimes no *one right* way of saying what is seen, for the additional reason that there may be no one right way of seeing it." [50]

Disunity, rather than unity, results from the object and our ways of seeing it. Austin says that his remarks apply only "for *special* cases." [51] But one may extend them by saying that the richness and complexity of things, persons, and events, and the differences between possible ways of seeing them, are among the factors which make possible the great diversity of all culture and certainly of theology. Things, persons, and events have so many aspects and dimensions, and they can be seen in so many different ways, that they can offer points of departure, examples and instances for a possibly infinite number of conceptual superstructures.

Similar objections could be made, of course, against any attempt to establish a unity among New Testament theologies by considering them as different solutions to the same problems. Here again, a point of unity is posited which is outside of those theologies themselves; this theory again even presupposes the disunity of these theological solutions. Moreover, the problems of Christian theology changed as much with the situation as did the "facts." Every generation had different problems. Similarly, communities in different locations had different problems: the Jewish converts had the problem of their relation to the Temple service of the Jews; the Gentile converts, the problem of their relation to pagan cults, etc. The solution from common problems is, in the end, merely a different formulation of the solution from common facts. Take the facts which have the greatest claim to being common and see them as problems, and one has attained the most common point possible for this particular attempted solution. Of course, that does not solve the problem of the *theological* disunity.

THE MEANS OF THOUGHT AND COMMUNICATION

I have shown that the theologians of the New Testament, in the construction of their theologies, used schemes, literary forms, images, titles, terms, and words which they had received from their milieus. One can fairly say that there is no theology of the New Testament which is not somehow dependent on these means of thought and communication. Also these means are not used systematically. For instance, Paul uses various schemes for his "enumerations of cosmic-worldly powers"; and, as Otto Michel says: "Paul could apparently bind together different schemes according to the particular purpose." [52]

Paul uses a great number of *images:* major ones such as the body or the bride of Christ for the community; and minor ones such as a house for the community; or, for the Christian life, a footrace. These images cannot be systematized. Christ's bride cannot be his body, etc.

Paul and all the New Testament theologians borrowed *technical terms* from many different spheres of the world around them. There are terms of Jewish preaching, of Gentile pagan preaching, of the Jewish and pagan religions, of law, and even of sports such as boxing. Paul, as is well known, can speak in Jewish terms to the Jews and in Gentile terms to the Gentiles. Most of these terms also cannot be synthesized with one another: the terms borrowed from the Jews often carry implications which contradict radically those carried by pagan terms. An obvious example would be the contradiction between the term "God" as used by a Jew and as used by a pagan. But, most often, these terms are simply set next to each other with no thought to their incongruity.

I have shown that a number of irreducibly different schemes were used to try to explain the meaning or significance of Jesus: the schemes of adoption, of exaltation, of the descent and ascent of a heavenly creature. All the titles applied to Jesus came also from certain very definite contexts: "Christ" or "the Messiah" was a title which belonged to a definite figure of speculation at that time, as were "Son of Man," "Son of God," etc. The theological interpretation of Jesus was just this application of various schemes and titles to him and to the events of his life. Again, all of these schemes and most of these titles were incompatible with each other. Jesus could not be both preexistent and nonpreexistent; equal to God and not equal to God. Yet, some of these incompatible schemes and titles are often used by the very same theologian.

A great deal of the theological disunity of the New Testament comes from this use of incompatible schemes, titles, etc. The Christian theologians were apparently following the methods of the Jewish missionaries to the Gentiles, who employed almost any means which their environment offered to help communicate their message.[53]

One cannot deny then that the New Testament writers use certain means of thought and communication and that this is a cause of much theological disunity. But just because these schemes, etc. are *means,* they are not *ends* in themselves. They are only instruments in the hands of their users. Their importance is therefore merely *relative.*

This is one of the reasons why some theologians have attempted to solve the problem of theological disunity by finding a point of unity in the facts,[54] in the object,[55] or in the motives,[56] or interests,[57] of the New Testament writers. The means of expression, they argue, are not important—only one of the above factors really counts.

However, I have shown that these attempts cannot solve the problems of theological disunity precisely because they abandon theology and seek their point of unity on another level.

One could however present the following argument: the New Testament writers use certain means of thought and communication. These means have only relative value and must be interpreted. Could it be that there is a unity of theology in the New Testament and a disunity of the means of expressing it? Ramsey claims: "Each metaphor can only describe one aspect of the nature of being of the Deity, and the inferences which can be drawn from it have their limits when they conflict with the inferences which can be truly drawn from other metaphors describing other aspects." [58]

This argument is interesting because it bases itself on two valuable insights: the New Testament writers use means of thought and communication, and those means must be interpreted. These insights imply, in fact, a whole new approach to language.

I shall examine the nature and use of such means in the New Testament, the way in which they should be interpreted and the new approach to language such an analysis implies. Then I will be in a position to criticize this attempted solution to the problem of New Testament theological disunity.

*The Nature and Use of the Means of
Thought and Communication*

MODELS

A great deal of philosophical study has been devoted recently to the role of models in human thinking: Ian T. Ramsey has begun applying those studies to theology.[59] A model is used as an aid to understanding and articulating something which could not otherwise be understood. A model is required when "a theory [is] needed about an object that is too big or too small or too far away or too dangerous to be observed and experimented upon." [60] God would be an example of an object which, in several ways, eluded our direct observation.[61] These models of a thing allow one to discuss that thing, which could otherwise not be so discussed. An example of such a model would be the model of the hull of a ship. One can put this model into a stream of water and see approximately how well the actual hull would cut through the water. Another example would be that of the atom as a core surrounded by little planets, or a large plastic model of a molecule.

At one time, such models were considered to be veritable pictures of what they modeled. The model hull was a true pic-

ture of the real hull; the atom was really a little planet surrounded by satellites. But this "could never have been more
than a fool's paradise." [62] Two fatal objections were made
against this theory: 1) a model was not and could not be a simple picture reproduction of a thing; it was essentially different.
Even for the most exact scale model, "change of scale must introduce irrelevance and distortion . . ." [63] 2) Scientists found
that, in many cases especially of those objects which were not
directly observable, they could use a variety of models for the
same thing. For instance, one theory of light based itself on the
model of particles; another based itself on the model of waves.
Neither of these models can be reduced to the other; there are
not particles in the waves or waves in the particles. In fact,
light is neither waves nor particles. But the model of waves and
the model of particles are helpful in constructing a theory for
the phenomena of light. Each model, or the theory based on it,
can be used according to need or desire, often according to the
mathematics with which the scientist prefers to work. Such
models were thus seen to be, not real pictures of a thing, but
rather conceptual schemes constructed simply because they
helped articulate a certain problem. The model one constructs
is thus purely formal, and therefore a multiplicity of models is
possible. [64]

But, it may be asked, what is the connection between the
models used and the thing to which the models are applied?
One can say only that the sole observable connection is that the
models are *useful* in explaining the phenomena or some of the
phenomena of the thing. Apart from scale models of observable
objects, no comparison with the thing itself is possible. Otherwise a model very often need not have been used.

It might be objected that that very usefulness shows that
the model somehow *is,* in fact, a picture of the object. This
objection is answered by showing that two irreducible models
are equally useful, just in different ways, for the purpose at
hand. The object could not be pictured by both of these models
at the same time. As Ramsey asks: "For what could it be that
was a build-up from them all?" [65]

What the thing itself is, in such cases, remains a mystery. All one can know is that certain models help one to understand it. One cannot even know the exact relation of the model to its object, because one cannot compare it with the object itself. The model itself, and possible future models, are all that are left. As Ramsey concludes: "The cost to the scientist is that he must be ready to allow an ultimately mysterious and elusive character to that which he essays to understand; the cost to the theologian is that he must be ready to live and to make do with theological uncertainties." [66]

Let me now examine how the schemes, images, etc. of the New Testament theologies act as models. First, as the reader does not need to be reminded, there are many different schemes, images, titles, etc. in the New Testament. We have already enumerated many, but by no means all of them. Moreover, we have already seen that not only are they different, but often contradictory.[67] Therefore, just as for scientific models, I can conclude that the schemes etc. used in the New Testament theologies are not perfect pictures of their objects or references. Just as light cannot be waves and particles, so the church cannot *be* "Christ's body," "Christ's bride," a "people," and a "rest." Jesus cannot be the "Messiah," the "Son of Man," and "God"; nor can he have been "exalted" *and* "returned." All of these schemes, images, and titles are models taken from the milieu of the New Testament theologians and applied respectively to Jesus and to the community in order to help explain him or it, in order to be able to say something about him or it. When one called the community Christ's body, one could say a number of things about the community by using that model: for instance, it is made up of different members in an ordered structure belonging to Christ. The bride of Christ model allowed one to say other things: that Christ loved the community. The community was neither Christ's body nor his bride, but those models were useful in articulating something about the community. Nor obviously could either of those models be reduced to each other. They were irreducibly different. Therefore, the community could not have *been* literally one or the other. They are both, one must conclude, models. One must also interpret critically the model of "the people of God," applied to the community. Do Christians all belong to a same race? Do they all live in the same country?

All models, therefore, apply only partially. No model can exhaust its object. Also each model has its advantages and disadvantages which cannot be replaced by, or reduced to, those of another model.[68]

Just because no model is absolute, either in relation to other models, or in relation to the object of which it is a model, each model can be only partially applied: one must not fall into the well-known error of pressing an image.

No theologian has ever looked for real noses, eyes, and ears on the body of Christ, but some have assigned different members to different orders within the church. One conservative theologian during the Second Vatican Council denied the right of laymen to participate in the council in spite of the fact that they were part of the body of Christ because the feet do not participate in the deliberations of the head. Paul himself pushes the image to absurdity in I Corinthians 12:23–24: Paul wants to say that the weaker members of the community should receive more honor because they need it (a curious endeavor in itself for a Christian). He naturally reaches for the body model and applies it methodically: the despised parts of the body are compensated for the lack of honor they receive from common opinion by the special honor of the clothes which they are allowed to wear.[69]

Most cases of the pressing of models are more serious. For instance, Paul uses a financial model for the redemptive history in I Corinthians 6:20: "For you were bought for a price." Johannes Weiss points out the uselessness of asking "how then the process of buying is imagined in detail. Who was the former owner? The demons? Satan? . . . And to what extent could the price that was paid (the death of Christ is certainly meant) be an adequate means of payment? For all these questions, there is no answer because the thought—at least at this moment—is not thought through in all its consequences." [70]

Ramsey has shown in an important chapter [71] how all theology of the atonement, the redemption, the salvation, etc. of man by God is determined by the particular model that is used; each model has its advantages and disadvantages; none can be reduced to the other; and yet, when one or other model has been pressed, isolated, or taken as the exclusive model, division in the church has resulted.[72] Not a few people have gone to the stake for one model rather than accept or recognize another.

Models, therefore, by their very nature, demand to be used critically. One cannot escape the necessity of interpreting them, of choosing among their many aspects, those which should be applied to the object. For instance, in the model of a price being paid for us by Jesus on the cross, the aspects which one would naturally prefer to develop would be Jesus' action for us, his giving of himself on our behalf. One might perhaps wish to develop what this model has to say of the situation we were in before Jesus ransomed us by his action. But how many aspects of this model would one not want to develop! Such as, the power of Satan; Jesus paying off the demons, etc. How little one would want to develop the possible aspect of a God who demands blood. In fact, a disadvantageous aspect of a model may, at one time or another, become so obvious that the model can no longer be effective, becomes indeed dangerously misleading, and must be abandoned.

How, we may ask, can we interpret a model? How do we know which aspects are those which should be applied and developed, and which not? Some help, of course, is given by examining the context or contexts in which the model was first used. For instance, the nationalistic aspect of the model of Messiah was not developed by the first theologians who applied the title to Jesus. The body model was usually applied to the corporate life of the community. On the other hand, we may not agree with the original use, or may have found others. There are also many cases where such clear guidelines are not to be found; how did the earliest Christians use the model of the Son of Man or the model scheme of the descent and ascent of a heavenly creature? For most cases, the final criterion of the interpretation of a model can be nothing else than the individual interpreter's own theology, or that of his community. The title-model "Son of God" was interpreted essentially differently by Christian converts from Judaism than by Hellenistic converts. The problem of such models is precisely that they demand to be interpreted and yet offer themselves no principle by which they can be properly interpreted.

THEORETICAL CONCEPTS AND AXIOMS

In constructing a model or a theory, one often uses what are called theoretical concepts. For instance, one can introduce multiple dimensions into the solution of a problem, not because there "exist" more than three (or four), but simply because more dimensions are useful for solving the problem. Science abounds with such theoretical concepts as energy, entropy, quantum, neutrinos, and atom. These are not things that exist in the world, they are not objects which can somehow be found or observed: they are merely invented mental entities which are useful in formulating a certain theory.[73]

That New Testament theologies use such constructs is clear, but sometimes disputes arise as to whether particular things, persons, or events alluded to in Scripture are real or just this type of mental construct. In many cases, all would agree: in I Corinthians 8:5, Paul posits the existence of many gods, first hypothetically, and then absolutely;[74] but few would argue from this verse that Paul was a polytheist. In I Corinthians 15:45, he posits not one Adam, but two; at the beginning God created two Adams, each of which has his role in redemptive history;[75] but few would therefore make it an object of their faith that God did, in fact, create two Adams. Paul, all would agree, is simply using, for his own purpose in the argument, a theoretical construct.

Also, angels are used in some parts of the Old Testament to avoid involving God too closely in the mundane doings reported; God sends an angel and remains himself at a certain distance. In Exodus 3:2–6, an *angel* is said to appear in the burning bush, but then Yahwe "sees," "speaks," etc. from the bush. One need not ask whether the angel is in the bush, or Yahwe, or both at the same time. To say that the angel is there is not to use language which has the function of describing, but rather language that makes a particular point: it preserves the separateness of Yahwe. "The angel," in this case at least, is simply a construct; and one falls into absurd confusions, if one takes it to be a description of something real in the world.

A similar analysis could be made about a good number of "entities" in the early Christian theology, such as the virgin birth, hell, the devil, natural law, etc.

Not only theoretical constructs can be so questioned; the principles, the axioms, as it were, of theology can also be questioned as to their function inside a total system. Is the principle "God is all good" a description of God, or does it have a different logical function? Kuss discusses the motivation of Paul's argument in Romans 3:4: "God should show himself as true, but every man as a liar." Kuss explains: "God shows himself as true while the whole untrueness, the whole lie, is on the side of man." [76] "The recognition of the essential trueness of God and the essential falseness of man takes place in order that the 'justice' of God in his words, that is, in his revelation, in his leadership, in his promises . . . be revealed and in order that he thereby emerge as victor from the trial to which man brings him . . . In the confusing situation in which man finds himself, he tends ever again to protest against God, simply to absolve himself and to apportion the total responsibility to God alone. At the same moment, however, he experiences that he has, in fact, struck not God, but himself: the image of God acquires, fatally, demonic characteristics, and man's apparent freeing of himself from the bonds of impenetrable guilt becomes a total slavery without hope. The indispensable presupposition of a true freeing of man is to guard the image of God from every stain and to assume the guilt entirely; more exactly: to recognize one's own guiltfulness, even when it remains ultimately a mystery."

Kuss himself would probably not want to label this proposition "God is good" an axiom with a logical function within a theory. To say that the principle "God is good" is not necessarily or exclusively descriptive is not to say of course that God is not good; one simply realizes that this proposition works in a certain logical way within a certain system. That an exegete would recognize, in description at least, this very specialized linguistic function is another indication that the conclusions of exegesis and of linguistic philosophy converge.

RHETORICAL FORMS

Similar problems of interpretation arise concerning the rhetorical forms used by the theologians of the New Testament: how much is rhetoric and how much point? In several cases, Paul seems simply to have entangled himself in a fully inappropriate rhetorical form. In II Corinthians 8:10, Paul writes to the Corinthians that "they began first not only to do but also to desire [to do]." Since one would expect the doing in this context to be more important than the desire to do, one must conclude that Paul has simply been caught in the rhetorical form "not only—but also . . ." and been thus led to an unintended climax.[77]

At times, Paul's use of a rhetorical form seems to imply a point which he does not in fact intend. In Romans 4:25, he speaks of Jesus "who was handed over because of ['dia'=causal] our sins and raised because of ['dia'=final: 'for'] our justification." The use of the word "dia" in two very different senses already shows Paul's desire to construct a parallelism despite any resulting ambiguity. The sentence would seem to be saying that Jesus died only because we have sinned and he was raised only for our justification. That is, Christ's death and Resurrection would receive discrete functions, and his death would have nothing to do with our justification. Theologians have built on the distinction seen here. But the difficulties involved—especially the great conflict with Paul's usual teaching—plus Paul's use of the word "dia," indicate rather that he has simply constructed a "synthetic parallelism," "which divides a single thought into two parts in parallel disposition."[78]

Sometimes, however, Paul's use of a rhetorical form decisively changes or disturbs his intended meaning. For instance, in Romans 9:31, the parallelism which he is desirous of constructing traps him into saying that Israel "did not attain the Law." However, Paul's whole point is that Israel did attain the Law, but thereby neither the perfection of the Law nor justification. He has simply followed his parallelism consequently to the end apparently without noticing that it reversed his intended point.[79] This happens more than once in Paul's letters.[80]

The most theologically important example of a rhetorical form possibly forcing Paul to say something which he had not intended is found in Romans 5:12–21, the text on which the doctrine of original sin is primarily based.[81] Paul apparently wants to show the superabounding graciousness of God in Christ. He does this by using the Adam-Christ comparison which was familiar to his readers: as sin came to men through Adam, so salvation came to men through Christ. But in carrying out his parallelism, Paul, because he wants to show the ineffable greatness of God's action, raises the ante by adding "all" to men. This would imply that *all* men were sinful just because Adam was, and that *all* men were in actuality saved already, simply in view of Christ. Few theologians have developed the latter point, but the former has been developed into the doctrine of original sin. The sin of Adam is passed down to all men regardless; they are sinful from their birth.

Does Paul really intend to say this, or is this point just a side effect of the rhetorical parallelism he is constructing? No one would deny that this point could not be Paul's main interest here. In all such parallelisms, he is mainly interested in the second member of the parallel, which is put in the position of the climax.

Furthermore, there are also strong indications that the point of sin coming to all men through Adam is, in fact, merely the result of the rhetorical form. Firstly, Paul begins the passage grandiosely: "Therefore, as through one man, sin came into the whole world, and through sin death, and as death came through to all men . . ." (Romans 5:12). Paul then leaves this sentence hanging and adds "because all men have sinned." He has begun his parallel by climaxing the one member at "all men." Then, seeing that this point contradicts his usual view, he breaks off his sentence, leaves it simply unfinished, and adds as a corrective "because all men have sinned." (The expression translated as "because" here is from the late, vulgar Greek. Augustine, applying the rules of classical Greek, mistranslated it as "in whom." He then constructed his teaching of original sin —which was to have a decisive effect on later theology—on this mistranslation.)

The next verses are a curious mixture of the parallelism which Paul is constructing and the technical terms of the theology of justification, a theology which presupposes a certain individual responsibility for sins. The parallel, as Eberhard Jüngerl says, is thereby "demythologized." [82]

In verse 16, Paul is trapped by a subsidiary parallelism into saying that grace came "from [out of] many sins," when his point is that it came through Christ. In verse 18, Paul is again forced by the form of his parallelism to say that *all* men *are* saved. Kuss explains: "That 'all men' are spoken of as being on the side of salvation as well as on the side of damnation, occurs under the force of the chosen form; one may not simply press that theologically . . ." [83]

Possibly, Paul is using here a rabbinical device, which provided for the danger inherent in such parallelisms—of tending to identify as closely as possible the two members of the comparison—by stipulating that: "The correspondence as such will be accepted insofar as the correspondence idea is theologically corrected." [84] Paul could have counted then on his contemporaries correcting any theological exaggerations into which he might have been forced by the rhetorical form of parallelism which he was using.

There are many, of course, who would not accept the above analysis, but one can see on this example the problems of interpretation and judgment raised by the use of rhetorical forms by the New Testament writers. How can one decide, in these cases, what the real intended point of the author is and what is due merely to the chosen rhetorical form? Historical analysis is an aid up to a certain point, but most often, the final decision will rest on the personal, theological views of the individual interpreter or his group. In any case, the need of some interpretation and decision becomes inescapable the moment such rhetorical forms are employed.

WORDS

These problems arise not only from the larger schemes, images, rhetorical forms, and from the more important titles and terms. They arise even from the ordinary words of language as well. Words share certain of the characteristics of models in that they are not formed *ad hoc* to fit a precise thing, person, situation, or event, but are rather prior to the situation and can only be partially applied to it. Words are generic. Except for a few very special exceptions, words apply to *classes* of things. They do not therefore indicate what is *unique* or individual in what is referred to, but are based rather on certain elements which it has in common with other things grouped in the same class. Thus words are *general* and vague.[85] Most words have, in fact, large fields of reference within which there need not be even one common denominator.[86]

Words are also most often ambiguous: they have more than one meaning or reference.

Moreover, such classes and words are formulated through the history of a language, express a particular way of dividing up reality, and therefore help transmit a more or less fixed cultural world view.[87]

The generic nature of words is an obvious disadvantage when something unique is to be expressed; just as the fact that they have inherited meanings and uses is a disadvantage when the thing to be expressed is new. Thus vocabulary and language can be inadequate and in certain cases fail to serve effectively.[88]

Thus, the New Testament theologians used a number of devices to stretch the possibilities of their language. They used "in one situation words appropriate to another; and no problem arises provided the circumstances are known."[89] "Adjustor words," such as "like," were used to adjust a familiar language to an unfamiliar situation.[90] Especially in the later theology, "operator words" were used, such as "infinite" or "eternal," which did not have the logical function of describing something, but rather of indicating how a word or model should be operated or employed.[91] A common word could be expressly or implicitly redefined.[92] New words were coined. Words could be borrowed from another language, or technical terms from any number of specialized terminologies.[93] Another device was "The inventiveness of Christian usage."[94]

Ogden and Richards point out that Bonaventura, for example, drew the proper conclusions "from the nature of language itself" about the possibility of speaking about God: "(i) Nomen proportionem et similitudinem aliquam habet ad nominatum [the name ((word)) has proportion and some similarity to the named] (but God is infinite and language finite); (ii) Omne nomen imponitur a forma aliqua [every name is determined by a certain form] (but God is without form); (iii) Omne nomen significat substantium cum qualitate [every name signifies a substance with quality] (but in God there is mere substance without quality)."[95] This medieval realization of the infinite gulf between theological words and their object resulted in the so-called "negative way," whereby finite predicates applied to God were immediately qualified as being really completely inappropriate to their infinite object. This qualification did not prevent the medieval theologians from elaborating great systems and invoking sanctions against those who did not submit themselves to them. The theologians of the negative way recognized the limitation of symbolism as a whole, but realized less that all individual symbols, or models, are themselves limited with their advantages and disadvantages, and, therefore, need not be simply reduced to each other, synthesized, or used as norms for other symbols or models.

Words, then, as well as models, rhetorical devices, and so on, demand criticism. They are generic; they are most often vague and even ambiguous. They can be, and indeed often are, misleading. They cannot be simply accepted, but must be interpreted.

The Old and New Approaches to Language

All this leads one to realize that "Christian doctrine will never give us a blueprint of God. It will talk of God as best it can, but never in terms of more than models, metaphors, key-ideas and the rest . . ." [96] The nature of the means of thought and communication determines the nature of the discourse. All the expression, that is the theology of the New Testament, is thus essentially conditioned by the means employed. Once the use of literary or rhetorical forms in the New Testament is admitted, as one must (and as almost every church authority has), all the rest follows. The dependence on one form is an example of the total dependence on all.

The description of theology which we have given in this chapter reflects, in fact, a whole new approach to language. Uriel Weinreich states as one of the agreed principles of all modern linguistic studies: "The semantic mapping of the universe by a language is, in general, arbitrary, and the semantic 'map' of each language is different from those of all other languages." [97]

This is radically different from the older view that language is a *mirror of reality,* that "the structure of human speech reflects the structure of the world." [98] The origin of this view was "primitive word-magic. To classify things is to name them, and for magic the name of a thing or group of things is its soul; to know their names is to have power over their souls. Nothing, whether human or superhuman, is beyond the power of words. Language itself is a duplicate, a shadow-soul, of the whole structure of reality." [99]

Thus to study language was to study reality itself. Ogden and Richards write, quoting Whewell: "There are two ways . . . of comprehending nature, 'the one by examining the words only and the thoughts which they call up; the other by attending

to the facts and things which bring these notions into being
. . . The Greeks followed the former, the *verbal* or *notional*
course, and failed.' " [100]

From this old view of language comes the temptation to
solve a problem simply by labeling it. Molière made fun of the
doctors of his time who spent their energies inventing elaborate
names for illnesses they could not cure. Pascal ridiculed the scientists of his day for occupying themselves with words instead
of with phenomena. This pseudo-method of solution is far from
dead today; many theologians have attempted to solve the contradictions in the New Testament and in the history of theology
by applying to them the label "development," but taking care
first to empty it of any meaning it could possibly have.

People, with such a mentality, identify words with the
things to which they refer: "At all levels of intellectual per-
formance there are persons to be found to whom any suggestion
that they could change their symbols comes, and must come, as
a suggestion that they should recant their beliefs." [101]

Furthermore, if one believes that language is the picture of
reality, one will tend to conclude that all words must refer to
something real in the world. So all words, even the most abstract, must have some reference. The universe was thus peo-
pled with a myriad of beings: "forms," "essences," "substances,"
etc. Similarly, if there are two words, one would hold that they
must convey some real distinction, even though they might
seem to be referring to exactly the same thing and to be used
absolutely equivalently.

Moreover, the *structure* of reality must be mirrored by the
structure of language. If a noun is qualified by a predicate, a
"substance" must "receive" "accidents," etc. A great deal of
philosophy was constructed on purely verbal grounds.

A change in theory was bound to come once the scientific
study of language had begun. Ludwig Wittgenstein had mean-
while constructed the ultimate philosophical formulation of the
picture theory of language, in his *Tractatus Logico-Philosophi-
cus*. He himself abandoned this theory, as is well known, when
a friend of his made a typically Italian gesture and asked him

what form of words could possibly form a picture of it. Wittgenstein then went on to construct many of the philosophical arguments used to prove the impossibility of the old, picture theory of language and to show that language is purely a matter of convention, an organic system of conventional symbols.[102] I will indicate here just a few objections to the old theory of language.

Two languages will have a different word for the same thing. This shows that a word itself is purely conventional. There is no necessary connection between a word and the thing to which it refers.[103]

Moreover, the structures of different languages are not the same; therefore, they could not reflect the structure of reality.[104]

Furthermore, many words do not refer to something in the world, do not describe anything, but are merely linguistic devices; the most obvious example being the word "not." Daitz asks: "Does 'not' name an element in the world? If it does, how odd an element; if it doesn't, how do we describe the difference between 'This is red' and 'This is not red'?" [105] Universals are also such linguistic devices.[106]

One must conclude with Daitz that pictures and language are "two vastly different modes of signification: the iconic and the conventional." [107] To speak of language as a picture of reality is "a *misdescription* of language . . . It is clear that sentences do not show, but state." [108] This has important consequences for all the attitudes and procedures which were based on the old view of language as a descriptive reflection of the structure of reality.[109]

The New Testament can be properly understood only by following rules of interpretation which are based on this new approach to language. The writers of the New Testament did not think and communicate differently from other men; rather, they thought and communicated as all humans do, in the way which this new approach describes.

*Objections to a Solution from the Means of Thought
and Communication: Reduction*

I must now ask whether this view of language allows us to
unite the theologies of the New Testament. I have shown that
New Testament theologies use means of expression. Those
means introduce a good deal of disunity into the New Testament and demand to be interpreted. Could it be that the observable disunity results only from these means and that proper
interpretation could reveal a unity of point, a real unity of theology, behind those means? Could it be that the New Testament
writers wanted to say the same thing but just said it in different
ways?

The problem of disunity would be solved then simply by
reducing what the New Testament theologians wrote to what
they really wanted to say. This is a well-known technique in
theology and the one most used by Ramsey to reinterpret apparently outmoded doctrines.[110] Examples of reduction can
often and easily be found in the New Testament itself: to give
just one example, in Romans 2:25, Paul reduces the physical
circumcision to its spiritual significance.[111] But in everyday life,
certainly, one becomes suspicious when one hears someone say:
"Now what you really mean is . . . ." In the historical sciences,
to interpret a text in this way is a breach of good method. I will
give a few reasons why this is so.

Firstly, the writers probably did mean to say just what
they in fact said. The philosopher Paul Ziff pleads: "It seems
that nowadays hardly anyone pays any attention to what a man
says, only to what one thinks he means. But virtually no such
exegesis, virtually no such interpretation, virtually no such con-
strual, is called for here. If I say what is stupid, do not say
'What he must have meant is such-and-such': I almost certainly
meant what I said and if it was stupid then I was being stupid
at the time whether I meant what I said or not." [112]

Ramsey admits, but nowhere fully faces, the problem that
the final sense of theological phrases reinterpreted by his logical

reductions is most often essentially *different* from the sense originally intended by the historical writers and even more by their traditional interpreters.[113] He can only repeat that one *must* reduce the phrases, if they are to remain at all viable.

Secondly, the point which an author intends is often difficult, if not impossible, to separate from the means with which he expresses it. What the writer wished to say is inextricably bound to his model of reality, to that which he, in fact, believed to *be* reality.[114] If one removes the means of thought, one removes the point itself.

Similarly, a point of argument often depends utterly on the sense of a particular word or on the structure of a particular model. The point *is,* in fact, to apply this word or model to the object. Paul's whole argument in Romans 8:3 depends on the use of the Greek word "homoioma." [115]

Linguistic philosophers and Biblical scholars have therefore come to the conclusion that it is impossible to separate an intended point from its means of thought and expression without in fact changing the point.[116]

Such reduction is always arbitrary. One can, in fact, reduce everything to almost anything. One can reduce the use of the title "Messiah" either to the point that Jesus is "God" ("What the writer is trying to say in inadequate categories . . .") or to the point that Jesus was "a good man" ("Using the mythical categories of his day, the writer wishes to express simply that . . ."). Taking the literal sense of a scheme, image, or title, etc. as a starting point, one can construct increasingly generalized senses in all directions. For instance, "Son of Man" originally means a mythical personage who would arrive on the clouds at the end of time. First reduction: the Son of Man is really Jesus who will arrive on the clouds at the end of time. Second: the Son of Man is Jesus who will arrive at the end of time. Third: Jesus is the Son of Man in that he has in his life a direct connection with the heavenly sphere. Fourth: Jesus is the Son of Man because he is somehow "spiritual." Fifth: Jesus was called the "Son of Man" by the early community because they thought he was "important." Or one can reduce this title in a completely different direction, if one so chooses. First reduction: Jesus *is*, in truth, the Son of Man, a heavenly creature, who will arrive, etc. Second: Jesus, the Son of Man, being a heavenly creature, must exist before his future arrival and even before his life on earth. He must be preexistent. Third: in view of his central function, Jesus, the Son of Man, must have been the first of all preexistent creatures. Fifth: Jesus is God.

Which one of these directions one takes, and at which point one pauses, is purely arbitrary. All are equally possible once one has decided to reduce the original sense of the title to its "true" or "inner" meaning. The true point of the doctrine of life after death might simply be that the human being "matters." [117] All Christology might be reduced simply to the proposition that Jesus is important.[118]

Such interpretative reduction neither does the original justice nor exhausts it. Ferré criticizes Cox's attempt to reduce the proposition "God exists" to "Some men and women have had, and all may have, experiences called 'meeting God.' " [119] Argues Ferré: "What the existence of God means to the theist cannot be reduced, without residue, to experiential terms." [120] This can be said of any reduction to any terms. So much for reduction in general.

As regards the New Testament itself, one could claim that, in certain very limited cases, reduction could be used: for example, however, one might choose to phrase it, "I in Christ" and "Christ in me," which "seem to be mutually exclusive," [121] can be reduced "to the mystical conception of being *in Christ, inside a new sphere of experience and spiritual existence . . .*" This is not so much a case of reduction as of partial explanation.

In any case, no one could claim that all the New Testament contradictions could be so resolved. The point of the evilness of the Roman government, which the writer of the Apocalypse expresses in many schemes and images, contradicts the point that all government per se is good and from God, a point which Paul defends with the means of the idea of natural law. True, means are being used to make points here; but those points themselves contradict each other. I need not give further examples, nor would they give pause to those theologians determined to reduce all things to a unity no matter what the cost. The ultimate reduction of the whole Bible would possibly be "God is other," but justice would not thereby be done, for instance, to his "nearness in experience." I have already criticized such attempts to generalize away or reduce the theologies of the New Testament to some abstract formula. I need not repeat those criticisms here.

I can, however, in the light of what we have learned here about theology, make one further criticism of these efforts. Theology, I have argued, is essentially the application of models, etc. to a reality which cannot be known or discussed by any other means. Those points, to which we reduce the models of other theologies, are themselves models: "God is other," for instance, applies the similarity-dissimilarity-, and perhaps the distance-, model to God. Reduction, then, is ultimately trading models for models. A notorious case of this is the substitution of the depth model ("God is our ground of being," "deep within us") for the height model ("God is up there"). One model is thought, for one reason or another, to have more advantages than another, so all other models are reduced as much as possible to it. But these models themselves *are* theology: to theologize is to construct models. Therefore, what reduction is, in fact, is what one would have suspected all along: the substitution of one theology for another. That this cannot be done "without residue" is obvious, as is the fact that such a method is contrary to any historical understanding of a text. Reduction is not a means of understanding, but rather a device for conforming the theologies of others to our own. One can, of course, and indeed must, form one's own theology, but one need not reduce all other theologies to it.

CREATIVITY IN NEW TESTAMENT THEOLOGY

Throughout this chapter, it has become clear that the work of the New Testament theologians was essentially creative.

Christian theology did not exist before they created it. They had things, persons, and events to explain which were new and unique, for which models had to be found, accepted, or invented, and always qualified. Those things, persons, and events had somehow to be placed within many different total contexts of meaning, each of which had its own design, ideals, history, and expectations. The writers themselves were living in and experiencing a situation which was not only rich and new, but perpetually changing. New problems were continually arising and new solutions had to be invented for them. One does a serious injustice to those writers in their struggle when one assumes that they were simply unfolding some sort of deposit of truths or receiving the sort of supernatural aid which would spare them from contradicting others and even themselves. Those very contradictions bear witness to the humanity, and also to the creativity, of their labor. What the dogmatician uses as scientific propositions, the exegete understands as arduous and personal expression.

Paul had to create "a formulation for realities which were absolutely new; to master them in language, the apostle had indeed also to conquer new territory." [122] He did that "not without strain." [123] Paul becomes confused and corrects himself.[124] His sentences break apart: "The thought runs hastily forward and overruns the exact logic of the construction." [125] He skips necessary steps,[126] introduces points too early.[127] He bursts the bounds of his chosen rhetorical form.[128]

In Romans 5:6–8, Paul is seeking desperately to express himself. "Paul attempts somewhat stumblingly to give his thought an appropriate form; he makes several essays . . ." [129] Paul tries first "The mild expression 'weak' . . . , but it is explained and sharpened by the following designations: 'godless' . . . 'sinful' . . . 'hostile.' " [130] He finally fights his way through to a satisfying expression: "Verse 8 expresses in flawless formulation what V. 6, formally, left still to be desired . . ." [131] Again in Romans 5, one should "understand verses 15, 16, and 17 as parallel, and yet ever wider-ranging formulations of the same thought." [132] When, in verse 18, he has finally molded his means of expression as he wishes them, "Paul sets the three concepts in both parts of the verse like blocks next to each other, and relates them to each other only through the prepositions." [133] "Paul constantly attempts new formulations." [134]

The situations which Paul encountered were on the most practical level new, and he had to invent solutions for them. As Weiss says: "That the Lord did not give directions about mixed marriages is natural; Paul now, *on his own,* applies here the general prohibition of divorce to this case as well." [135]

Since most of the practical problems of the community were religious, they had to be solved theologically: to bring order into the services of the community, one had to construct a theology of the spirit which would allow and encourage order.[136]

The theological problems were new and had to be solved theologically. Weiss describes Paul's toil in I Corinthians 16:12–20: "The restless change of thoughts and motifs in this section, the relative imperfection of the logical exposition, the difficulty of understanding, which is conditioned notably by the peculiar use of [the Greek word "body"]—all this shows Paul's *struggle* for a truly conclusive refutation of the libertinistic view in the Corinthian community; for a refutation from the deepest religious convictions of Christianity. One sees how completely new and, till then, as yet unthought of, these arguments are; they are therefore not completely perfect in form and not completely unobjectionable." [137]

Some models of course were already to hand, such as the sermons of the Jewish missionaries among the Gentiles, sermons which castigated the epoch in its sinfulness. But Paul had somehow to make these models express a new message: "All that is not new. New, however, is the ordering of this criticism of the age into categories—the projection of it into a system of coordinates—which is constituted through the cross." [138]

In Paul's case, he also had certain Christian predecessors, but he could not simply content himself with what they had said. He had to broaden their conclusions in directions which they never would have imagined: he applies the old Christology to the Christian and then to his own personal situation.[139] He had learned a certain Christian teaching about baptism, but himself related baptism to the Crucifixion and Resurrection of Jesus as no one before him had ever done.[140]

He sometimes even achieves insights which are totally new. For instance, in Romans 1:18–3:20, Paul is assuming the teaching that Christ brought salvation and that, before him, there was no salvation in the world. The problem is then raised: what was the situation of the world before salvation? Looking at his own contemporaries and into history, Paul sees the fact of individual sins, a fact admitted by both the Jews and the Hellenistic peoples. Paul, basing himself on received teaching and on his own observation of the world, breaks through to an idea which is completely new: that those individual sins were the revelation of the wrath of God.[141]

Also, Paul had received a number of different schemes of redemptive history, but he could accept no one of them absolutely. He was led, by his own insights and experience, to form his own, new and original design. In fact, every writer of the New Testament formed his own outline of the history of salvation; each saw God working differently in the world. Of course, they also had inherited other schemes, many other ones; but none could entirely satisfy them. They learned from them, certainly; but, in the end, the scheme in which they themselves believed had to be one which expressed, not only what they had been taught, but also what they themselves had personally experienced and intuited. Naturally, there was never such a scheme already at hand; they had to create new ones.

How shallow, then, is the view that their efforts were merely "the human means." They were not just human means, but human thoughts, insights, and action.

We ourselves are, in all essentials, in the very same situation as they were. We are living in a new situation which is perpetually changing. We have received solutions which we can no longer totally accept. We also must search for models in our world to express something which is ultimately beyond us. Our labor is equally difficult and doubtful. But whatever we do construct, we must do justice to our new experiences and insights. Because of the nature of our situation, our object, and our means, our struggle, just as that of the New Testament writers, must necessarily be creative.

Notes

[1] J. L. Austin, *How to Do Things with Words,* ed. J. O. Urmson (Oxford: Clarendon Press, 1962). Also his "Performative Utterances" in his *Philosophical Papers,* ed. J. O. Urmson and G. J. Warnock (Oxford: Clarendon Press, 1961), pp. 220–239.

[2] Carl Brockelmann, *Hebräische Syntax* (Neukirchen Kreis Moers: Verlag der Buchhandlung des Erziehervereins, 1956), sec. 41d., p. 40.

[3] E.g., Kümmel, *op. cit.,* p. 519; Käsemann, *op. cit.* (Begründet), p. 217; Ogden-Richards, *op. cit.,* p. 130.

[4] Scott, *op. cit.,* pp. 26 ff.; Ramsey, *op. cit. (Religious),* p. 215; Frederick C. Grant, *The Earliest Gospel* (New York: Abingdon-Cokesbury Press, 1943), p. 167.

[5] Kümmel, *op. cit.,* pp. 161 f., 168.

[6] Dibelius, *op. cit. (Formgeschichte),* p. 7. See also pp. 8 f.

[7] Austin, *op. cit. (How),* p. 52. See also p. 20. See also his *Sense and Sensibilia,* ed. G. J. Warnock (Oxford: Clarendon Press, 1962), p. 118. This is also one of the concerns of existentialism and phenomenology.

[8] Norman Malcolm, *Ludwig Wittgenstein, A Memoir,* with a biographical sketch by G. H. v. Wright (London: Oxford University Press, 1958, paper, 1962), p. 93: "Ein Ausdruck hat nur im Strome des Lebens Bedeutung."

[9] Ogden-Richards, *op. cit.,* p. 141. See also pp. 142, 154 ff.

[10] Käsemann, *op. cit.* (Sackgassen), p. 44

[11] H. H. Farmer quoted in Frederick Ferré, *Language, Logic and God* (London: Eyre & Spottiswoode, 1962), p. 96.

[12] Ogden-Richards, *op. cit.,* p. 203. See also Willard Van Orman Quine, *Word and Object* (Cambridge: The M.I.T. Press, 1964), p. 8. See also John Ciampa, "The Synanon Game," *Los Angeles, FM & Fine Arts, Southern California's Entertainment Magazine,* Beverly Hills, December, 1966, pp. 4–11, p. 10: "If the group desires, the leader may read short passages from some

text to assist an individual who is re-living an experience of trying to come to grips with a confusing set of feelings." See also Louis Orizet, *Les Vins de France,* Que Sais-Je, Le Point des Connaissances Actuelles; 208 (Paris: Presses Universitares de France, 1964), p. 106: wine-tasting is a question of "the eye, the nose, the palate. Certainly, even the layman is capable of pronouncing a summary judgment on these three aspects, but, most of the time, his vocabulary is quickly found to be deficient for the expression of all his sensations. Indeed, our purpose is to furnish him with the references which will enable him to order and explain his emotion, his pleasure, or his disappointments. It is perhaps because the professionals have not sufficiently normalized the terminology of the subject of wine-tasting that the layman hesitates to hazard into the domain of the appreciation of wines, for fear of appearing ridiculous or just simply for lack of being able to express his sensations." See also pp. 103, 121 (for the terminology). For an example of wine-tasting terminology, see Art Buchwald, "It Puckers Your Mouth," column in the *International Herald Tribune,* July 23, 1968, p. 14: " 'It has a texture all its own,' I said. 'It tastes like cotton.' Lichine kicked me in the leg. 'What he means,' he said to the master, 'is that it tastes like velvet.' "

13 Ferré, *op. cit.,* p. 96.

14 Now in Robert Short, *The Gospel According to Peanuts* (Richmond, Va.: John Knox Press, 1965), pp. 36 f. (I clearly disagree with Short's interpretation.) Similar criticisms can be made of any philosophy or theology which seeks to base itself on some experience: e.g., Ramsey's disclosure experience.

15 See Cobb, *op. cit.,* pp. 225–228, on exponents of the new hermeneutics.

16 Odgen-Richards, *op. cit.,* p. 126. Also pp. 93 f., 152 f., 224 ff., 233 f.

17 See Kuss, *op. cit.* (*Römer*), pp. 386 f.; *op. cit.* (paulin. u. nachpaul.), pp. 123 f.; Bultmann, *op. cit.* (*Theologie*), pp. 143 f.

18 Grant, *op. cit.,* p. 12. Also pp. 164–167.

19 *Ibid.,* p. 167.

20 Ramsey, *op. cit.* (*Christian*), pp. 20 f.

21 Antony Flew, "Philosophy and Language" in his (ed.) *Essays in Conceptual Analysis* (London: Macmillan, 1963), pp. 1–20, pp. 6 f., 18. Stephen Ullmann, *The Principles of Semantics,* Glasgow University Publications; 84 (Oxford: Basil Blackwell, 1963), pp. 12–15.

22 E.g. Austin, *op. cit.* (*Sense*), pp. 62 ff.

23 Flew, *op. cit.* (Philosophy), pp. 4 f.

²⁴ *Ibid.*, pp. 5 f. See also Ullmann, *op. cit.* (*Semantics*), pp. 167 ff. on polysemy; pp. 180 f. on homonyms as causes of ambiguity.

²⁵ See, e.g. Willard Van Orman Quine, "Meaning in Linguistics" in his *From a Logical Point of View, 9 Logico-Philosophical Essays* (New York and Evanston: Harper Torchbooks, Harper & Row, 1963), pp. 47–64, pp. 61 f.; also his *op. cit.* (*Word*), pp. 77 f.

²⁶ Ullmann, *op. cit.* (*Principles*), pp. 156–170; *op. cit.* (*Semantics*), pp. 244–253, 312–321.

²⁷ Ullmann, *op. cit.* (*Semantics*), p. 245.

²⁸ See *ibid.*, p. 248; *op. cit.* (*Principles*), pp. 159, 163 ff.

²⁹ Ullmann, *op. cit.* (*Semantics*), p. 248. Also pp. 246 f. and *op. cit.* (*Principles*), p. 169.

³⁰ Ullmann, *op. cit.* (*Principles*), p. 159.

³¹ *Ibid.*, p. 163. Also pp. 310 ff., 319; Malinowski in Ogden-Richards, *op. cit.*, p. 328.

³² Ullmann, *op. cit.* (*Semantics*), p. 51.

³³ See Barr, *op. cit.*, chaps. 2–7.

³⁴ Nor can the language of the Bible provide "an authoritative standard on the syntactical level of theological discourse for the Christian religion" (Ferré, *op. cit.*, p. 93). At least, it could not provide a uniform standard.

³⁵ Ullmann, *op. cit.* (*Principles*), pp. 12 f.

³⁶ Ullmann, *op. cit.* (*Semantics*), pp. 193 f., 248, n. 1.

³⁷ Quine, *op. cit.* (*Word*), p. 8. See also p. 13.

³⁸ Ullman, *op. cit.* (*Semantics*), p. 22. Also pp. 21 ff.

³⁹ G. von der Gabelentz quoted in Ogden-Richards, *op. cit.*, p. 152. See also pp. 218, 224 ff., 233 f.

⁴⁰ C. F. Hockett quoted in Ullmann, *op. cit.* (*Semantics*), p. 22.

⁴¹ S. I. Hayakawa, *Language in Action* (New York: Harcourt, Brace, 1941), p. 65. Italics his.

⁴² Ogden-Richards, *op. cit.*, pp. 152 f. But see Ullmann, *op. cit.* (*Principles*), pp. 62–65.

⁴³ Willard Van Orman Quine, "Two Dogmas of Empiricism" in his *op. cit.* (*Logical*), pp. 20–46, pp. 39–42.

⁴⁴ See e.g. Martin Dibelius, "Glaube und Mystik bei Paulus" in his *Botschaft und Geschichte, Gesammelte Aufsätze,* Vol. 2, ed. G. Bornkamm, etc. (Tübingen: J. C. B. Mohr [Paul Siebeck], 1956), pp. 94–116, pp. 108, 115. C. H. Dodd, "The Appearances of the Risen Christ: An Essay in Form-Criticism of the Gospels" in D. E. Nineham, ed., *Studies in the Gospels, Essays*

in Memory of R. H. Lightfoot (Oxford: Basil Blackwell, 1955), pp. 9–35, p. 29. Scott, op. cit., pp. 22 f.

[45] Scott, op. cit., p. 23.

[46] Dodd, op. cit. (Appearances), p. 29.

[47] Ibid. Also Scott, op. cit., pp. 22 f.

[48] Ogden-Richards, op. cit., p. 156. See also pp. 154 f.

[49] Austin, op. cit. (Sense), p. 100. Italics his.

[50] Ibid., p. 101. Italics from ". . . or in . . ." to ". . . total situation . . ." are mine.

[51] Ibid., p. 101, n. 1.

[52] Otto Michel, Der Brief an die Römer (Meyer; 4) (Göttingen: Vandenhoeck & Ruprecht, 1963), p. 219. See also p. 219, n. 1, and p. 218.

[53] See Martin Dibelius, "Die Christianisierung einer hellenistischen Formel" in his op. cit. (Botschaft), pp. 14–29, 23 f., 27 f.

[54] E.g. Scott, op. cit., p. 23.

[55] E.g. Martin Dibelius, "Paulus und die Mystik" in his op. cit. (Botschaft), pp. 134–159, p. 152. See also Kümmel, op. cit., pp. 335 f.

[56] E.g. Grant, op. cit., pp. 12, 164 f.

[57] E.g. Barth, quoted in Kümmel, op. cit., p. 468.

[58] Ramsey, op. cit. (Religious), p. 190. This is symptomatic of Ramsey's tendency to systematize. Models are subsumed under "dominant models," which are subsumed under the "super-model" of "person." See his op. cit. (Christian), pp. 82–86.

[59] Ramsey, op. cit. (Religious), pp. 55–102; op. cit. (Christian) esp. pp. 28–60; also his Models and Mystery (London: Oxford University Press, 1964), passim.

[60] Apostel quoted in Ramsey, op. cit. (Models), p. 12.

[61] Ibid., p. 15.

[62] Ibid., p. 6. See also pp. 1–6.

[63] Max Black quoted in ibid., p. 6.

[64] See ibid.

[65] Ibid.

[66] Ibid., p. 21.

[67] Ibid., p. 20. See also Ferré, op. cit., pp. 152 f.

[68] Willard Van Orman Quine, "On What There Is" in his op. cit. (Logical), pp. 1–19, p. 17; Ramsey, op. cit. (Religious), p. 191.

[69] See Johannes Weiss, Der erste Korintherbrief (Meyer; 5) (Göttingen: Vandenhoeck & Ruprecht, 1910), pp. 305 f. Paul is

usually as bad at choosing and using images as Charlie Brown is at flying kites. In Rom. 6:19, he must apologize for introducing an inappropriate and offensive image (Kuss, *op. cit.* [*Römer*], p. 390). After unraveling a most confused and pressing Pauline use of a rural image in Rom. 11:16 f., 23 f., Lietzmann, *op. cit.* (*Römer*), *ad loc.*, made his famous remark: "Paul is a child of the city." See also I Cor. 9:24 (and comments of Lietzmann, *op. cit.* [*Korinther*], and Weiss, *op. cit., ad loc.*); and II Cor. 3:2. Paul sometimes manages to correct himself, as in I Cor. 15:37 f. (see Weiss, *op. cit.*, p. 369).

⁷⁰ Weiss, *op. cit.*, p. 167. See also p. 72, and Kuss, *op. cit.* (*Römer*), p. 452.

⁷¹ Ramsey, *op. cit.* (*Christian*), chap. II, "The Atonement," pp. 28–60. See esp. pp. 36–40, 43 f., 51 f.

⁷² Ramsey, *op. cit.* (*Religious*), pp. 184 f., 190–198.

⁷³ See, e.g., Peter Herbst, "The Nature of Facts" in Flew, *op. cit.* (*Essays*), pp. 134–156, pp. 142 ff. Quine, *op. cit.* (Two Dogmas), pp. 44 f.

⁷⁴ See Weiss, *op. cit.*, pp. 220 ff.

⁷⁵ *Ibid.*, pp. 374 f.; Lietzmann, *op. cit.* (*Korinther*), pp. 85 ff. (see also Kümmel's notes to Lietzmann's interpretation).

⁷⁶ For this and the following, Kuss, *op. cit.* (*Römer*), pp. 101 f.

⁷⁷ Lietzmann, *op. cit.* (*Korinther*), p. 135.

⁷⁸ Kuss, *op. cit.* (*Römer*), p. 195. See also p. 194 and Kuss's remarks on verse 4:12.

⁷⁹ Lietzmann, *op. cit.* (*Römer*), p. 90.

⁸⁰ See e.g., I Cor. 1:4–9 (Weiss, *op. cit.*, p. 6) and I Cor. 12:5 (*ibid.*, p. 297).

⁸¹ See Kuss, *op. cit.* (*Römer*), pp. 224–275. Günther Bornkamm, "Paulinische Anakoluthe im Römerbrief" in his *Das Ende des Gesetzes, Paulusstudien, Gesammelte Aufsätze*, Vol. 1, Beiträge zur evangelischen Theologie, Theologische Abhandlungen; 16 (Munich: Chr. Kaiser Verlag, 1963), pp. 76–92, pp. 80–90. Eberhard Jüngerl, "Das Gesetz zwischen Adam und Christus, Eine theologische Studie zu Röm 5, 12–21," in ZTK, 1963, pp. 42–74. Jüngerl takes the main lines of his argument from Bornkamm's article.

⁸² Jüngerl, *op. cit.*, p. 66.

⁸³ Kuss, *op. cit.* (*Römer*), p. 238.

⁸⁴ Jüngerl, *op. cit.*, pp. 60, 63. See also Billerbeck, *op. cit.*, p. 230.

⁸⁵ Ullmann, *op. cit.* (*Semantics*), pp. 118 f.

[86] *Ibid.*, pp. 118, 124 f.; Ogden-Richards, *op. cit.*, pp. 129, 146 f.

[87] Ullmann, *op. cit.* (*Semantics*), pp. 120–123.

[88] Austin, *op. cit.* (*Sense*), pp. 73 f., 130.

[89] *Ibid.*, p. 91. He is not referring specifically to New Testament writers, but his remarks can be applied to them.

[90] *Ibid.*, pp. 73 ff.

[91] Ramsey, *op. cit.* (*Religious*), pp. 55–102.

[92] See, e.g., Kuss, *op. cit.* (*Römer*), pp. 609 f.; Ullmann, *op. cit.* (*Semantics*), pp. 165 f.

[93] Kuss, *op. cit.* (paul und nachpaul.), pp. 134 ff.

[94] Nigel Turner, *Syntax*, Vol. 3 of James Hope Moulton, *A Grammar of New Testament Greek* (Edinburgh: T. and T. Clark, 1963), p. 262. See also ff.

[95] Ogden-Richards, *op. cit.*, p. 255, n. 2.

[96] Ramsey, *op. cit.* (*Religious*), p. 191.

[97] Uriel Weinreich, "On the Semantic Structure of Language" in Joseph H. Greenberg (ed.), *Universals of Language, Report of a Conference held at Dobbs Ferry, New York, April 13–15, 1961* (Cambridge: The M.I.T. Press, 1966), 2nd ed., pp. 142–216, p. 142. For theology, see the prophetic book of Tyrrell, *op. cit.*, p. 103: "The only remedy lies in a frank admission of the principle of symbolism." See also pp. 100–104, 213 f.

[98] Ogden-Richards, *op. cit.*, p. 32, explaining the view of Heraclitus.

[99] *Ibid.*, p. 31. See also Malinowski in *ibid.*, pp. 322–326; Ullmann, *op. cit.* (*Principles*), p. 66.

[100] Ogden-Richards, p. 34. See pp. 44 ff. for modern times.

[101] *Ibid.*, p. 216.

[102] E. Daitz, "The Picture Theory of Meaning," in Flew, *op. cit.* (*Essays*), pp. 53–74. George Pitcher (ed.), *Truth,* "Contemporary Perspectives in Philosophy Series" (Englewood Cliffs, N.J.: Prentice-Hall, 1964), pp. 4–14 (his introduction).

[103] Ullmann, *op. cit.* (*Semantics*), p. 60; Ogden-Richards, *op. cit.*, pp. 10 f.

[104] Flew, *op. cit.* (Philosophy), p. 6. See also Ullman, *op. cit.* (*Principles*), p. 16.

[105] Daitz, *op. cit.*, p. 57. See also pp. 68 f.; Austin, *op. cit.* (*How*), pp. 3–6, 12, 21 f., 46; *op. cit.* (*Sense*), pp. 3, 83; Flew, *op. cit.* (Philosophy), pp. 14 ff. Many more examples could be given.

[106] Ogden-Richards, *op. cit.*, pp. 95–101.

[107] Daitz, *op. cit.*, p. 67.

[108] *Ibid.* Italics are Daitz's.

[109] E.g. Ogden-Richards, *op. cit.,* pp. 67, 97.

[110] E.g. Ramsey, *op. cit. (Religious),* pp. 85, 94 f., 101, 136 f., 140, 183–187, 193–197, 201 ff.; *op. cit. (Models),* pp. 64 f. See also his *On Being Sure in Religion* (London: The Athlone Press, 1963), pp. 8–12, 16–20. See also Ferré, *op. cit.,* pp. 38 ff. For similarities see Quine, *op. cit.* (Two), pp. 25 f.

[111] See Kuss, *op. cit. (Römer),* p. 89.

[112] Paul Ziff, *Semantic Analysis* (Ithaca: Cornell University Press, 1960), pp. vii f.

[113] Ramsey, *op. cit. (Sure),* pp. 20 f.

[114] Ramsey, *op. cit. (Christian),* p. 47.

[115] Kuss, *op. cit. (Römer),* pp. 491 ff. Comp. Flew, *op. cit.* (Philosophy), p. 5, on J. S. Mill.

[116] E.g. Kümmel, *op. cit.,* pp. 486 ff., 491.

[117] Ferré, *op. cit.,* p. 123.

[118] See, e.g., Bultmann, *op. cit. (Theologie),* p. 46.

[119] Ferré, *op. cit.,* p. 39.

[120] *Ibid.,* p. 41.

[121] Turner, *op. cit.,* p. 263, and for the following quote.

[122] Otto Kuss, "Zu Röm 6, 5a," in his *op. cit. (Auslegung),* pp. 151–161, p. 156.

[123] *Ibid.*

[124] E.g. I Cor. 4:3–5. See Weiss, *op. cit.,* p. 97.

[125] Kuss, *op. cit. (Römer),* p. 18 on Rom. 1:12. Also p. 85 on Rom. 2:19–22.

[126] Rom. 7:25. See *ibid.,* pp. 459 f.

[127] Rom. 10:16. See Lietzmann, *op. cit. (Römer),* on this text.

[128] Rom. 6:5. See Kuss, *op. cit. (Römer),* p. 303.

[129] *Ibid.,* p. 207.

[130] *Ibid.,* p. 208.

[131] *Ibid.,* p. 210.

[132] *Ibid.,* p. 237.

[133] *Ibid.,* p. 238.

[134] *Ibid.,* p. 297. See also pp. 108 f., 296 ff.

[135] Weiss, *op. cit.,* p. 179. Italics are Weiss's. See also pp. 192 f., 339 f., 342 f.

[136] *Ibid.,* pp. 297, 341. Also Kuss, *op. cit.* (Enthusiasmus).

[137] Weiss, *op. cit.,* pp. 168 f. Italics are Weiss's.

[138] Kuss, *op. cit. (Römer),* p. 56.

[139] II Cor. 13:4. See Lietzmann, *op. cit. (Korinther),* p. 161, and the additional notes of Kümmel.

[140] See Kuss, *op. cit.* (*Römer*), on chap. 6, and also his *op. cit.* (vorpaul. Tauf.), *op. cit.* (paul. u. nachpaul.), *op. cit.* (Todestaufe).

[141] Otto Kuss, "Die Heiden und die Werke des Gesetzes (Nach Röm 2, 14–16)" in his *op. cit.* (*Auslegung*), pp. 213–245, p. 228. See also his *op. cit.* (*Römer*), p. 44.

10

The Systematization
of the
New Testament

In view of the great mass and importance of the theological contradictions in and between the theologies of the New Testament, one might well ask how they were ever leveled into the various modern dogmatic systems or syntheses.

The historian is aware that contradictions also exist in tradition. Newman has shown conclusively that the formula of Vincent of Lerins—the faith is that which has been believed always, everywhere, and by all—cannot, in fact, be applied to the fathers.[1] Newman's theory of development was an attempt to solve the problems posed by this disunity. The same objections made against applying that theory to the contradictions of the New Testament could be made against applying it to the history of theology: the differences run too deep. In any case, the phenomenon of the constant, historical disunity of the history of theology forbids one's speaking of *the* tradition, just as the theological disunity of the New Testament forbids one's speaking of *the* teaching of the New Testament. In fact, the history of theology is subject to the very same rules of human thought and communication which were followed in the New Testament: partial models are used, each of which has its advantages and disadvantages.[2] Of course, the later Christians created means for imposing order, such as excommunication, which did not exist in New Testament times; [3] but this did not, and could not, result in the absolute uniformity desired. Even if the historian chooses to confine himself to those theologies labeled orthodox, he can find evidence enough of irreducible, and even at times consciously undecided differences. But he will most likely not so confine his view and will discover the value of so-called unorthodox theologies and sometimes the injustice of their condemnation, even on orthodox terms.

Moreover, the many contradictions between the New Testament and important doctrines of the church today need hardly even be mentioned. The later doctrines which are contradicted range from those of the divinity of Christ, the personality of the Holy Spirit, and thus of the whole doctrine of the Trinity; to the teaching that the hierarchical church was founded by Jesus; that the sacramental system is, in any way, cultic; that there were any established and generally practiced Christian services other than baptism and the common meal of the community etc., etc. A host of smaller, but no less discrediting, contradictions could be mentioned: for instance, that in Mark 14: 23–24, Jesus pronounces the so-called "words of institution" after the apostles have drunk the wine. Mark could therefore have had no idea that these words were somehow to change the wine, as the later doctrine of transubstantiation defined.

That the enormous effort of systematizing all of these contradictions was undertaken is only comprehensible in light of the faith in the old theory of the unity of the New Testament being the foundation of the unity of theology, which, in turn, unites the church. According to this theory, no contradictions could possibly exist in the New Testament itself, between the New Testament and the later tradition, or within the tradition itself. The problem, therefore, for those who would maintain such a theory is to deal somehow with the contradictions within those areas.

These problems arise, of course, for any religion which bases itself on a supposed revelation which should be somehow contained in a historical book and/or tradition. The rabbis constructed such a theory with the Old Testament as the record of revelation and the rabbinic tradition as its unfolding or explication.[4] Naturally, the rabbis were then forced to overinterpret Scripture and to posit an in fact nonexistent continuous tradition from the times of Moses to their own. No conflict within or between the Old Testament and the supposed tradition could be admitted; this led, quite naturally again, to systematic violence being done to the text and to history. The theory was particularly hard to maintain as new situations arose and had to be met. But the rabbis preserved a certain perspective: "When the exigencies of the time seemed to demand it, the rabbis in council or individually did not hesitate to suspend or set aside laws in the Pentateuch on their own authority, without exegetical subterfuges or pretense of Mosaic tradition." [5]

One of the interests of this example is that almost all Christians accept the fact of contradictions in the Old Testament and would therefore condemn any attempts at suppressing them. But those same Christians often use the very same methods to interpret the New Testament.

For the rules of "systematic" interpretation are everywhere the same; they are the very opposite of the rules for scientific historical interpretation. These rules are also a direct result of an adherence to the old view of language. If language is a picture of reality, and if all that is written in Scripture must be a true picture of reality, then the New Testament pictures must be able to be synthesized into a larger picture which would contain all of the individual ones and put them in their place. Therefore, just as the new approach to language provides rules to interpret accurately and historically the different New Testament theologies, so the old theory of language, coupled with the presuppositions of the old theories of unity, provides rules for distorting the intended meaning of a historical text.

I will now examine very briefly just a few of the methods of systematic interpretation. But first I should point out that many of the false interpretations of the New Testament arose from simple misunderstandings. I have mentioned that the later Gentile converts were often unacquainted with the Palestinian background presupposed in many of the traditions which they received. Thus points of parables, sayings, and stories could be misunderstood. Similarly, later theologians thought that the title "Son of Man" referred to the "humanity" of Christ and "Son of God" referred to his "divinity."

Nevertheless, very often a text is simply forced to express what the interpreter wishes it to say. Paul merely follows rabbinic method when he twists Old Testament texts to suit his purpose, even when the sense which he imposes on them may be directly contrary to what their authors had originally intended.[6] Paul does this by adding or subtracting words, by changing them around, by combining texts, by taking a statement from one context and putting it in another; and also by reduction, allegory, and so on.

Not even the most orthodox theologians have ever, to my knowledge, suggested that his interpretations be accepted as normative for the church.

The oldest and most blatant method of reading an unintended meaning into a text is allegory: the elements in the text stand for something else.[7] Paul and the early Christians used allegory extensively. Allegory can take on many forms, which we need not so name. Some Protestants thought that their system of ecclesiastical government was indicated in the New Testament by the word "presbyter." Some Catholics found theirs in the word "episcopoi." But these words mean, respectively, "elder" and "overseers." Later definitions and connotations are applied to words at a stage at which they had not acquired them. Few would condone such methods today,[8] simply because they falsify the historical meaning of a text and allow one to read into it anything one desires.

There are, however, subtler ways of unifying theologies: for example, one can argue from words as if they were technical terms and thus always had the same meaning or reference. I have shown how Dodd claimed that *kerygma* and *didaché* were technical terms for two very different things and then used this supposed difference as the basis for his projection of the dogma-private opinion distinction into the New Testament.[9] The fatal objection to such an attempt is that such a technical use of these words cannot be found in the New Testament.

Of course, once one defines these words as technical terms, one can find a remarkable unity between the different theologies of the New Testament: did they not all use the same words, which are technical terms with always the same meanings? Did they not therefore share exactly the same ideas? Thus the temptation arises to discuss, always word by word, "the basic concepts" of earliest Christianity.

Uses can be read into a word. A word can be used in very many contexts; thus the temptation arises to consider all those contexts as somehow included in the word. Thus some theologians speak of words being "Christianized" because they have been used by Christian writers. By finding "in the word" all the contexts in which it has been used, one can find very large unities indeed in the New Testament.

A similar method of reading into a text is that of using, in one's explication of it, terms which possess connotations which are inappropriate because they are anachronistic or introduce nuances or contexts foreign to the text. For instance, speaking of the New Testament stereotyped formulas as "creeds" is very misleading.

Another method is based on the phenomenon of meaning change. Ullmann writes: "Objects, institutions, ideas, scientific concepts change in the course of time; yet in many cases the name is retained and thus helps to ensure a sense of tradition and continuity." [10] Many theologians have constructed modern theologies that contained just the same words in just the same contexts and in just the same relationships to each other; only all those words were given new and modern definitions. A lulling semblance of continuity was maintained, while something new was created. Let those with ears hear; and those with eyes, see.

There were, of course, many disadvantages to this method. The continuity was often merely that of a verbal facade. The original meaning of the word had disappeared without a trace leaving only the form of the word behind: "the cherished resemblances no longer clothe the beloved object." [11] Those who use this method would most probably claim that their definition of the word revealed its "real meaning." In other words, advocates of these definitions almost inevitably use the method of reduction as well.

Another disadvantage of this method is that it twists a new theology onto an old form. The old words are turned into cumbrous circumlocutions. For instance, let us imagine a theology which articulated the relations between man and God according to the model of personal intercourse. God speaks to us; we speak to God. We encounter each other as persons. Now, let us suppose that the author of this theology felt, for one reason or another that he had to use the term "grace" in this theology. To follow this model perfectly, he would have to translate the word into personal terms, say, the "graciousness" of God. But let us suppose further that this theologian felt bound to use the word "grace" just as it is. He is then forced to use expressions which are capable of including the word "grace": "God gives us his grace"; "We have received his grace." But our theologians did wish to speak in personal terms! His only recourse is to somehow "define" "grace" emphatically and incessantly as "personal": "the deepest, innermost element of a person," "personality as such," etc. Then, if someone asked him why he just did not say: "We encounter God as a person" instead of saying "God gives us his grace, which is, as always, the innermost, deepest, most profound element of his person as such"; his only answer could be that he must somehow find a place for the word "grace." What is happening here is, clearly, that our theologian is trying to use a personal model as a means of expression, but expressing that means of expression through another which is its exact opposite: a nonpersonal model is taken as the means of expression for a personal one. He would surely not be so roundabout, if he felt he could avoid it.

A third great disadvantage of this method is that it is, in practice, not very successful. *Newsweek* reports: "Protestant pastors have been living in a world of 'semantic double-talk,' charges Presbyterian minister Carl Thomas of San Mateo, California. 'We haven't changed the words, so Mrs. Jones in the pew will stay there. But we've changed the meaning, hoping that when the man comes in off the street, he'll recognize the differences. But it doesn't work.' " [12]

I need not discuss again the method of pressing images, nor that of reduction. The latter method has been employed extensively, and most often consciously, throughout the history of theology; the best known example being Aquinas' many reductions of Augustine. Countless later theologians have realized that Aquinas had twisted Augustine's teachings to conform to his own, but this has not led them to reevaluate the theory of unity which caused Aquinas to feel he had to do so; nor to reconsider their own uses of this method.

All of these methods are the *Doppelgänger,* as it were, of the rules for historical interpretation; they are all designed to suppress the point originally intended by the author. I am far from denying that the richness of a writing may give rise to many different interpretations. But let all those interpretations be truly historical, be true attempts at understanding the richness that is the author's; not merely impositions of the interpreter himself on what he should be interpreting.

Needless to say, once one has used these methods to read certain points into texts, one can then draw conclusions from those points, extrapolate from them, use them in fact as the bases of a whole system.

The easiest method of systematization is that of simply combining elements. Ephesians 5:5 speaks of "the kingdom of the Christ [the Messiah] and of God," thereby simply joining two irreducible eschatological representations.[13]

Another method of synthesizing a contrary view into a proposed system is to add new elements to that view. We have seen how II Thessalonians gets around the eschatological view of I Thessalonians simply by adding elements to it: through them, an entirely new eschatological scheme is created. Of course, the old view is thereby essentially changed.

Another such method is to subordinate one view to another. For instance, the exegete Ernst von Dobschütz attempts to synthesize two theologies which he finds in I Corinthians 15: 4–5. In the passive "he was raised," the activity of God is indicated; but in "he appeared," the activity of Jesus is expressed. Dobschütz synthesizes these two theologies by formulating thus: "God determined that Christ, awakened through his might, is now also seen . . ."[14] The Christocentric theology is merely subordinated to the Theocentric. Also, Bultmann has a tendency to take one representation as a category under which he gathers various other views: [15] the choice of the representation which will be the category for the others must remain, of course, arbitrary.

Another method is to unite two theologies through a principle which is foreign to both of them. Bultmann unites two representations of the spirit—that it is God's gift and that it is Christ's—through the principle that "the gift of the [spirit] was effected through the redemptive event which was executed in Christ." [16] But this principle does not belong necessarily to either of these views and can only be imposed on them from without.

Even Käsemann asks "from what unified center" the various antinomies of Paul's theology of God's justice can be understood.[17] He discusses the idea of God's justice as "gift" and as "might," [18] and finds their "unified center" in the principle: "Might becomes gift when it takes possession of us and enters us . . ." [19] Many criticisms can be made of this attempt at synthesis. Most fundamentally, "gift" and "might" are two models, each of which allows us to articulate different things: to put it simply, the "gift" model allows us to speak of God's justice in terms of his love; the "might" model allows us to speak of it in terms of his rule or power. These models need not be, and in fact are not, reducible to each other. Käsemann attempts to reduce them by subsuming them under a principle which is extraneous to both models and the points each one is trying to make. As Käsemann formulates the principle, one can doubt that it is even genuinely Pauline. What Käsemann does ultimately is to subsume the "gift" model under the "might" model, to make one model the tool of the other.

When even exegetes convinced of the disunity of Scripture nod, one need not wonder that others make grosser attempts at systematizing. Such attempts remain the greatest dangers for a true, historical understanding of the text.

Eventually, such additions and introductions of foreign principles lead to full-scale speculative superstructures which attempt to solve all possible contradictions.[20] The New Testament speaks of Jesus as being both subordinate to God and equal to God. A speculative structure is constructed to accommodate both of these views: Jesus had a full, concretized human nature (which was, of course, subordinate) and a full divine nature (which was, of course, equal). Then the question arises, how are these two full natures united? The answer is produced: the divine nature is the person. Then the problem arises, how can a full, concretized, individuated human nature, which possesses, after all, an intellect and a will, not also be a person? A host of modern theologies seeks to establish some initiative, etc. for "the human nature" of Christ. The contradiction between the original theologies to be systematized has not been resolved; it has simply been moved to another level; it has been hidden deep inside a system. Instead of realizing that each of the original theologies was using a model, the later systematizers took each one as a literal picture of the object. Because they knew that truth was one, they tried to design a larger picture of the object which could somehow accommodate the two irreducible models used of it. That this was ultimately impossible is obvious.

Similarly, if Jesus *is* God and is, admittedly, also distinct from God, the problem arises as to how this identity and distinction can both be accommodated. The doctrine of the Trinity defines God as three persons but one God. But does personality not necessarily entail individuality, and thus three Gods? The answer is given that, in this case, personality does not do so. The contradiction is not resolved, but merely transposed.

Dogmatic theologians call this process "placing the mystery." The mystery of God is said to reside where their speculative superstructures break down: where a full, concretized, individuated human nature is not also a person; where personality does not entail individuality. What these theologians call "placing the mystery" is, in fact, merely transposing the contradiction. Most of those troubled by the original contradiction will be satisfied by the first answer: "Oh, I see, two natures, so one aspect is equal and another subordinate." Few will ask the next question; and one must be very well acquainted with the usually rather complicated superstructure to be able to continue asking until one meets the contradiction in its final form, which is then labeled a "mystery." By then, one has usually been converted to the superstructure itself. We do not lack theologians who would rather resign themselves to the impossibilities of their explanations than abandon themselves to the incomprehensibleness of the mystery.

These systems, then, do not resolve contradictions; rather, they use sleight of hand to make them disappear.[21]

These theoretical superstructures, just as the theologies of the New Testament, posit conceptual entities. Many belong to the philosophies on which the superstructures are based. Problems arise of course when those philosophies are no longer tenable.[22]

Many such posits have been constructed according to theological need. Just as the Jews and the early Christians posited hell to settle the accounts of the wicked, so the later theology posited limbo to accommodate less obvious cases. Just as Luke posits a virgin birth to account for the Hellenistic understanding of the title "Son of God," so the later theologians posit a *vow* of virginity to account for that virginity itself and a miraculous birth to resolve any further complications. Even the popular tradition, in its innocence, posited a great age for Joseph. Many such posits originate in the much used theological principle of "appropriateness": it was appropriate that Jesus be born of a virgin, etc.

One's judgment of what is real and what merely a posit depends on one's own theory. He who has constructed a theory on "grace" will regard it as real. He who has constructed his theory on "person" will regard "grace" just as a convenient posit. Similarly, the unbeliever will regard "God" as merely a posit in a certain theory to which he does not himself subscribe.[23] Quine goes so far as to say: "Everything to which we concede existence is a posit from the standpoint of a description of the theory-building process, and simultaneously real from the standpoint of the theory that is being built."[24]

Systematic theology is then the attempt to systematize or

synthesize irreducible models or theologies.[25] Of course, the first systematic theologians would not themselves have so described their efforts. They believed that they were constructing a real picture of their object, and this belief lends dignity to their endeavors and controversies. However, for those who have realized that theology is essentially the construction of models which are neither pictures of their objects nor necessarily reducible to each other, several important objections arise against the very practice of systematic theology.

Firstly, the practice of systematization ignores the nature of models. They need not, and indeed cannot, be reduced without residue to each other. The attempt to reduce or to systematize models inevitably falls into the methodological errors discussed earlier in this chapter.

Secondly, models, of their nature, cannot be solid bases for systems because their necessary use introduces the element of uncertainty previously discussed.[26]

Thirdly, such superstructures tend to stifle or confuse prayer, worship, and a personal attitude toward God and Jesus.[27] The doctrine of the Trinity, if it is really the center of Christianity, should surely be centrally important in the conscious lives of most Christians. This is notoriously not the case. Theologians preach incessantly the need of making this doctrine the center of our lives, but seldom tell us how to do so. When the Third Person of the Blessed Trinity was "revived" a few years ago, most people found that the only method of giving him more attention seemed to be to honor him somewhat as one did a saint. This, exclaimed the theologians, was not the way one honored the Holy Spirit. Nonetheless, most people did not seem capable of extracting much spiritual nourishment from the speculative definitions which the theologians proffered. On the contrary, where the doctrine of the Trinity does arise, it is most often felt as a disturbance. Many Catholics find that the Preface of the Trinity intrudes on the mood created in the Mass up to that point.

One can be so impressed by the greatness of Paul's image of God as personal and acting, and then distressed by the enormous and inhibiting complications introduced by the apparatus of the doctrine of the Trinity. Can we imagine the God of Paul and of the Old Testament as really being three persons acting somehow as one? Or are we more deeply impressed by their vision of one personal God? Elaborate explanations only diminish, sometimes fatally, the powerful impression of God which one can receive from the theologians of the Old and New Testaments.

Similarly, few can pray to Jesus in terms of the doctrine of the Hypostatic Union. The moment the mechanics of that doctrine intrude on our image of Jesus, many find it difficult to find a point of personal contact: am I praying to Jesus in his humanity? Only to the Second Person of the Blessed Trinity? Can I make some contact with the whole? Supersophisticated explanations of how this can be done leave most people stumbling in their dust.

As just one example of the confusions introduced by this superstructure, I might mention the following curious story. At my university, a graduate student (later an Anglican priest) was conducting a survey on a subject in religious psychology. I was one of the tested. He first gave me a card with the word "mother," and I was to answer a series of questions using that word to fill in the blanks: for instance, "——————loves me?" "——————wishes me well?" etc. After answering all the questions for "mother," I was given a card with the word "father." After answering all the questions for "father," I received another card on which was written the word "God." As my tester apparently thought I looked puzzled, he took me on tiptoe into the next room and asked in a whisper: "When you think of God, do you think of God the Father, Jesus, or the Blessed Trinity?" I hesitated to tell him that he had not exhausted the possibilities.

The above considerations are admittedly subjective, and one should not put too much weight on them even in one's personal theology. But the final objection against systematization is purely objective: that the very source of Christian theology, the New Testament itself, contains theological contradictions which cannot be properly systematized. One pole of a contradiction can be suppressed, veiled, forgotten, misunderstood, or forced; but it cannot be synthesized to the opposite pole. Any consistent system must reject certain New Testament theologies and accept others. But the strongest motive and ultimate purpose of the usual systematizer are thereby vitiated: he can no longer construct a total synthesis of all the elements of New Testament theology. He must place his own system next to all the others as just one theology among many.

Moreover, when one realizes that whatever one *does* systematize is, from that very fact, changed—by being placed in another context, added to, given a new set of coordinates, etc.; then one must question the very validity of any such synthesis. One is not explaining or revealing "the real meaning" by systematizing; one is merely transforming the original elements. One could no more synthesize Aquinas and Kant without radically changing them than one could so systematize Gilson and Maritain. In philosophy and theology, as well as in literature, the original work is not transformable. Aquinas must be understood on his own, not through his later commentators. Luther is being continually disentangled from the later Lutheran theologians. A textbook survey of a *Summa* is on a par with plot outlines of Shakespeare's plays. Nothing replaces the original because nothing can reproduce it.

Theology for centuries has been just this attempt at total systematization. Theology is forced, then, either to content itself with several systematizations of only parts of the New Testament, or else to discover a whole new procedure. Since even partial systematizations have the disadvantage of necessarily distorting everything they touch, a new procedure would seem to be demanded, the first concern of which would be to respect, appreciate, and care for the individualities of the many theologies which have preceded it; to be humble before the toil of earlier theologians. Such a procedure does not yet exist; it must be created.

Notes

[1] Newman, *op. cit.* (*Development*), pp. 9–27.

[2] See Ramsey, *op. cit.* (*Religious*), pp. 197 ff.

[3] Ehrhardt, *op. cit.*, pp. 170 f.

[4] George Foot Moore, *Judaism in the First Centuries of the Christian Era, The Age of the Tannaim*, Vol. 1 (Cambridge: Harvard University Press, 1927), pp. 251–262.

[5] *Ibid.*, p. 259.

[6] See Lietzmann, *op. cit.* (*Korinther*), pp. 112 (II Cor. 3:13), 138 (II Cor. 9:7); 160 (II Cor. 13:1). Kuss, *op. cit.* (*Römer*), pp. 87 (Rom. 2:24), 182 (Rom. 4:6 ff.). See also Weiss, *op. cit.*, p. 285. Ramsey, *op. cit.* (*Religious*), p. 137.

[7] See the remarks of Overbeck in Kümmel, *op. cit.*, pp. 255 f.

[8] But see Ramsey, *op. cit.* (*Christian*), p. 16.

[9] Bultmann also bases arguments on supposed technical meanings of word. See, e.g., his *op. cit.* (*Theologie*), p. 152.

[10] Ullmann, *op. cit.* (*Semantics*), p. 198. See also pp. 199, 209 ff.; *op. cit.* (*Principles*), p. 211. Odgen-Richards, *op. cit.*, p. 216.

[11] Rignano, quoted in Odgen-Richards, *op. cit.*, p. 42.

[12] *Newsweek*, January 3, 1966, p. 31.

[13] Bultmann, *op. cit.* (*Theologie*), pp. 81, 84.

[14] Dobschütz, *op. cit.*, p. 22.

[15] Bultmann, *op. cit.* (*Theologie*), pp. 87 f. See also pp. 197 f.

[16] *Ibid.*, p. 155. See also p. 165.

[17] Ernst Käsemann, "Gottesgerechtigkeit bei Paulus" in his *op. cit.* (*Exegetische* 2), pp. 181–193, p. 184.

[18] *Ibid.*, pp. 184–189. Käsemann's argument for God's justice being God's might is that it is rhetorically personified, just as certain other terms, in several passages in Paul's letters (pp. 185 f.). In spite of possible parallels, arguments from rhetorical forms are, of course, very vulnerable. Bultmann offers similar arguments: e.g. *op. cit.* (*Theologie*), p. 208.

[19] Käsemann, *op. cit.* (*Gottes*), p. 186. Also, p. 187.

[20] On the following, see Ramsey, *op. cit.* (*Sure*), pp. 87 ff.

[21] Odgen-Richards, *op. cit.*, p. 40. See also J. J. C. Smart,

"Metaphysics, Logic, and Theology," in Antony Flew and Alasdair MacIntyre, ed., *New Essays in Philosophical Theology* (London: SCM Press, 1963), pp. 12–27, p. 22.

[22] Ramsey, *op. cit. (Religious)*, p. 215. See also Kümmel, *op. cit.*, pp. 93 f.

[23] J. J. C. Smart, "The Existence of God," in Flew, *op. cit. (New)*, pp. 28–46, p. 41. See also pp. 40, 45.

[24] Quine, *op. cit. (Word)*, p. 22. See also p. 24.

[25] See Ramsey, *op. cit. (Religious)*, pp. 147 ff., 175–216. The problem is simplified for Ramsey in that he regards the different models, theologies, or languages to be systematized as "complementary" (p. 196). See also Ferré, *op. cit.*, pp. 83 f.

[26] Ramsey, *op. cit. (Sure)*, pp. 22 ff.

[27] See, e.g., *ibid.*, pp. 72, 85 f.

11
Conclusions

Exegetes have pursued their researches without considering their consequences for theology.[1] In fact, the very possibility that historical research of any sort could raise objections to theological teachings has not been envisioned. That the evidence must corroborate, or at least not be able to contradict, religious convictions has simply been assumed. Thus the theologian finds himself before a new problem: that of defining the relationship between theology and the results of historical research.

An analogy can be found in the gradual definition over the last centuries of the relation of the results of the natural sciences to theology. As a result of the Galileo and Darwin controversies, the field of competence of theology was radically restricted. No longer was theology the ultimate court of appeal for all sciences. The results of a nontheological science wrought an essential change in our view of theology.

One need not be surprised, then, when the results of a more related science cause equally great changes in one's view of theology. New Testament scholarship investigates the base on which all later theology is supposed to be constructed. The results of its investigations must have an immediate and profound effect on theology.

Ogden and Richards write: "As a rule new facts in startling disagreement with accepted explanations of other facts are required before such critical analyses of what are generally regarded as simple satisfactory notions are undertaken. This has been the case with the recent revolution in physics." [2]

In the case at hand, the "accepted explanations" are the Catholic and Protestant assumptions of the unity of the New Testament as the foundation, or one of the foundations, for the unity of theology; which is, in turn, the foundation for the unity of the church. The "new facts in startling disagreement with accepted explanations" are the theological contradictions discovered in the New Testament. However much one may disagree with some of the examples which I have given, one cannot disagree with them all or with the many other examples to be found in the New Testament. These contradictions—and it is useless to try to deny, suppress, or resolve them—disconfirm the old explanations, the old theories. Those theories demanded in the New Testament a theological unity, at the very least, on the most important points of Christian theology. As we have seen, that unity does not exist in the New Testament: rather disunity is everywhere to be found. A more direct refutation of theories could not be imagined: at their very foundation, they are disconfirmed.

The theological disunity of the New Testament is a fact, not a problem. Rather, it poses a problem: one must discover the modifications which one's view of theology and therefore of the church must undergo in light of these findings. A completely new theory of theology and of its role in the church is needed. The confirmed results of New Testament scholarship have, in fact, ushered in a whole new period of theology.

There may be some theologians who will seek to modify somehow the old theory in order to accommodate the new findings, just as Lessing modified it by restricting the field of inspiration. As Quine says: "Any statement can be held true come what may, if we make drastic enough adjustments elsewhere in the system." [3] But how drastic must the changes in the old theory be before it can accommodate these phenomena! The old theory demanded a unity in the New Testament; it has already abandoned textual and historical unity. Now that it must abandon theological unity as well, what remains? Can unity be somehow redefined in order not to exclude disunity? There comes a point at which the drasticness of the changes made reveals obviously special pleading; such desperate attempts at salvage cannot be convincing. Theories are useful only insofar as they aid in understanding the phenomena. When they no longer do so and are thus no longer useful, they must not be allowed to become hindrances to understanding. The old theory of unity cannot help one to understand the disunity of the New Testament any more than the old view of language can help one to understand the disunity of human thought. Both must be abandoned.

There may be also theologians who attempt to deny that the Catholic and Protestant teachings on the unity of the New Testament and theology are, in fact, theories; who might claim that that unity was an article of faith that had simply to be believed. There are, however, too many similar cases of such theories being held as articles of faith until they had to be abandoned in the face of disconfirming facts: the theory of the incorruptibility of the text of Scripture had to be abandoned when Richard Simon definitively established its corruption; the theory that all truth, even historical, was guaranteed by inspiration had to be abandoned when Reimarus and the English Deists demonstrated historical contradictions in the New Testament. Now that the theological disunity of the New Testament has been not only accepted but established by scholars as a principle of interpretation, the theory of the theological unity of the New Testament must be abandoned as well. A person can believe something about which the facts are doubtful or unclear, but he cannot believe something which the clearly confirmable phenomena contradict. Nor has this sort of belief been demanded by most churches.

Moreover, no one could deny that each correction of our view of theology which has been occasioned by newly discovered evidence has brought us nearer to understanding the nature of theology. What appeared, at first, to be painful losses were found in the end to be significant gains.

We now find that theology is neither unified nor a picture of its object. We are not yet sure what theology then can be. We can only hope that the correction of our view demanded by these newly discovered phenomena will prove ultimately as fruitful as the previous corrections. But our first task is to undertake that correction itself. Catholics and Protestants are united and equal in this task, since the traditional assumptions of each have been disconfirmed. We must remember also that the difference between their two views of theology has been a major obstacle to ecumenical reunion. Now that a new view must be created, we may hope that one of its possible fruits will be an improved prospect for the unity of all Christians.

In the next section, I will sketch briefly some aspects of a possible theory and discuss some of its consequences. That I leave many questions unanswered, many problems unraised, and even many fields untouched, goes without saying. I hope, however, that this sketch will be useful in indicating some of the areas which must be explored and in emphasizing again the absolute necessity and advantage, in view of the situation, of the creation of some new theory of theology and of its role in the church.

Notes

1 Kümmel, *op. cit.*, pp. 131 f., 226 f.
2 Ogden-Richards, *op. cit.*, p. 13.
3 Quine, *op. cit.* (Two), p. 43. See also p. 42.

III
A NEW
THEORY

"This is sure
to befall a man
when he
directs the attention
of a friend
to any truth
which hitherto he has
thought little of.
At first,
he seems to be
hazarding a paradox,
and at length
to be committing
a truism.
The hearer is
first of all startled,
and then disappointed;
he ends by asking,
'Is that all?' "

JOHN HENRY NEWMAN

12

Old and New
Theories

The old theories of unity assumed a certain view of language. However, just as the old theories of unity have been disconfirmed by the findings of Biblical scholarship, so has that view of language been disconfirmed by the findings of linguistics and philosophy.

That view could not enable one to understand the New Testament in its disunity. On the contrary, it not only did not provide the means of understanding that disunity, but, when coupled with the old theories of unity, necessarily distorted the different New Testament theologies.

The findings of linguistics and philosophy, which have disconfirmed the old view of language, are being used to formulate a new approach. I have argued that philologists and exegetes have anticipated in their own work many of its principles. If one wishes to understand the New Testament, one must accept this new approach to language, on which the proper principles of understanding are based. Only those principles allow one to understand the disunity of the New Testament and of all thought.

The present problem arises from the fact that the old theories of unity were basic to the old theories of theology. In rejecting the old theories of unity, one has rejected the theories on which one's practice of theology has been based. The present problem is, therefore, to provide a new theory of theology.

On what can one base that new theory?

I propose to base it on the new approach to language. I do so for the following reasons:

The old theories of theology assumed the old view of language. It would seem natural now to use the new approach.

Most important, the new approach to language allows one to understand the New Testament, which is supposed to be the base of all later Christian theology. At the very least, the New Testament is an *example* of Christian theologizing. If any area of Christian discourse were to transcend the rules of human discourse, it would be the New Testament. But the disunity of the New Testament shows that its writers also were subject to those rules. The whole history of theology displays that disunity, which can and must be understood in the same way as that of the New Testament.

Let me recall briefly various positions of the old theory of unity and of the old view of language, the phenomena which disconfirmed them, and the explanations of those phenomena which the new approach to language was able to provide.

The old theory of unity posited a revelation of truths, of a body of doctrine, a deposit of faith, at the beginning of Christianity. The fact is that such a deposit or body of doctrines cannot be found in the New Testament; rather, only a great variety of contradictory theologies. The doctrines of revelation and inspiration must either be radically revised [1] or simply rejected as no longer useful or intelligible.[2] Inspiration and revelation would seem to be simply theoretical constructs of the old theory.

The old theory demanded that all theology be a reinterpretation of the original, revealed deposit. But such contradictory theologies could hardly be considered mere reinterpretations of one unified body of truths. Moreover, successive changes give rise to theologies and theological positions which are simply new and radically different from everything which preceded them.

Basing myself on the new approach to language, I was able to show how this disunity arose from the efforts of different theologians in different and changing situations, etc., and with different and changing means, to come to grips with objects and experiences which were not only vague and rich, but were themselves constantly changing or varying in importance. Theology was not reinterpretation but constant creation.

The old view of language considered language and thus theology to provide a picture of reality which was to some extent certain. However, so many different pictures are offered by the theologies of the New Testament that they could not at least all be pictures of reality. Rather, they must be considered models which are partially useful in enabling one to be articulate about objects which are ultimately beyond one. Theologies, because they are or use models, cannot give one a picture of God. An unavoidable theological uncertainty replaced the qualified certainty of the old theory. Thus, the theologies or models of the New Testament do not provide foundations for systems which attempt to claim for themselves a degree of authority which could only be granted to a system which was, in fact, certain. Needless to say, the conclusions or consequences drawn from models provide even less certainty than the models themselves.

Moreover, models, of their very nature, need not be, nor can they be, reducible to each other. When one sees further that language changes, that individual contexts determine meanings, that no thought system can be fully reproduced, and so on, one realizes that disunity is an inevitable and even a necessary consequence of the process of human thought.

Not only is disunity inevitable and necessary, but, in view of the partiality of all models, it is desirable. Each different model enables one to articulate differently. Each different model has its advantages. Disunity should be, not suppressed (which is, in any case, ultimately impossible), but fostered. Thus, the very usefulness of attempted systematizations of theology is put in serious doubt.

Finally, according to the old theories of unity, theology, or church teaching, was to be simply accepted. But models, because of their very partiality, demand to be criticized. A model is only partially useful, is only partially to be applied. The problem, then, is to decide which parts of the model are to be used.

To judge the New Testament theologies critically entails judging all theologies critically, because those theologies are supposedly based on the New Testament. One cannot even take refuge in church tradition and dogma because they also reveal disunity; and because one is forced, in any case, to criticize the theories on which that tradition and dogma have been based: the old theories of unity. Moreover, one has no absolute, external criterion according to which one can make one's criticisms: ultimately, one can only make them from the point of view of the theologies which one has himself, consciously or unconsciously, created.

This description of the process and practice of theology —a description which the new approach to language enables one to make—is, I believe, more accurate than the one provided by the old view. In point of fact, theologians have always theologized in the way I have just described; only they have taken great pains to cover their tracks. They have used reduction, forced readings, and all the other methods of antihistorical interpretation, which I have described, in order to keep up to the pretense that theology was continuously the same. Theologians have almost always been aware of the incorrectness of these methods and of the artificiality of this continuity, but this awareness has apparently not led them to reconsider the theory on behalf of which they were engaged in such curious obfuscations.

The new approach to language, which alone enables one to explain that disunity, forbids on principle the methods which have been used to preserve the façade of the unity of the history of theology. Those methods were calculated to distort the authentic sense of the theologies which they sought to harmonize. Simple respect for the theologies of one's predecessors demands, not that one distorts them, but rather that one *understands* them as accurately as we can.

Indeed, the ultimate reason for one's need for a new theory of theology is the fact that one's old view of language has been replaced by a new approach. One can no more build one's theory of theology on an outmoded theory of discourse than one can speak of God living literally in the sky. In Alfred de Musset's *On ne badine pas avec l'amour,* the baron remarks suddenly to a priest: "I have an idea!" "Oh," says the priest. "Which one?" [3] In that question lies the fundamental error of the old view of the nature of human thought and discourse. Human thought and discourse, just as every other truly human work, are not reproducible, but variable, creative, and infinitely nuanced.

In the next chapters, I will discuss a few of the advantages, problems, and consequences of this proposed new theory of theology.

Notes

[1] See, e.g., Ramsey, *op. cit.* (*Religious*), pp. 123 f.; Ferré, *op. cit.,* p. 100; Scott, *op. cit.,* p. 17. Kümmel, *op. cit.,* pp. 74 f., 80 f.

[2] Kümmel, *op. cit.,* pp. 62 f., 74 f., 80 f., 389, 393. Related: pp. 69 f., 116 f., 128 ff., 132 f., 135, 138, 140 ff., 173. Gerald Downing, *Has Christianity a Revelation?,* The Library of Philosophy and Theology (London: SCM Press, 1964).

[3] Alfred de Musset, *On ne badine pas avec l'amour,* Act I, scene II.

13
Aspects
of a
New Theory of
Theology

One may ask whether theology is at all necessary. One can, indeed, no longer use theology in many of its former functions. It can no longer function, for instance, as the norm of inclusion in a church.

But theology still retains certain irreducible functions. Christianity, insofar as it bases itself on a certain historical person and set of events, must speak about them. They can no longer be directly observed. One must use words; but, necessarily, one must choose them. Even for statements about the observable, this can involve interpretation. Certainly, the moment one wishes to claim or communicate a relevance or meaning for that person or set of events, one is involved in interpretation: that is, theology. Christianity must use theology to perpetuate itself. Even, say, good example cannot replace theology. One may be deeply impressed by the apparent goodness of a person, but if one wishes to learn *why* he is so good, one must ask him, and he must use words to explain himself.

Similarly, one must hear words in order to learn about Christianity. One is dependent upon theology when one wishes to become a Christian. Nothing can replace theology in these two of its functions.

Once one is a Christian, theology, models, images, etc. may also be means of understanding: of relating various aspects of Christianity to each other and to one's life, and so on. Words can also be needed to express one's faith, say, in community, in worship, or as witness.

But theology is not absolutely necessary for understanding, and one need not always express one's faith in words. The usefulness of theology for these last functions can vary. It *can,* however, be significant at times.

Nevertheless, since theology *is* necessary for transmitting Christianity and learning it, one is forced to confront the problems of theology. One theologizes because one must. But one must also understand as best one can what theology is. One has been forced to abandon one's old theories of theology; one must now construct a new theory.

THE DISUNITY OF THEOLOGY

The fact of the theological disunity of the New Testament destroys forever the *possibility* of a unified Christian theology. My description of the process of human thought, as manifested in the New Testament, has shown that disunity is natural and inevitable. I have also argued that it is *desirable.* All models and theologies are partial; each one has its advantages and disadvantages. A plurality of models and theologies provides therefore more possibilities for articulation.

Even *extreme* models and ways of speaking can have their advantages.[1] Thus, one should not be surprised that the New Testament contains theologies which are truly extreme. Paul, for instance, constructs in Romans 2:9, a "damnation history" with "Jew first, then Greek."

The means of expression used in the Apocalypse are surely as extreme as possible. Yet the Apocalypse *was* included in the canon, and one should realize that its means also have their advantages as well as their perhaps more obvious disadvantages. Most obviously, they were able to reach many who would have otherwise remained uninterested in the new sect. Moreover, apocalyptic writings could not only say differently what other theologies also said in their own ways; apocalyptic writings were uniquely capable of expressing and communicating total views or contexts in striking and often even visual terms. Christian literature would be poorer without its apocalyptic element.

Gnostic theologies or theological elements were useful for communicating with people of gnostic tendencies or convictions.[2] Technical terms, schemes, and models were borrowed by the New Testament writers from Gnosticism as important aids in articulating theologies of the Christian services and of Jesus himself. Gnosticism has lost neither its fascination nor its usefulness today.

Extreme expressions can be useful for certain people. Reform-school members have been encouraged to translate New Testament stories into their own jargon. The Good Samaritan became the "cool square." [3] Needless to say, to translate a message is to transform it. These delinquents are, in fact, creating a new theology, giving new interpretations of statements and placing them in totally new contexts. Terms such as "cool" and "square," and phrases such as "make it" and "get with it," have nuances which can be found in no others. Christian theology has been given a whole new set of models which opens up new possibilities of articulation and new perspectives of understanding. The work of these delinquents is one example of the process of all theology.

One is tempted to say even that some theologies are powerful just because they are so extreme. An extreme emphasis on the principle of "God alone" can be very moving; an emphasis on the dignity and worth of man can also touch us. Often a theology creates its effect just by letting one model or principle override another. Each of these theologies is rendered much milder when its main principle is coolly balanced against another. One often needs the extreme emphasis simply because one thinks partially; one can only with difficulty hold two models or principles in one's consciousness at once. One's usual method is to concentrate one's thoughts on one or the other, or else to use the one or the other as the occasion demands.

A good example of two principles or models being emphasized each to the exclusion of the other is the controversy between Pelagianism and Augustine. The Pelagians emphasized the activity of man in his own salvation, and Augustine, the exclusive role of God. Now either of these partial principles, when pushed to an absolute, creates an impossible problem. If man does all, then why or how does he need God's help? If God does all, what is our own personal initiative? The first alternative returns to a Judaistic legalism, the second to such impossible solutions as that one cannot even respond to God's initiative without a further initiative by God, without a further initiative by God and so on to infinity.

The Catholic Church opted officially for the position of Augustine, and many theologies were constructed to explain how man, at every step of the way, could do nothing at all as a person. Very mechanistic views of "grace" were devised. Man could refuse on his own to respond (that is, he could do evil), but he could not decide on his own to respond. Then, other problems of other models intruded. God was all powerful; therefore, irresistible; therefore, his grace could not be resisted. What was the impulse then which man rejected when he refused to respond? A theory was devised by which that which man resisted in refusing to respond was different from that which led him irresistibly to respond. And so on.

In point of fact, the suppression of one model in favor of another and the absolutization of the favored one always lead to an impasse. Each model allows one to say different things. Pelagianism allows one to speak of man's own effort or response; Augustinism allows one to speak of God's initiative. Even today, one uses the one model to articulate some points ("We must make an effort to live a better life!" "We cannot get to heaven without striving!"); and the other to make other points ("God alone . . ." "All that we have has been given to us by God."). Thus most of the old condemned heresies can be found in one form or another in popular and even official church language, simply because those heresies were or used models which had their advantages; advantages which are still required today.

That such models were suppressed arose from a mistaken view of theology: the theologians of the time thought that one must be a true picture of reality, and the other, a false one. They therefore decided for one and rejected the other. They thereby curtailed their field of possible articulation and forced themselves to press one model absolutely.

One is more accustomed today to the idea that two sides of a controversy can both be right in some ways and wrong in others; just as one is accustomed to say "You look at it your way, and I'll look at it mine." The mediating theologians of the Reformation—such as Erasmus, Bucer, and Melanchthon—are more appreciated today than they have been in the past. One has learned in practice to appreciate the principle that all theories are partial.

Some contradictions between the theologies rest on ultimately unresolved tensions in the earliest Christianity itself. For instance, the pendulum of theological interest and emphasis has swung fairly regularly between the sacred and the secular. A church settles itself too comfortably into the world, and a prophet such as Newman or Barth arises to proclaim the sacred. A church becomes too otherworldly, and men of holy worldliness slowly turn it back toward its work among men.

This serious difference between the sacred and the secular is present and unresolved in the earliest Christianity. The first Christians thought that they would be taken from the world at any minute by the Parousia. The theology by which they resigned themselves to staying in the world was a stopgap measure. The members of the earliest Jerusalem community may have considered the ritual Temple cult an essential part of their Christian lives. At least one of the antiritual theologies of early Christianity was constructed by those who were *not allowed* to take part in the Temple cult.

Similarly, the Christians thought that they were already saved, but found that they had to make efforts to persevere. Paul simply joins the two inconsistent standpoints: we *are* saved, but we *ought* to strive toward our salvation. Small wonder, then, that these two views have often been resurrected as poles in controversy. They are inconsistent; and, when one is not prepared to admit inconsistency in theology, one must suppress one pole in favor of the other. Of course, one is thereby led inevitably to one or other of the well-known historical positions. Thus many of the great controversies or even divisions in the history of theology can be seen as manifestations of an original inconsistency in Christianity itself; and, so to speak, the possible limits of what can be called Christian are considerably widened.

Disunity can be found, not only at every stage in the history of theology, but also between the successive stages. These revolutions take place most often in regard to the means of thought and expression. An old philosophy is rejected; a new one is found. The old theology must be translated into the terms of the new philosophy. Such translations cannot be accomplished, of course, without corresponding transformations of the theology "itself." Thus the conservative forces of the Roman Catholic Church manifest a certain natural sagacity in seeking to impose one philosophy on all theology within their church. Even more liberal theologians can be discovered attempting to establish "Hebrew categories of thought" as somehow normative. But philosophies simply change, and after a time the strain of adhering to a philosophy which, however great its interest, has become outmoded, becomes unbearable.

Profound changes can occur not only in the means of thought and expression, with all that implies, but also in the whole structure of theology, in its rank of interests and emphases. The first emphasis of Christianity was laid upon the imminent coming of the Parousia. That near expectation *was* Christianity. When the Parousia was delayed, the main accent had to be laid elsewhere. The much derided absence of eschatological interest in the many later centuries of Christianity was perhaps a truer reaction than the rather precious revival of eschatology in Christianity today.

What profound successive changes have characterized theologies of the church! of the services! of the Christian life! One may no longer veil the differences between the various stages in the history of Christianity.

One may expect such changes in the future. Many seem to

be commencing in our own day. The new interest in the secular, the revived use of the "GOD IS DEAD" model, the ecumenical movement within Christianity and between it and other religions; each of these and many more movements or tendencies contain possibilities of radical restructurings.

That the New Testament is a theological disunity has the most serious *practical* consequences for the churches today: they may continue to demand theological unity as the criterion of church unity and membership only at the price of contradicting one or more theologies in the New Testament. A church can no longer claim *both* to be a theological unity *and* to be based on the New Testament. To make the one claim is to abandon the other. To abandon either one is to transform radically or even replace the theory according to which churches have acted until now. A church has the choice either of not accepting the New Testament as a whole and of thus preserving its theological unity, or of accepting somehow the New Testament as a whole and of finding some theory by which it can explain the theological disunity to which it has thus opened itself. The first solution could, however, lead only to an illusory unity.

Clearly, the whole function of creeds must be reconsidered.[4] Creeds are certain theological formulations which are imposed as authoritative on the members of a church. One theology or model suppresses others.

Important objections can be brought against this procedure. Firstly, creeds are almost always results of systematization; therefore, all the objections which can be made against systematization can be made against creeds.

Secondly, since there are in almost every church widely divergent theological persuasions, creeds are almost always in practice given very different and even contradictory interpretations. Ever since the bishop Eusebius was able to interpret the decree of the Council of Nicaea to mean exactly what it sought to condemn, theologians have found ways of getting around creeds. Using the right methods, almost any writing can be interpreted to mean anything. While certain disadvantages of creeds are thereby discreetly circumvented, the very purpose of a creed has been vitiated. Why have a creed if it is open to such contradictory interpretations? What could its function then be? Our doubts are increased when ambiguous words and phrases are inserted into creeds and decrees so that the possibilities of contradictory interpretations are deliberately increased! At times, the very *right* of contradictory interpretations has been defended.

Thirdly, creeds always evolve into burdens and must be either ignored, frankly revised, or somehow reinterpreted. In the Roman Catholic Church very elaborate methods of reinterpretation have perforce been devised. Whole new theologies are reared on a quibble: the final revision of the decree on revelation proclaimed by the Council of Trent states that revelation is contained "both" in Scripture "and" tradition; the earlier version read "partly" in Scripture and "partly" in tradition. Aha! say a number of theologians, this is quite different, and a very different theology of revelation is constructed. Liberal theologians use as antihistorical methods to reinterpret magisterial documents as conservatives do to interpret Scripture. They both follow, in fact, the old theory of unity, whereby no contradictions are allowed. The elaborate subterfuges to which these theologians are thus forced indicate both the extent to which that old theory is a burden and the artificiality of the facade of unity which must be erected if that theory is to be maintained. Ordinary people today tend to be rather impatient with such strained evasions.

On the other hand, if a creed must be revised, as many Protestant churches are doing, why should a creed be formulated at all? Should I live by, and perhaps even die for, a creed that will be revised two hundred years from now? When the Presbyterians formulate a new creed which omits two cardinal propositions of the old one—inspiration and predestination —one might well ask whether any sort of creed is necessary or useful.

Fourthly, creeds or creedal statements are increasingly difficult to formulate. Recently, a group of Lutherans could not agree on a formulation of justification. The Second Vatican

Council composed its decrees simply by setting side-by-side the many alternative and often mutually exclusive formulations proposed by theologians of different tendencies. In sum, where the distinctions between formulations are felt, the construction of a creed is impossible. Where those distinctions are ignored, a creed or decree is possible, but will be inconsistent.

Finally and most important, the theological disunity of the New Testament itself forbids any consistent creed which would pretend to include the theologies of the New Testament. To formulate a consistent Christian creed necessarily entails rejecting several New Testament theologies. The first Christian systematic theologians did not realize this, of course; but one can today. If one wishes, in spite of this awareness, to continue formulating creeds, one is placed before two possibilities.

Firstly, one might retain one's view of the nature and function of creeds and devise a theory to justify one's rejecting any New Testament theologies which contradict it. I can see no very good reasons why anyone should accept such a theory.

Secondly, one might revise one's view of the nature and function of creeds. Instead of their being considered exclusivistic, irreformable, absolutely authoritative, they would be regarded as informal guidelines, general directives, common tone-setters, etc. But these are, of course, no creeds at all in the old sense and could not be used as norms of unity. A church would not be unified by a creed.

In other words, the whole theory of orthodoxy has been revealed as inapplicable. Orthodoxy has hoisted itself on its own petard.

The difficulty arises that most churches have used creeds as one of their most important criteria of unity and membership. A whole new basis for unity and membership would have to be found or devised. I myself can think of ·no criterion as handy as that of theological conformity. But then again, the theological unity in most churches has proved to be illusory. On the other hand, if teaching cannot be a criterion of exclusion, what could be? Is anything else sufficiently important to cause or allow the exclusion of someone from the community?

Should not even great scandal on the part of one member lead his coreligionists to seek all the more to incorporate him into the community?

Moreover, the question of membership and nonmembership is not only difficult to decide, but is in many ways repugnant today. True, most Christians no longer believe that those who do not belong to their churches are going to hell, but *any sort* of membership mentality demands some sort of exclusivism. To concentrate on the joys of belonging smacks of selfcongratulation. More important, any choice of a criterion is bound to be arbitrary and impossible to establish with complete certainty. Finally, any exclusion of groups, tendencies, theologies, etc., is bound to impoverish the church which excludes them.

For these reasons, I myself become increasingly convinced that our whole idea of the church as a closed community must be revised or abandoned. Augustine has said that many who seem to be in the church are really outside it; and many who seem to be outside are really inside. There are already loopholes in our membership theories which allow good pagans to be really "in the church" in that it is "through the church" that they get to heaven. Even according to this "old theory," then, the criteria of membership were ultimately intangible. One may therefore ask if visible membership or observable criteria are really indispensable.

In any case, whatever criterion one chooses, it cannot, without the grave difficulties discussed, be that of theological unity.

Rather, for a church to be ideally effective as a teacher, it should contain a variety of irreducible models and theologies, each of which has its advantages. Only with the full spectrum of possibilities and with an openness toward the new possibilities which successive changes bring can a church be even capable of reaching the very diverse people and peoples whom it wishes to serve. Even extreme or one-sided models or theologies can be useful insofar as their disadvantages lend force to their advantages. A church should not have one, necessarily partial theology, but a whole wealth of theologies, each of which donates its advantages.

The idea of one group allowing great differences of opinion is comprehensible and even congenial to us today. A group which does not allow such differences condemns itself in the eyes of most men. Nor are these human reactions of repugnance merely instinctive. Men did not always so react. Rather, the idea has sifted down to the great mass of men that no formulation or system can be complete; that every suppression of contrary opinions is a persecution that contradicts the very nature of man himself; and that such a persecution ends, ultimately, by impoverishing the persecutor himself. Neither human thinking, nor whatever is being thought about, can be simplified into an absolute ideology without being distorted or destroyed. The very lack of neatness and of clear distinctions which results from abandoning authoritative creeds is much truer to the nature of man's thought and of his object than the stifling and artificial systems to which he felt he must conform himself and others.

My conclusion is that no church can demand theological conformity today. This can legitimately be considered a proclamation of freedom or an attempt at making a virtue of necessity. I would prefer to regard this conclusion simply as an attempt to conform our practice to our best understanding of the nature of human thought and communication, and thus of theology.

This conclusion has, of course, most important consequences for the ecumenical movement, which finds itself currently in an impasse. The benefit of a united church seems to be denied us because of our theological differences. True, some of those differences may be found unreal, reducible, or unimportant; but no one could claim that *all* the theological differences between the churches could be so disposed of. If the churches are to be united, theological disunity must be accepted.

One must be mature enough to recognize one's necessary limitations and to welcome as comrades and helpers in the search all those who feel that they should contribute to it. What church could help but be proud to number among its members geniuses of such divergent persuasions as Augustine, Aquinas, Luther, Butler, Newman, Kierkegaard, Barth, and Bultmann? If the differences between the views of these great Christians seem too great for one church to contain, let us recall that each church already claims to include teachings which contradict each other just as deeply: those in the New Testament.

The criterion of the worth of a theology for a church is not its conformity, but rather, that which has made certain theologians, each in his own way, great. That all those theologies —despite their divergences, or even, in fact, because of them —are deeply valuable for us, must convince us in the end that theological disunity, which we cannot avoid in any case, is an advantage for the church, rather than a hindrance to its unity.

THE LIMITS OF THEOLOGY

Since models are not pictures of their objects, an element of uncertainty has been introduced into theology. Ferré argues, however, that, if certain models are useful, "we may ask *why* this happens to be the case. And if some models are capable of providing greater coherence and adequacy than others, we may begin to suspect that this tells us something not only about the models but also about what reality is like . . ." [5] Ferré proposes the model of person, just as Ramsey has proposed the model of personal love. Both Ferré and Ramsey place a great deal of confidence in these models.

However, certain serious objections can be made to these models and to their use as supermodels around which to group others as subsidiary. Firstly, the New Testament and Christianity have used models which cannot be reduced to the model of person. For instance, *im*personality is an important part of one idea of the spirit used to understand the phenomena in the early community. To reduce models to one supermodel is, in the end, just a more sophisticated method of systematizing.

The person-model has great advantages, to be sure. It also has one of the most notorious disadvantages in all theology: if the person-model is taken as a picture of reality, one is immediately faced with the classic problem of evil. If God is a person and loves us, why does he not help us more? Why does he not *act* as a person who loves us? etc. None of these questions have been satisfactorily answered; nor can they be. For the whole difficulty arises because theologians have pressed, absolutized, or used as a picture, the model of person. Thus the person-model, just as any other model, has a very circumscribed field of competence. When one misuses the person-model, one falls into the very same sort of problems that arise from every misuse of a model.

To articulate somehow the evil in the world, most theologians have supplemented or qualified the person-model with a series of other models, such as the fall, or posits, such as the devil. These supplements are obviously inadequate. Most Christianity, just because it has taken the person-model as a picture, has been, and still is, ludicrously unable or even unwilling, to come to grips with the problem of evil. Christian theologians will be able to offer something other than evasions only when they accept the fact that the person-model is also a model, with its advantages and disadvantages. Even the medieval theologians recognized that "person" was not predicated univocally of God. Theologians must also have the humility to accept models which orthodoxy has condemned or suppressed, just because they were and are so effective at articulating the problem of evil.

Moreover, one of the advantages of the person-model is that modern philosophy has been very interested recently in the phenomenon of person. To speak of "person" has also become, to a certain extent, modish. Therefore, a theology which uses the person-model has some very new and interesting material on which to base itself and also "speaks to the modern world." Nothing allows one to think, however, that the person-model is the last or the best that will ever be devised. Fashions and interests change, and for all one knows, a new appreciation of impersonality may be the next vogue. This is not to deny the very real advantages of the person-model; it is merely to recall its natural limitations.

Thus, as I have said before, uncertainty is inevitable in theology. One must accustom oneself to the idea that many problems will remain unsolved, many questions unanswered. The object of theology will remain mysterious.

The realization of the limitations of all and each language about God is of the most practical importance. Mystics have often emphasized the impossibility of expressing their experiences in words. It is significant that so many Christians try not to listen to the Sunday sermons. Theology is often much more a hindrance than a help.

The best example of this I know is that of a Danish girl, a very good social worker, who grew up without religion in a society for which religion had lost all meaning. Nevertheless, she felt in herself a need to go to church "just to sit alone and think." She gradually became very interested in religion and Christianity but felt that she had to avoid going to church services because what was said there turned her against everything religious. From my other acquaintances, I know that her case is not atypical.

The only remedy for such cases is to put theologies in their proper places as partial, limited, and uncertain theories. The realization of the gap between theology and its object distinguishes both the religious man and the great theologian. The greatness of a theology lies in its ability to remind one of its own inadequacy by suggesting to one something of the mysteriousness of its object. The purpose of theology is self-defeating only in the strictest sense. As a Belgian theologian has said, ignorance has its areas of competence as well as knowledge. To realize our ignorance, to recognize the true relation of theology to its object, can enable us to understand problems for which our supposed knowledge has rendered us tragically incompetent.

THEOLOGIES AND CONTEXTS

I have shown that a great number of different models and contexts have been used to construct theologies and that they were often not chosen, but almost forced on the theologians who used them. Christian writers had to find some way of using the models and contexts of their hearers because they could only be reached by means of those which were somehow meaningful for them.

This is also true today. Different peoples use different models or contexts as means of understanding. Theologies must be created for such contexts as, for instance, those of existentialism, evolutionism (Teilhard de Chardin and the process theologians), historicism, relativism, secularism, positivism, scientism, and even perhaps atheism. Needless to say, each of these contexts will give rise to schools of irreducible theologies; and each theology or school of theologies will have its advantages and disadvantages. What can be said in one context, or according to one theology, will not be able to be said in another. Each context imposes certain limits of possibility, and one's attitude toward those limits will depend on one's attitude toward the context. Thus, the theology of one context will be useful and meaningful for those who accept that context, but may be utter nonsense for those who do not. Aristotelians will not find Chardin very useful, nor will Chardinians find Aristotle satisfying. Many individuals will of course be eclectic, taking something from one context and another from another. In fact, an analysis of the usual presentation of the doctrines of any church would reveal a wide variety of contexts; most theologies which depend heavily on tradition are, for that very reason, syncretistic.

The person who holds one context will naturally regard it as *the* context and will often be tempted to suppress others in favor of it. He considers his context to be a picture of the real and, once he sees that other contexts are irreducible to his own, will tend to regard his context as the true picture and others as false or inadequate ones, the only valid aspects of which are already contained in his own. Thomists will find all of historicism contained in Aquinas' teaching on prudence; historicists will explain Aristotelianism, perhaps, as an attempt to describe a frozen stage of development. The relativist will see "the good points" in both.

Each context is naturally open to criticism. Most criticism of a context is often simply that it is not another context. Empiricists criticize metaphysicians for not restricting their statements to those which are empirically verifiable. Thomists criticize non-Thomists by pointing out that they have "neglected" one of the distinctions which Thomas makes. A context can be criticized on internal grounds: is it consistent? Is this important? A context can also be criticized on external grounds: can the context in question accommodate this or that phenomenon? The consideration of these mutual criticisms will naturally be important for the individual in his choice of a context or in his construction of a new one. Those mutual criticisms and a short survey of the history of philosophy teach one also not to claim an absolute authority for any one context.

In any case, it is clear that one can make certain statements in one context which one cannot in another. If one wishes to make those statements, one must use that context. If one wishes to reach people who believe in that context, one must speak within the framework of that context. It is useless to talk to them in terms of another context, which they do not hold themselves and to which they may refuse to be converted. One of the great problems of traditional theology today is, of course, that it operates within a context or contexts which are no longer meaningful to many people today. There was indeed a time, and perhaps it is not yet over, when to become a Roman Catholic was also to become a Thomist. A book professing a new appreciation for the Angelic Doctor was *de rigueur* for every convert of some intellectual reputation. However, a broad variety of new contexts has by now been introduced into, and has often formed, the theologies of almost all churches; but one has lacked the means of understanding why and how those different theologies can coexist within one church. The old theory of theology did not provide for this eventuality.

I will now discuss, as an example, the advantages and limitations of one modern context: that which limits itself to statements which can be empirically verified.

A theology which works within this context will necessarily limit itself to statements which can somehow be verified in experience. Otherwise, a statement will be meaningless in this context.

One advantage of the method of this context is that it allows one to test whether a statement refers to something observable. Since most contexts sometimes use language which appears to be descriptive, one may be interested in discovering whether that language describes in fact something which can be observed. For instance, one can test the proposition: "The cosmos bears Christological traits." When one asks what those traits are, one finds that this proposition depends on a particular view of the universe, a view which itself cannot be verified by observation. One can then say that this proposition is not meaningful in the context limited to statements which can be observationally verified. The question which the user of the proposition must then face is whether he can accept the world view which alone justifies the proposition. Of course, the user of the proposition can say that he *believes* that "the cosmos," in its real, never to be defined form, bears Christological traits. The peculiar logic of the phrase "believe that . . ." is that it allows almost any statement to be placed after it. Nonetheless, the user of the proposition must then realize just what sort of statement he is making.

A number of other statements are more closely dependent on the observable. For instance, the proposition "The Bible is the source of our theology" can be tested: does the theology in question originate, in fact, from the Bible? If it is found that the Bible *contradicts* the theology in question, then the proposition must either be abandoned or redefined: "source" in the sense of inspiration, "general source," "beginning of a long development," etc. Some of these remarks will also admit of empirical testing. If they also are disconfirmed, then thcy must also be abandoned or redefined, and so on. Refuge can always be taken in a redefinition which does not admit of empirical testing. But the empirical method has proved useful, in any case, either in allowing a proposition to be more accurately formulated or in helping us realize that it is not a proposition about the observable.

The proposition "The theological unity of the New Testament is the basis of the unity of theology" also admits of empirical testing. *Is* the New Testament a unity? This method could also be applied to such propositions as "We have formed our lives on Jesus," "God works in history," "The real is basically trinitarian," and so on. If thesc propositions cannot be verified by observation, then one knows that they do not belong to the context under discussion. They must belong to another context, and the question arises whether one desires to accept that other context. One may, of course, choose to *believe* that, say, God works in history, although that working cannot be observed. But then one must realize that one is believing in a working that cannot be observed. Or one might prefer to draw completely different conclusions from the fact that it cannot be observed.

Of course, the disconfirmation of a proposition can itself be very useful. I have mentioned, for instance, some of the advantages which result from a disconfirmation of the old theory of unity.

Another advantage of this context is that it does allow one to make certain statements which themselves have certain advantages. For instance, one may be able to state that "Jesus is my teacher" and verify this proposition by indicating certain elements of Jesus' teaching which have helped one to formulate similar propositions in one's own theologies. Or one might say "Jesus was a prophet" in the sense that he had a certain insight into needs which one feels and that his teaching is able to help one deal with those needs. Or one might wish to say "Jesus has freed me from a legalistic view of religion."

These propositions are valuable simply because they are so modest and personal. One can verify whether these propositions apply to oneself by asking whether one *has* learned from Jesus or whether he *has* freed one from a legalistic view of religion. In this context, theology comes very close to autobiography, with all the advantages (and, of course, the disadvantages) involved. It will be very interesting to see what theologies will be formed within this context.

Of course, this context has its limitations; one of the most important is that it does not allow one to make all the statements which one might wish to make. Most notoriously, one cannot verify the principle of verification itself. One may also wish to make, for instance, the statement that "Jesus, as all good men, was persecuted." One cannot verify that Jesus was good or that all good men have been and are persecuted. Nevertheless, the model of the good man being persecuted can be helpful in speaking about Jesus. There may be moments or discussions in which one will want to make this statement even though it cannot be verified.

The great mistake of most theologians who have tried to work within the empirical context is that they have attempted to reconstruct *all* traditional theological propositions in its terms: the Trinity, the Hypostatic Union, doctrines of grace, and so on. These theologians have then been forced either to posit some very curious experiences ("I experience the Trinity"; "I feel grace"; "In my worship, I encounter Christ as God and man") or to exercise on those traditional theological propositions some alarming reductions ("God exists" becomes "Some men and women have had, and all may have, experiences called 'meeting God.' ").[6] Moreover, perhaps because attempts at constructing theologies within the empirical context have usually been bound to discussions of the possibilities of "natural theology"—the theology which, some hold, can be constructed from purely natural data—attempts have been made to prove somehow the existence of God from experience! But no experience of "meeting God" can indicate any more than that a person has had such an experience: one cannot prove that there exists, in fact, a person, God, from the fact that one has had "the experience of meeting him." Obviously, the limits of the empirical context have not been respected. Anyone who wishes to restrict himself to that context will content himself with a much more modest theology, if he feels he requires one at all.

One may choose to use other contexts as well as the empirical one; of course, these other contexts have their own disadvantages, but if one wishes to make certain statements, one must necessarily resort to them. Thus I return again to the need of disunity in theology. Different theologies in different contexts will be meaningful for different people at different times. A plurality of contexts must be used as bases for theologies, if all people are to be reached.

Two sorts of attempts can be made to restrain this plurality: 1) one may attempt to impose a certain theology which entails imposing a certain context; 2) or one may claim that a certain context is the only valid one.

The first attempt can be seen in the argument that if one or other traditional theological statement cannot be made within a certain context, then that context must be inadequate for theology. This argument ignores of course that all contexts are somehow inadequate and assumes that a certain theology and the context in which it is made can be norms to which all other theologies must conform. This assumption itself arises from an ignorance of the limits of theology. One must accustom oneself to a plurality of contexts.

The second attempt is continually made by those philosophers who would restrict the label "philosophy" to a certain brand or method of philosophy, not unsurprisingly, their own. One can hear from some of these philosophers remarks such as "Pascal is very interesting, of course, but he's no philosopher." Naturally every philosophical school doubts the credentials of every other. Some Thomists are firmly convinced that they are the only genuine philosophers in the whole world. Some existentialists consider the Oxbridge philosophers grammarians. Some among the Oxbridge philosophers themselves have been known to refuse to grant to existentialists and others the right to label themselves philosophers; and this from philosophers who have established the essential arbitrariness of all such labels! The simple fact is that there are many schools of philosophy today and that there will be many more schools in the future, just as there have been many in the past. The individual must simply choose which school, or which aspects of which schools, seem most convincing to him.

In any case, one task of the theologian is to see that the theological possibilities of all these schools are plumbed. He must only remember the limits of those contexts and of the theologies which he constructs within them and not make claims for them which transcend those limits. He may not claim, for instance, that his is the final context or theology, nor that his theological propositions refer to the observable world when they do not. He must above all remember that his theology has all the limits of any model or theory and is not a picture of its object. That realization is the ultimate corrective for the one-sidedness and inadequacy inevitable in any model, context, or theology.

THE USES OF THEOLOGIES

From what I have said of the limits of theologies, certain conclusions may be drawn about how they should be used, for ourselves and for others.

Most obviously, one should never allow a theology to become a hindrance rather than an aid. Theologies were created for man, not man for theologies. When a theology is no longer useful for one, one should feel free to reject it and either to accept or to create another. One may even elect to forego one altogether. The limits of all theologies make this a perfectly viable alternative. In one's decisions, the only ultimate authority can be one's own conscience; and the only ultimate guarantee, one's own honesty.

Needless to say, one should never seek to impose a certain theology on others. Even for purely practical reasons, one should work within the context or contexts which are meaningful for a certain person: one should follow Paul's practice of becoming Jews to the Jews and Greeks to the Greeks; realizing all the while that one's theologies as Jews are different from one's theologies as Greeks and that these theologies need not be, and—if they are at all effective within their particular contexts—cannot be, reducible to each other. One must speak in sacred terms to some, in secular to others. For some, one must be consistent; others will regard consistency as suspect.

One's first purpose in offering theologies to others should be, of course, primarily to help them. One must offer them a theology which they will be able to use. One must have the insight to realize which theology, model, or proposition can be useful to this person at this moment; and one must have the tact not to impose more than they can bear.

One may, of course, seek to enlarge the perspectives of the people with whom one is speaking; one may offer them means of understanding which they have perhaps not considered. But one may not impose upon them propositions which, for one reason or another, are meaningless for them. One's first duty is to respect the limits within which people have chosen to operate. One must be joyful for that which they feel they can believe; and not be chagrined that they may not believe all that which one may believe oneself. One should not beat people over the head because they may attribute a unique importance to Jesus, but not divinity. Nor should one castigate Christians who take part in the Christian services, but do not believe in transubstantiation. Needless to say, a limited but sincere belief is more worthwhile than an unconvinced or unexamined submission to the fullest creed. Any attempt to slight the belief of a person reveals, at the least, a gross misunderstanding of the limits of theology and the crassest insensitivity to the relation of the individual to his beliefs.

In offering a theology to someone, one's final objective can be only to aid them in ultimately forming their own theology. No two people have exactly the same theology, just as no two people have exactly the same philosophy. Even if they use the same words, their understanding of them will be different.

Moreover, each thinking person is continually at work creating and re-creating his views. Few people ever achieve a final philosophy or theology. By offering them what theologies one has, one can hope at most—and that is very great—to help them in some small way in their effort of creation. They must criticize the theologies which one offers them, just as they must criticize all theologies. Only they can judge in the end what is useful to them and what not. They must *use* the theologies which we offer them, just as we have had to use the theologies which we ourselves have received.

The most important criterion of a theology is, then, whether it is useful for ourselves and/or others.

Notes

1 Flew, *op. cit.* (Philosophy), p. 3. Comp. Ramsey, *op. cit.* (*Religious*), pp. 108 ff., 157 f.

2 Bultmann, *op. cit.* (*Theologie*), p. 167. See also pp. 178, 184 f.

3 *Time*, March 5, 1965, p. 61. See also f.

4 See Ramsey's discussion in *op. cit.* (*Sure*), pp. 81–88.

5 Ferré, *op. cit.*, p. 165.

6 *Ibid.*, p. 39.

14

The Theologian

and

His Work

Every person must theologize. He does this consciously or unconsciously. The very fact that he must create his own
theology—either by constructing a new one or by understanding an old one in his own inescapably individual way—
is an important disconfirmation of the old theory of theology.
This new theory understands that, because man must theologize, the freedom to theologize cannot be denied him. The ines-
capability of the individual's theologizing not only necessitates
a freedom, it imposes a responsibility. One is duty-bound to
understand as best one can and to communicate one's understanding as best one can to others. Therefore, the problems of
the theologian are those of every Christian insofar as that
Christian is fulfilling his mission of understanding and transmitting his faith.

I will now discuss the personal factors of a theologian, his
relation to his object and to other theologies, and theological
creativity. I will necessarily be brief. Each of these subjects is a
study in itself. My only intention here is to apply some of the
more obvious consequences of what I have already discussed to
our view of the process of theology.

PERSONAL FACTORS

I have already mentioned the influences which personal
factors such as individual situation, experiences, interests, and
so on can have on a theology. All the factors that form him as
a person will help to form his theological understanding. Nevertheless, people cannot be exhaustively explained by their

backgrounds. Two people will react very differently to the same thing. The final reason why they react differently is not analyzable in terms of causative influences; people are irreducibly individual, free, and creative. The course and result of the evolution of an individual are also unpredictable. Thus, in theology, as in any human endeavor, one encounters as broad a range as possible of personalities and reactions.

Some theologians have radically reformed their situation, either by prophetic action (such as Paul) or by a whole new theology (such as Luther). Others have depended heavily on the means which their situation offered them (such as Aquinas). Some theologians agree with the views and tendencies of their time (such as the new secular theologians). Some are highly critical of their age (such as Kierkegaard). The relation of a theologian to his time cannot therefore be standardized. Every reaction is possible and, depending on many factors, valuable. The theologian who is at one with his time can incorporate its advantages; the theologian who criticizes his time can reform it or introduce a new age.

Similarly, a variety of attitudes is possible toward one's individual experiences. One may live from them, distrust them, reject them. One may follow one's interests, or one may mortify them.

That all personal factors are a real influence on the individual cannot be doubted. But the effect of those influences, the individual's reactions to them, the use which he will eventually make of them, cannot be predicted.

As one reaches the final cause of any theology, the individual in his inescapable freedom, one also returns to the ultimate reason why theologies will always be irreducible to each other: because people are irreducible.

Theological understanding, just as all understanding, is necessarily personal. Theological communication also is always, to some extent, personal expression. Language communicates not only an impersonal meaning, but always also the person who is using that language. Often one is more impressed by the person speaking than by what he says. I myself have, on occa-

227   The Theologian and His Work

sion, been deeply moved by a sermon, with every point of which I disagreed. The saints are reputed to have been able to say the same old things in the same old words, and yet they became suddenly very meaningful. The role of personal influence, an influence that cannot be measured simply by referring oneself to the words which the person in question used on this or that occasion, could be the object of a very enlightening study.

Theology remains a very limited means. The theologian will never be able to articulate fully either his object or himself. But sometimes one can feel the finally inexpressible person behind the theology and divine the ultimately mysterious object beyond it.

THE THEOLOGIAN AND THE OBJECTS OF THEOLOGY

The question as to the object of theological explanations —that of which theology is a means of articulation—cannot be avoided. I will only list a few aspects of this problem here.

Of course, Christian theology has several objects which it seeks to explain, and they can present very different problems. The problems of understanding raised by a present situation are different from those raised by historical events. Therefore, when a theologian deals with a current event, his method will be different from that which he uses to study a historical personage. Theologians have borrowed the methods of historical scholarship to deal with historical objects, but some branches of theology have yet to develop a method to any great extent. At the Second Vatican Council, theologians were generally stymied as to how they should compose a decree on the modern world. The development of different methods is, therefore, an urgent task for theologians today.

The various models and theologies themselves can also become objects. A theology will be cleaned of its minor inconsistencies; a principle will be qualified; the system will be applied in new areas. All of this can certainly be interesting and exacting work.

Also, new models will be constructed; theological propositions will be transposed from one context to another.

Of course, the most discussed problems of object in theology are those of the object God. One can phrase the three main problems as questions: 1) Can we know with certainty that God exists? 2) Can we know with certainty something about God? 3) What can we say about God?

A not uncommon opinion is that we can know with certainty that God exists; the existence of God can, at least hypothetically, be proved. We can also know with certainty certain things about God, and those are the things we can say. This is the view of those who hold that a natural theology is possible: God can be known through nature.

In my opinion, certain convincing objections can be made to this view. Firstly, any argument for the existence of God from nature must depend on a context in which the existence of God (of whatever sort) is already presupposed. If one argues from the contingency of the world to the need for something absolute—God—then one bases one's argument on one's view of the world as contingent, a view which already presupposes the need for *something else* which would be absolute— which is then named God. Similarly, if one argues from the finitude of the world to some necessary infinite—God— then one has based one's argument on a view of the world as finite, a view which again already presupposes that there must be something else which is infinite, which one then calls God. In other words, one's view of nature is dependent on one's opinion about the existence of God: if one believes that God is the absolute, one will believe that nature is contingent; if one believes that God is the infinite, one will believe that nature is finite. One cannot prove that nature is contingent or finite. In other words, all arguments for the existence of God from nature necessarily presuppose in their view of nature that which they are seeking to prove. Or again, one can only prove the existence of God within a certain context and that context itself cannot be proved.

Similarly, any deductions about the nature of God will depend on the context within which one is working and will thus be necessarily as uncertain as that context itself.

A new attempt has been made to establish the existence of some certain knowledge of God by referring to experience: a person has the experience of meeting God. But, as I have argued before, such an experience can only allow one to be certain that one has had such and such an experience, not that there really is an ontological reality, a real being, "at the other end" of the experience. No one can deny that such an experience can be extraordinarily convincing for a person and may lead him to believe in the real existence of that which he feels he has met. But, because he cannot argue necessarily from the experience to the reality of that which he has experienced, his conviction remains a belief.

I can only conclude that one cannot know certainly that God exists; one can only believe that he does. Belief is, in all cases, necessary.

Similarly, one cannot know anything with certainty about God. The person who may have had the experience of meeting God may, because of the quality of his experience, prefer to speak about God in one way rather than another. But, just as he cannot prove the existence of God from his experience, so he cannot prove that his manner of speaking about God is more appropriate than another. He can only say that he finds that this or that way of speaking is truer to his own experience.

This is, in fact, all that anyone can say. The Christian believes in God; and what he believes about God, that is, his theology, will depend on all of the factors I have discussed before: his situation, his experience, his interests, his context or contexts, his own insights and creativity, and so on. The process by which he forms his view of God is exactly the process which I have been describing: the process of the creation of a theology. Similarly, I have been answering, as best I can, the question of what one can say about God.

This view, that one must believe in the existence of God and that one can only claim that this or that expression or model is more useful in speaking about him, is, I believe, more accurate than the view that one can know God certainly and know some things about him with certainty. At least, that certainty was not shared by the New Testament writers, who disagree so profoundly about God, nor by most theologians of the past, the present and in all likelihood the future, whose views conflict or will conflict just as radically.

The realization that one must depend on faith can itself be, I believe, very useful. At the very least, it can help convince one of the uncertainty of all one's theology. I have argued already how useful this realization could be; one may be confident that the realization of the uncertainty of one's belief itself will prove equally positive.

THE THEOLOGIAN AND OTHER THEOLOGIES: INFLUENCE AND CREATIVITY

I have already discussed at some length various improper methods of using other theologies: forcing meanings, pressing models, reducing theologies, systematizing them, and so on. Both Protestant and Catholic theologians were forced to resort to such methods because of their theories of theology. Roman Catholics have had to produce absurd arguments to establish the presence of the doctrine of the Assumption in Scripture. Protestants have been embarrassed at the difficulty of proving the existence of the practice of infant baptism in New Testament times.

The disingenuity of such distorting methods can no longer be veiled. Aside from the fact that this procedure is profoundly disrespectful of the texts which it handles, the theologies constructed on such distortions cannot be convincing. With unhistorical methods, one can only build an "illusionary theology." [1]

The theologian must understand other theologies historically; the questions then arise: how should he deal with those theologies? What is their value for him? In what sort of continuity does he stand to them?

The theologian realizes that he can neither systematize nor reproduce them. Other theologies remain irreducibly different and other. Every theologian must create *his own* theology or theological understanding. But what is his relation to other theologies as he does this? Of course, he learns a variety of models, techniques, and possibilities from them. The reader of the previous chapters will be able to realize how valuable such learning must be. But what is the relation of the theologian to other theologies themselves?

Theologians seem, at first, to accept one proposition from one theology and reject another from another. As Scott writes: "Such a gospel was capable of many interpretations. No one could take in the whole of it and each believer was drawn to that aspect of it which had most significance for his own mind." [2] This would certainly *seem* to have been the method of the New Testament theologians. They accepted the Old Testament, but not the absolute authority of the Law.[3] They accepted the teaching of Jesus, but eventually rejected his restriction of his attention to the Jews and were forced to "reinterpret" his faith in the imminent coming of the kingdom. All the churches would seem to use this method to a certain extent. For instance, the Second Vatican Council would seem to have rejected the position of John's Gospel that the Jews as a people were responsible for the execution of Jesus.

Important qualifications must be made, however, of this attempt to formulate the relation of a theologian to other theologies as one of picking and choosing among theological propositions.

Firstly, this formulation is based on a view of theologies as collections of divisible, isolable propositions. But this, as I have argued, is not the case: each theology is constructed within a context and each proposition of a theology qualifies the others and is qualified by them. A proposition which has been isolated from its context has been voided of all the connotations, purposes, nuances, and so on, which it had within its original context. To take a proposition from one theology and insert it into another context or into a different set of propositions is somehow to transform it. A proposition is qualified in quite a different way; something new is created. In other words, a theological proposition is no more reproducible than a theology. A proposition taken from Paul is no longer the same when it is in another theology. The opinion of John that the Jews as a people were responsible for the death of Jesus is bound up with the whole of John's theology and with his whole method of presenting everything in the most absolute terms. Jesus' call to repentance is qualified by his expectation of the imminent coming of the kingdom. Other theologies can contain *similar* propositions, but they obviously cannot contain *identical* ones.

The other side of the coin of this indivisibility of a proposition from its context is that certain propositions, just because they might have been used so often in a certain context or with certain associations, tend to continue to connote them. Thus, a writing can remain a more or less loose bundle of very heterogeneous material. This is certainly true of many New Testament writings and certainly of portions of Paul's letters. Sometimes, someone will deliberately use two irreducible propositions; [4] for instance, the formulators of compromise creeds merely join irreducible theologies.

There is also the special case of propositions which one could call loose: those that have been or are so generally used that they are no longer necessarily bound to a particular theology. An example of this type would be: "Jesus brought salvation." But this proposition will, of course, be qualified in different ways in whichever theology it appears. Each theology will mean something different by "salvation." Thus this proposition is not identical in the different theologies in which it is used.

Even behind the loosest collection of propositions, there is most often some attitude or general context which gives those propositions a certain, even if often not complete, unity. In a theology which has been consciously and personally constructed, the parts will find their significance in the whole. Almost every line of Newman's can be related to his basic insights and thus to every other line, though his thought certainly developed. Aristotle's theory of babbling can be related to his doctrine of the soul. No theology is really understood unless it is understood as a whole. No portion of a theology can be understood unless the whole has been understood.

One cannot speak then of picking and choosing. One simply cannot reproduce others' propositions in one's own theologies. Rather, one may formulate *similar,* but *not identical* propositions. My theology may *resemble* another theology at certain points, but it cannot be identical with it. Each theology will qualify those points somehow differently. One can, certainly, speak of rejecting certain propositions, but one cannot mean literally that one "accepts" others.

Thus other theologies can obviously be an aid by helping or inspiring one to formulate similar propositions. We often speak of our "getting ideas" from other theologies.

However, since a theology is best understood and appreciated precisely as a whole, the question naturally arises as to the relation of the individual theologian to these *whole* theologies.

Faced with this question, one realizes the great practical limitations of the view of theologies as collections of divisible propositions. For this view, the question is irrelevant. Moreover, when a totally different or new theology appears, the theologian who shares this view will tend to be baffled or simply miss the point. For instance, the Roman Catholic controversialists of the time of the Reformation were confused by the new *total* theology of Luther. As the historian Joseph Lortz writes: "Not a couple of new, unimportant or interesting math problems were given by Luther to theology; it was a matter of understanding in a completely new way the meaning of Christianity, of man and his place in the process of salvation." [5] The theologians who hold such a view will also tend to misunderstand individual statements of a theology either by not appreciating their context or by assuming that they mean exactly what they would if they were said within the contexts of the critics themselves. Also such a critic tends to condemn a theology as a whole simply because it does not contain one or more favored propositions. Theologies which used Kant's philosophy were condemned because they did not hold the idea of substance necessary for the doctrine of transubstantiation. Chardin is condemned because Jesus cannot occupy the same position in an evolutionary scheme as he can in a static one. Moreover, such a view renders historical understanding impossible.

How then does one learn from theologies as wholes? One method which has been attempted is simply to reduce the "central insights" of a total theology to propositions and to pick and choose among them: to take from Luther the proposition of justification through faith alone; from Newman, his emphasis on the personal; from Kierkegaard, his emphasis on sincerity. Here again, one meets all the objections which can be made against the method of picking and choosing.

More important, a whole theology cannot be reduced to propositions. A whole theology is more than its unitive insights; it is those insights applied and qualified by a *whole world* of objects and problems. A whole theology *is* a whole world; it is a way of looking at things and those things themselves as they are looked at in that way. It is also the *process* of insight and application, of the revision of vision occasioned by the problems of application. A whole theology is its failures and disadvantages as well as its triumphs and advantages. It is the result of a person thinking in a world. In understanding a theology, one understands how a person attempted to understand the world, and one is enabled to understand the world, to a certain extent, as he understood it. One appreciates and repeats his effort.

Somehow, by understanding a total theology or philosophy, one learns. What one learns is not easy to define. One is not learning a set of propositions which then may or may not appear in one's own theologies or philosophies. One may, in fact, learn a great deal by achieving an understanding of a theology or philosophy with which one in no way agrees. One can always read Plato and Aristotle with great profit, even if one does not agree with them at all. But in what does that profit consist?

Everyone has a more or less conscious total world view.

That view is being continually developed. By learning to understand another world view, one learns to see the world in a different way. One sees that there are other possible ways of looking at the world. The range of one's possibilities has been widened. More important, in understanding another's world view, one is participating in the process of his forming of that view through experiences, insights, received information, with various means of thought and communication, and with much effort. One recognizes the kinship of his process with one's own; although one will most probably start from very different points and create totally different views. Nevertheless, one learns, at the very least, techniques, methods, and procedures of thought. One also learns about possibilities and problems. But most important by first participating in another person's creation of his world view, then by understanding and, to a certain extent, living in it, and finally by criticizing it and transcending its limits, one learns not only how to understand and to create a view, but also how to transcend whatever view of the world one has received or created oneself. To speak in terms of space, one sees the inevitable distance between a world view and the world, and, in that vacuum, the possibility of new creation is offered.

Creative change arises when an old world view or solution is, for any number of reasons, no longer adequate. In the inadequacy of that view or in the shortcomings of a solution, the need for the creation of a new view or a new solution is felt. In the vacuum created by the rejection of the old view, the possibility of the creation of the new is given. An effort *must* be made to look at the world or the problem, not through the picture which the old view or solution gives of it, but rather, as much as possible, blankly, in order that a new view or solution may arise: that is, be created. This "fresh look" at a problem or the world is a look emptied, as it were, of the "stale look." One makes oneself ignorant. One deprives oneself of one's former solutions. The great creators are those who are able to free themselves from their old pictures and solutions and, perhaps only for a moment, to leave themselves free to see things differently, to create another view or solution. Just because this crea-

tion arises through a certain emptiness, it often appears similar
to the process of memory, especially sudden remembering, or
of religious inspiration.

Jean Charlot writes that the painter

> *of today, unless he be of the strongest, will ease himself by*
> *leaning on an academic knowledge of the art styles of the*
> *past. All he knows, from Altamira to Miró, will be in-*
> *geniously put to work in pictures whose only defect will be*
> *a lack of creativeness.*
>
> *True creation must start from nothing. For the artist*
> *who only approximates this godlike attribute, true creation*
> *must at least start from little. The real painter approaches*
> *his work as nakedly now as he did in the prehistoric cave.*
> *This emptying of himself, this vacuum cleansing which is*
> *the first step of creation, is the absolute opposite of the*
> *data gathering and file ordering of the critical type.*[6]

Creation is a result of just this knowledgeability, passivity
(or receptivity), blankness, and action. Harvey Cox has described well the passive, receptive factor in theological creation: "Rather than clinging stubbornly to antiquated appella-
tions or anxiously synthesizing new ones, we must simply take
up the work of liberating the captives, confident that we will be
granted a new name by events of the future." [7]

Luther indicates the active factor: "Who knows [but] that
without pride or at least the appearance of pride something new
would never be produced? So they should expect from me not
the sort of humility (that is, hypocrisy) that they would presume
that I must first question them for their advice and opinion before I publish something." [8] The kind of "pride" which Luther
is discussing here has never, as far as I know, been investigated. His own analysis of it is definitely within his theological
context: "My work should be accomplished not through human
advice and cleverness, but rather through God's advice. Then,
when the work comes from God, who wills to hinder it?" Lortz

writes that "for the first time, he signs himself: Martinus Eleutherius (= the Free)!"

Of course, one cannot really *learn* from others to create. On the contrary, other views can become hindrances, in that they block our "fresh look." Nevertheless, one of the few ways in which one can even begin to understand the creative process in theology is by beginning to appreciate theologies as totalities.

One of the advantages of this new theory of theology is precisely that it allows one to appreciate theologies as wholes and as they really are. It makes one realize that they are more than bundles of propositions and forbids one to distort them. Indeed, to understand them truly, one must understand them as wholes. Precisely, in this way, does one learn what is most fundamentally important. So one can appreciate Luther for what he is and not worry about how much one may agree or disagree with him. One can appreciate Aquinas, although one may not become a Thomist. One can leave a text problematical, unsynthesized, contrary to one's own opinions—that is, one can allow a text to be what it is—and realize that to do so is to allow oneself to begin to learn from it something which one might otherwise never know and which is ultimately of the greatest usefulness.

Once one has realized what it is to appreciate theologies as wholes, one can understand better the process of acceptance and rejection. One realizes that one cannot reproduce a theological proposition or position in one's theology, but rather that one can formulate *similar,* but not identical, propositions or positions. One can also reject a proposition or position for one's own theology and yet appreciate it and learn from it. This is, I believe, a fuller and more precise understanding of the actual process of adoption and rejection than the view of the theologian picking and choosing among the propositions of different theologies.

Therefore, I would formulate the relation of a theologian to other theologies in the following way: the theologian, having studied other theologies, in the way I have just described, then creates a new theology which bears certain resemblances to other theologies and differs from them in certain ways. Of course this formulation could describe equally well the relation of the theologian to other solutions of particular problems.

The key to understanding the relation of the theologian to other theologies is thus to realize that the theologian must necessarily be creative. There are, of course, *degrees* of creativity. In some theologies, the creativity will be almost accidental: the necessary result of the juxtaposition of two propositions in a different context. Some might prefer to label such theologies "different" rather than "new," "original," or "creative," because we are accustomed to use those terms of works which are outstanding or very original.

Creativity can be more or less obvious. One person may use the same words as another but understand them in a very different way. The devotion to the Infant Jesus was for Thérèse of Lisieux a meditation on the Incarnation. The devotion to the Sacred Face of Jesus became for her an expression of her encounter with Jesus, of God's giving his love and attention to man. Deep understanding need not obviously ripple the surface. Many Christians lead lives of profound understanding and express their understanding most conventionally. Of course, unconventional expression can often conceal rather conventional understanding. But creativity or, if one prefers, difference must be to some degree present.

One must take this necessary creativity into account when one attempts to formulate the importance for the theologian of the history of theology. That history contains, of course, individual theologies which are useful in the way I have discussed.

The long tradition of theology can also act as a corrective. Each theologian has his particular limits and tends to see other theologies from within those limits. The plurality of theologies offers one the means of recognizing those limits and of creating theologies which go beyond them. For examples from other fields, each age has its interests in art and tends to view the history of art through those interests. The Surrealists resurrected Hieronymus Bosch; the Cubists, David. In literature, the Pro-

vençal poets were once supreme, and then Laforgue. The tradition of any humanistic field is rich enough to offer bases for almost any tendency and thus to act as a corrective for the limits
of any one. A new tendency, a reaction against the current interests, is usually heralded by an interest in a neglected but obviously great figure of tradition. Thus, an English critic can remind us that Victor Hugo is a great poet, or a new interest can
be awakened in romantic pianists. Käsemann can remind us
that Jesus is more than just a presupposition for the *kerygma* of
the later community, and a whole new theological tendency begins, radically different from the former one, which was forced
through its own logic to give Jesus that inadequate position.
Many revolutionary movements in theology have begun in a revived interest in Paul's theology; his teachings on the Christian's freedom from the Law will always be an interesting
corrective as long as churches tend to develop toward legalism.
Also, when one sees what revolutions, what profound restructurings, have taken place in the history of theology, one must
correct one's view of theology as static and be prepared for further revolutions and restructurings in the future. Indeed, mental
revolution seems to be an inherent human need, an expression
of the basic, necessary creativity of man's thought.

Similarly a study of the history of theology, just as one of
the history of philosophy, can reveal to one one's unconscious
presuppositions and thus enable one to free oneself from them.

It is in this context that the problems of the authority of
Scripture and of the canon should be raised. Does Scripture
hold a special interest? Is it especially valuable for the theologian, and, if so, why? [9] Is there any reason at all to mark out
these particular books in a special canon? If so, why have these
very different books been chosen? [10] Are this special authority
and this canon merely posits of the old theory of unity? In any
case, one should begin an investigation of these problems by
asking rather simple questions: such as, has Scripture been, *in
fact,* the center of our theologies? How have we been, *in fact,*
influenced by the various theologies of the New Testament? Is
it true that many writers are more relevant for us personally

than Scripture? After discussing these questions very factually, one could then proceed to more complicated ones: such as, how the theology of the New Testament, being a disunity, could act as a norm.

The recognition of the role of creativity in theology has important consequences also for any definition of theological continuity. That continuity must not be pictured as a serial reproduction of the same thing. The theologian is not the parrot of a perennial truth. The theology of Aquinas cannot be identified with that of John of St. Thomas, nor with any of those of the modern Thomists. Paul's theology or theologies cannot be identified with any of the later Pauline ones. A theology, just as any human work, cannot be reproduced. Revivals are always new creations. The Renaissance did not reproduce antiquity any more than Neoclassicism did. The Pre-Raphaelites are very different from the painters who lived before Raphael. The kind of continuity one must seek in the history of theology is the same as that which we find in the history of any creative field, such as the history of art.

Let us glance at some examples. David worked in the studio of Boucher, but broke away and formed a quite different style. In his painting "The Oath of the Horatians," we notice his suppression of the brushstrokes, his unpretty, almost acidic colors, the emphasis on solid form, the masculinity of the gestures. These elements in David's painting could be considered continuous to elements in the style of Boucher in that they were a reaction or even a revolution against them. On the other hand, the group of women in the picture shows traces of Boucher's positive influence in the relative softness of the colors, the delicacy of the folds of their robes, and the general charm of their gestures. Of course, all these elements are very different in David's painting than they would be in one by Boucher.

To take another example, the Mannerists adopted the rhythmic lines of Michelangelo's style, but not the bulk that filled those lines. Wagner took the melodic line of Beethoven, but it became something very different in his hands.

Similarly, in the history of philosophy, one can see how Aristotle influenced Aquinas, how he did not and how all the elements of Aristotelian philosophy were transformed by Aquinas.

The historical continuity of any one of these fields is not that of reproduction, but of *influence and creativity*. The influence and the creativity will be *different in every case*. No general formula or recipe can be given. Rather, each stage, each individual case, must be studied on its own.

This view of theological continuity is more useful, I believe, than that which discusses "To what extent Jesus himself, in the speech-event of the Pauline teaching on justification, *as* he himself comes *new* to speech." It allows of more precision than those which discuss succession as "encounter and interpretation," [11] or as "a series of finite lines," [12] or as "call and response." [13] This new view of continuity enables one to discuss it, not in abstract or emotional terms, but in highly concrete and historical ones.

That one cannot incapsulate the long history of theology in an easy formula is no cause for wonder. One has a great deal of work to do before one has even understood and appreciated any great number of Christian theologies; to establish the myriad lines of connection between them is an even greater project. In any case, the continuity of the history of theology will not be defined by abstraction, by ever vaguer theories, but by precise scholarship which is trained on the many problems presented by the vast history of Christian theology. One can be certain that the continuity scholars find will be that, not of reproduction, but of influence and creativity; and that the continuity will be different between every stage and for every individual.

CREATIVITY IN THEOLOGY

That creativity or even difference is not only inevitable, but essential to the process of theologizing is an important disconfirmation of the old theory of unity. The realization of the role of theological creativity opens, in fact, important new possibilities of understanding and practice. I will discuss a few of those possibilities.

Firstly, once one recognizes the role of creativity, one can appreciate much more fully the achievements of other theologians. They have been and are accomplishing more than "interpretations"; nor can they be simply explained by their influences. Aquinas seems today an almost inevitable chapter in the history of medieval philosophy. One forgets his protest against, his discontent with, previous philosophies and the striking originality of his attempt to think through the antinomous problems and solutions of his age. One forgets how dangerously novel he appeared to his contemporaries. In the same way, Paul, striking out into the Hellenistic world, appears, in the cliché, to be part of the long process of the Hellenization of Palestinian Christianity. His nearly desperate struggle to express himself and the scandal and misunderstandings which he caused among his brothers reveal how truly creative he had to be to accomplish his mission.

To recognize the role of creativity allows one to understand the shock which each new great creation in theology looses upon the world. A creation *is* different from that which preceded it. Those who feel they can admit only "interpretations" or reproductions will naturally be shocked at the newness of a creation. Indeed, no great new theology has ever been introduced without creating consternation. Jesus shocked his listeners, as Paul did his. Tertullian and Origen were continually embroiled in the bitterest controversies. Athanasius was repeatedly deposed. Nestorius and Chrysostom went into exile. Augustine carried on a set of running controversies. Abelard was condemned as was Aquinas. Ockham fled, and Bacon hid. One is usually surprised to discover that the august personages of our traditions were considered dangerous by their contemporaries. Later forgetfulness and antihistorical methods of interpretation have evened the jagged passage of history. Unevenness, however, is familiar to us from more modern times. All the great reformers were condemned and persecuted. Simon was condemned as were most of the early Bible scholars of all denominations. Kierkegaard was an outcast. Newman was held in constant suspicion. Tyrrell was excommunicated. Bultmann has been drummed out of Christianity. We have been warned against Chardin.

One must admit that those who were scandalized recognized the creativity of those new theologies more clearly than those who have tried to smooth out the history of theology into the usual view of continuity. Certainly, if theology *is* a unity, one *should* be scandalized by new theologies, because new theologies are inevitably different. Only if one changes one's view can one frankly admit that new theologies must be different; one may still be shocked by them, but for other reasons than simply their difference from the theologies which preceded them.

Great creations can also be shocking in that they make such rapid advances. In 1813, Gerber's New Lexicon stated of Mozart: "Artists were calmly proceeding, industriously and actively, along the sure and direct road of art and approaching their fulfillment, according to the laws of Nature—slowly, yet all the more surely and effectively; when suddenly *Mozart* appeared, and by the force of his genius brought about a general revolution in artistic taste." [14]

Another result of creativity is that the future of theology is never predictable. One can consider present factors and interests, but the creative theologian cannot be limited by these and will, in all likelihood, go far beyond anything that most of us can see at the present.[15] One is often tempted to consider historical figures such as Paul, Luther, and Aquinas as somehow inevitable; as somehow "demanded" by their times. In fact, they created their times; one considers them inevitable only because they created the history of theology, which one now, much later, mistakes for an inevitable process. The history of theology would have been completely different if they had not lived, but other creators had. One would then have regarded those others, and their very different contributions, as inevitable.

Another result of creativity in theology is that the history of theology will never end. Each theology, just because it is different, will add something different and new to that history. Nor may one expect this change to be somehow logically consistent with previous stages, or even to be predictable. Theology can surprise as much as life can.

In other words, one must accustom oneself to the idea of theology as a creative search. This will not be easy. One is so accustomed to thinking according to the old theory: one feels that the answers to one's questions, the solutions to one's problems, must somehow already be given, already be present in Christianity. One thinks only of finding them or reinterpreting them.

Not only are professional theologians imbued with this old view of theology, but many popular attitudes betray its influence as well. For instance, nuns speak of "finding their place in the modern world" as if that place already existed somewhere, and they had only to discover and occupy it. Surely this is an incorrect view of the situation or at least an incorrect way of speaking about it. That place does not exist; it must be created. Similarly, brothers and priests cannot "find" their "proper relationship" to other ranks of the hierarchy. Any number of relationships can be found in history and today. At the least, one must choose among them, but difference is inevitable. In fact, one must create a new relationship, which will resemble some of the preceding relationships and be very different from others. Unions of priests, or whatever they should be called, have not been found, but created. Similarly, many are beginning to realize that an adequate theology of marriage and sex does not yet exist; efforts to *find* one have been tragicomically disappointing. Such a theology also must be created.

The realization of the role of creativity in theology is therefore of the greatest importance for Christians today. The great majority of Christians are being faced with a great variety of new and serious problems. Accustomed to the old theory of theology, they are searching in the Christianity they have received for the solutions. When they cannot find them there, they are becoming discouraged.

The pain felt by a person in this situation is not simply the pain of loss. The pain arises in part, certainly, because one feels that one must lose all that one has believed and appreciated before. It arises also in part because one feels oneself dislocated and isolated, and because one does not know what one should do. But the reason why the old theologies are seen to be inadequate, the reason why their limitations are felt, is precisely that one has realized or sensed something which the old theologies cannot account for. This is the pain of insight. One must, in fact, advance beyond the old views; one must gain. In any other case, one would greet this insight. One would use it to advance. One would allow oneself to desire to appreciate what one had appreciated before *along with* what one had learned newly to appreciate. But the person who has deep insights, who sees very much more than the old theologies can account for, realizes at the same time how very different any theology must be which he himself would create to account for what he has seen. At this point, the old theory of theology causes a tragic inhibition. What allows one to create something new? Does not the inadequacy of the old theologies simply disconfirm everything which one has believed?

That inhibition must be removed. The old theory of theology which has been disconfirmed in so many ways must no longer be allowed to be a hindrance or to cause confusion and despair. Those who are troubled by doubts and problems must be allowed to realize that they have been privileged with a special insight, a special sensitivity; and that that insight and sensitivity call them and in fact oblige them to create. They *must*, in any case, create a new vision. If they understand the inevitability and desirability of creation in theology, they can realize, not only that they do not lose what they have appreciated before, but that they are fulfilling their roles as Christians of understanding their faith; and that they are also helping other Christians who themselves have similar insights and sensitivities and are thus similarly distressed. They will realize that what they are experiencing is nothing less than the act of theologizing, the pain of creation.

METHODS OF THEOLOGY

I will now discuss very briefly how this new theory of theology helps us to understand theologies today, and will offer a paradigm of the theological method which I have developed in our previous chapters and sections.

There are several new models current in theology. One is that of the Suffering Servant as portrayed by the author of Second Isaiah. Much attention has been given recently to the group of writings contained in chapters 40–55 of Isaiah, which were written at the time of the exile. These writings contain the so-called Songs of the Servant of Yahwe, which portray a good man, a servant of God, who suffered persecution and whose sufferings were for the good of his brothers and, according to some interpretations, of all men. Attempts were then made to establish the fact that some New Testament writers had used the figure of the Suffering Servant as a model for understanding Jesus. These attempts have not, however, been successful. There is too little evidence that the New Testament writers used this figure in their Christologies.[16] However, this makes it no less useful and effective a model for us today. In fact, the scholars who have attempted to reconstruct New Testament theologies using this model have been constructing *new* theologies, using exactly the same methods which the New Testament writers used with other models. An advance in knowledge has provided new means of understanding and articulation.

Another very popular and effective model used in modern theology is that of the death of God. "God is dead" is not an existential proposition such as "God does not exist"; nor can it be mistaken for a descriptive proposition, which supposedly reports the actual death of God. The sentence cannot be taken literally in any way. "God is dead" is, in fact, a new model.

That it has gained such wide currency shows that it is an effective model. But how should it be used? A number of possibilities present themselves: one can use this model as a means of forcefully articulating the irrelevance of God for us and for the modern world, the "post-Christian" age, the "distance" of God, loss of faith, and so on. Different people will use this model in different ways, because it enables them to make certain statements more effectively and forcefully than by means of any other model. The ludicrousness of persecuting anyone for using this model is evident. On the other hand, this is obviously as extreme a model as possible for theology. If one cannot forbid this model, what model *could* one forbid? The new theory of theology enables us to understand 1) why it is ridiculous to forbid the statement "God is dead"—because it is a model, a means of articulation; and 2) why one *should* use this model—because it allows one to make certain statements forcefully and effectively. Here, a new situation, among other things, has called forth a new model.

I have already discussed the theological method of constructing a theology within a context. This new theory of theology helps one to understand why the theologies constructed within these very different contexts will differ from each other, and enables one to accept that difference and thus not to feel obligated to formulate, within one context, statements which are only possible in another. The theologies within these new contexts are examples of new theologies being able to be constructed because of advances in knowledge.

Another method of theologizing is represented today by the new quest for the historical Jesus. The New Testament writers already had the *kerygma,* but they wrote the gospels just the same. The history of Jesus somehow had theological meaning for them. Of course, they used the method of inserting that meaning into the history of Jesus to express their own theologies. Scholars since have learned to employ historical methods which ensure as much as possible against reading personal views into history. The problem then arises as to what relevance history as such can have for theologies, for interpretations of that history.

I believe that this new theory can help in solving this

problem. Firstly, one must realize that the very separation of history from interpretation is an important advance, which frees one from false presuppositions and methods.

Secondly, this new theory provides a means of deciding which theological statements are historically accurate. One can discover which propositions, interpretations, or theologies which claim to be descriptive, can be disconfirmed by the historical evidence. For instance, the proposition "Jesus was all-knowing" can be disconfirmed as a statement about history by the fact that Jesus was mistaken about the imminence of the coming of the kingdom. One can, of course, choose to redefine the proposition "Jesus was all-knowing" in such a way that it would *not* admit of historical disconfirmation, but at least one has understood that this proposition cannot be used as descriptive of the observable without being false. Needless to say, to claim for a theology or statement that it is correct as a descriptive of the observable even though it has been disconfirmed is a contradiction in terms.

Thirdly, this new theory can suggest the relevance and usefulness of the many recent studies of the possibilities, limits, problems, and means of a philosophy of history. A philosophy of history is as important to theologians today as a philosophy of essences was to those of the Middle Ages.

Finally, this new theory enables one to realize that any theological interpretation of the history of Jesus must rest on faith; that the process of the formulation of that interpretation will follow the rules of human thought; and that the results will have all the natural limitations of a human intellectual construction.

In these ways, this new theory can be useful in attempting to solve this very new and complex problem of the possibilities of a theological interpretation of the historical.

I will now illustrate, by means of an example, the method prescribed by this new theory of theology. Let us assume that a theologian wishes to construct a scheme for the history of God's work among men, a history of salvation. He is aware of his presuppositions, of the process by which he will construct his scheme, and of all the natural limitations of his results.

On the one hand, he will study all the different contemporary and traditional schemes of the history of salvation. He will try to understand them as exactly as possible. He will appreciate them as they are and criticize them. He will not reduce, distort, or systematize them in any way. He will not speak of *"the* Biblical scheme of the history of salvation." He will recognize the plurality of those schemes and will not veil the contradictions between them. In so doing, he will learn from them in all the ways I have described. He will, of course, not allow himself to be hindered by them.

On the other hand, he will look at history itself. What facts must be accounted for? What have we learned since the last important schemes were constructed? Often new findings will be profoundly significant. The progress in Biblical studies, for instance, has rendered many, if not all, the old schemes untenable.

He will also look at his own time and very recent history. What will be the influence of, say, the two World Wars on any scheme of salvation? What, the influence of the ecumenical movement? or, of the "death of God" theologies? The sensitive theologian will not simply put these phenomena into pigeonholes; he will be influenced by them.

He will at every stage be aware of all the personal factors which play a role in his thinking. He will be aware of his own positions and insights.

Then, basing himself both on what he has learned from other schemes and on what he knows and understands of the phenomena, he will create a new scheme, which will be different from all others, and which will resemble some in some ways and contradict others in others. He will, of course, regard the differences between his scheme and others as perfectly natural.

This description of the process of theology takes account of the value for the theologian of other theologies, of phenomena, of all personal and technical factors, and of creativity. This method can be used in any field of theology or for any problem. Of course, each theologian will use this method with very different emphases on the different elements; but all of these elements will be present to some degree in each act of theological creation.

This method is really little different from the one which theologians have always used. It is, in fact, that very same old method, only stripped of its evasions. Theologians have always differed and created, but they have tried to hide the fact. They have used antihistorical methods to conceal what they were really doing and to preserve the illusion of the unity of theology. This new theory of theology frees one from the need of these evasions and allows one to understand more fully and accurately the process of theology.

It does this none too soon. Because of the flood of new considerations caused by the wealth of important new findings in Biblical and historical scholarship and in philosophy, all the old theologies and theological positions can be easily seen to be seriously inadequate. All Christians will recognize the need for new solutions. Theologians will be forced to be very creative. Only a more accurate understanding of the process of theology can enable us to theologize as intensively as we now must.

The differences which will necessarily result from the efforts of theologians to accommodate the new data of scholarship will be so great that efforts to uphold the old theory of theology by somehow explaining away those differences will be self-condemnatory. Theology will be brought into disrepute if it is not allowed to proceed honestly.

Even more important, those Christians who have only the old theory of theology will be tempted to regard the inevitable changes as a disconfirmation of all Christianity. The very first task of theology in this new situation is, therefore, to explain how change is inevitable, necessary, and desirable. Only a new understanding of theology itself can enable us to transform our present difficulties into occasions of advance and gain.

Notes

[1] Käsemann, *op. cit.* (amor fati), p. 227.

[2] Scott, *op. cit.*, p. 18.

[3] Bultmann, *op. cit.* (*Theologie*), pp. 111 ff.

[4] Scott, *op. cit.*, p. 292.

[5] Joseph Lortz, *Die Reformation in Deutschland*, Vol. 1, *Voraussetzungen · Aufbruch · Erste Entscheidung* (Freiburg: Herder, 1962), p. 137.

[6] Jean Charlot, "The Critic, the Artist and Problems of Representation" in his *Art from the Mayans to Disney* (New York: Sheed & Ward, 1939), pp. 117–142, p. 118. See also his "Art, Quick or Slow" in *ibid.*, pp. 143–150, pp. 145 f. See also Robert Craft (ed.), *Stravinsky in Conversation with Robert Craft* (Baltimore: Penguin Books, A Pelican Book A 517, 1962), pp. 29, 40 f., 138 f. Alfred Einstein, *Mozart, His Character · His Work*, trans. by A. Mendel and N. Broder (London: Cassel, 1946), pp. 133 f.

[7] Harvey Cox, *The Secular City, Secularization and Urbanization in Theological Perspective* (London: SCM Press, 1965), p. 168.

[8] Lortz, *op. cit.*, p. 422. Also, for following.

[9] See Ferré, *op. cit.*, p. 100. Kuss, *op. cit.* (*Römer*), p. 594.

[10] See Kümmel, *op. cit.*, pp. 389 f.

[11] Käsemann, *op. cit.* (Sackgassen), pp. 57 f.

[12] Ramsey, *op. cit.* (*Christian*), pp. 34 f.

[13] See Käsemann on Jeremias, *op. cit.* (Sackgassen), pp. 38–41. See also pp. 43–47.

[14] Quoted in Einstein, *op. cit.*, p. 133. Italics in the original text.

[15] Craft, *op. cit.*, p. 144.

[16] See Hahn, *op. cit.*, pp. 54–66. See also Martin Rese, "Überprüfung einiger Thesen von Joachim Jeremias zum Thema des Gotteskrechtes im Judentum," in ZTK, 1963, pp. 21–41.

Conclusions

The discovery of the theological disunity of the New Testament must lead to a reconsideration of all current theories and practices. I have tried to indicate in this book some of the consequences of theological disunity for the old theories of unity and have attempted to sketch some aspects of a possible new theory of theology.

Needless to say, I have not even mentioned many of the areas in which important consequences must be drawn. Tyrrell is credited with the following bittersweet story about the Baron von Hügel:

> THE BARON: *There can be no doubt that Our Lady failed to occupy her proper place at the Crucifixion; the evidence of the Synoptic writers makes this clear.*
>
> THE FRIEND: *Yes? But it is a long way from this to the Salve Regina.*
>
> THE BARON: *There can be no doubt that Our Lord's faith broke down on Calvary.*
>
> THE FRIEND: *Yes? But it is a long way from this to the Nicene Creed.*
>
> THE BARON: *There can be no doubt that St. Paul's teaching on the Eucharist is based upon certain forms of Syrian Nature-worship.*
>
> THE FRIEND: *Yes? But it is a long way from this to the Tantum Ergo.*
>
> THE BARON: *I hear the* Angelus; *I must go and make my evening visit to the Blessed Sacrament!"* [1]

Certainly, forms of devotion will be affected by the new findings. Spirituality will be influenced as well. On the other hand, this new theory is, in fact, in surprising agreement with many traditional forms of spirituality: in its emphasis on faith and on the limitations of theology.

Liturgy is already being influenced by the new Scripture studies; positively, in that many of the new theologies of liturgy attempt to base themselves on Scripture; and, negatively, in that, for example, many psalms are found not to have in the original the Christological significance which they had in the Vulgate.

In many cases, the new methods which followed from this theory were found to be nothing more than the old methods, only more clearly understood. As Wittgenstein quoted Nestroy in the preface to his *Philosophical Investigations:* "Progress is, on the whole, so, that it appears much greater than it really is." [2] To discover the consequences of these new findings and the values of former views is one of the many interesting theological tasks before us.

Without doubt, many of the examples of New Testament theological disunity which I have given in this book can be challenged. I myself would want to reexamine the usual view of the title "Son of Man." But no one could deny that there is *some* theological disunity in the New Testament, however much one may disagree about particular *instances* of that disunity. And *some* theological disunity suffices to establish my thesis.

One can also criticize my description of the process of theology and of creation. At the very least, much *more* must be said than the little which I have had occasion to say in this book. One of the advantages of this new theory of theology is, in fact, that we are rendered again radically dependent on the latest findings of scholarship. Progress has been made most often in theology when problems arose which demanded entirely new means of thought and communication for their solution. These new problems raised by the discovery of the theological disunity of the New Testament will not be able to be solved until we develop the means of solving them. But however one may disagree with my own description of the process of theology, one cannot escape the need to provide some such description, and one which will take into account the factor of disunity.

Similarly, one may disagree with the whole approach of

this attempted new theory of theology; but one must, in that case, provide another.

Some new theory of theology is necessary and must be developed. The one which I have presented here is simply the best which I myself can formulate at this time. I am perfectly ready to abandon it the moment a more useful theory appears. I certainly have hopes that one will, but I also suspect that any such theory, to be in any way adequate, would have to be the result of the teamwork of a number of scholars from many different fields.

In any case, theologians cannot begin too soon to formulate such a theory, which will be not only of theoretical but of the greatest practical importance.

Notes

[1] Quoted in Michael de la Bedoyere, *The Life of Baron von Hügel* (London: J. M. Dent and Sons, 1951), pp. 214 f. This story is no exaggeration. See Maisie Ward, *Unfinished Business* (London and New York: Sheed & Ward, 1964), p. 53: "The Baron, who in Scripture exegesis went all the way with the Modernists, was philosophically poles apart from them. He had an uncanny power of dividing his mind into two compartments, of which the right seemed not to know what the left was about. His friends said he would pass from writing Scripture criticism logically destructive of belief in Our Lord's divinity to an hour of rapt adoration in front of the tabernacle."

[2] "Überhaupt hat der Fortschritt das an sich, dass er viel grösser ausschaut, als er wirklich ist."

Bibliography

AUSTIN, J. L. *How to Do Things with Words* (ed. J. O. Urmson). Oxford: Clarendon Press, 1962.
————. "Performative Utterances," in his *Philosophical Papers* (ed. J. O. Urmson and G. J. Warnock), pp. 220–239. Oxford: Clarendon Press, 1961.
————. *Sense and Sensibilia* (ed. G. J. Warnock). Oxford: Clarendon Press, 1962.
BARR, JAMES. *The Semantics of Biblical Language.* London: Oxford University Press, 1961.
BARTH, KARL. *Die Auferstehung der Toten, Eine Akademische Vorlesung über 1 Kor. 15,* 3rd ed. Munich: Chr. Kaiser Verlag, 1935.
BEDOYERE, MICHAEL DE LA. *The Life of Baron von Hügel.* London: J. M. Dent & Sons, 1951.
BILLERBECK, PAUL. *Kommenter zum Neuen Testament aus Talmud und Midrasch,* Vol. 3, *Die Briefe des Neuen Testaments und die Offenbarung Johannes.* Munich: C. H. Beck'sche Verlagsbuchhandlung, 1926.
BORNKAMM, GÜNTHER. *Jesus of Nazareth.* New York: Harper, 1960.
————. "Paulinische Anakoluthe im Römerbrief" in his *Das Ende des Gesetzes, Paulusstudien, Gesammelte Aufsätze,* Vol. I (Beiträge zur evangelischen Theologie, Theologische Abhandlungen; 16), pp. 76–92. Munich: Chr. Kaiser Verlag, 1963.
BROCKELMANN, CARL. *Hebräische Syntax.* Neukirchen Kreis Moers: Verlag der Buchhandlung des Erziehervereins, 1956.
BUCHWALD, ART. "It Puckers Your Mouth," column in the *International Herald Tribune,* July 23, 1968, p. 14.
BULTMANN, RUDOLF. *Die Geschichte der synoptischen Tradition* (FRLANT;21). Göttingen: Vandenhoeck & Ruprecht, 1961.
————. "Karl Barth, 'Die Auferstehung der Toten,'" in his *Glauben und Verstehen,* Vol. 1, pp. 38–64. Tübingen: J. C. B. Mohr (Paul Siebeck), 1961.
————. *Theologie des Neuen Testaments* (Neue Theologische Grundrisse). Tübingen: J. C. B. Mohr (Paul Siebeck), 1961.
BUSHINSKY, LEONARD A. In a review of H. H. Rowley: *The Unity of the Bible.* Washington: *The Catholic Biblical Quarterly,* 1956, p. 178.
CAMPENHAUSEN, HANS FRHR. VON. *Tradition und Leben, Kräfte der Kirchengeschichte, Aufsätze und Vorträge.* Tübingen: J. C. B. Mohr (Paul Siebeck), 1960.
"Die Anfänge des Priesterbegriffs in der alten Kirche," in above, pp. 272–289.
"Die Askese im Urchristentum," as above, pp. 114–156.
CHARLOT, JEAN. *Art from the Mayans to Disney.* New York: Sheed & Ward, 1939.
"Art, Quick or Slow," in above, pp. 143–150.
"The Critic, The Artist, and Problems of Representation," as above, pp. 117–142.
CIAMPA, JOHN. "The Synanon Game." Beverly Hills: *Los Angeles, FM & Fine Arts, Southern California's Entertainment Magazine,* Dec., 1966, pp. 4–11.

COBB, JOHN B., JR. "Faith and Culture" in Robinson, James M. and Cobb (ed.), *The New Hermeneutic* (New Frontiers in Theology, Discussions among Continental and American Theologians; 2). New York: Harper & Row, 1964, pp. 219–231.

CONZELMANN, HANS. *Die Apostelgeschichte* (HNT;7). Tübingen: J. C. B. Mohr (Paul Siebeck), 1963.

COX, HARVEY. *The Secular City. Secularization and Urbanization in Theological Perspective.* London: SCM Press, 1965.

CRAFT, ROBERT (ed.). *Stravinsky in Conversation with Robert Craft.* Baltimore: Penguin Books, A Pelican Book A 517, 1962.

CULLMANN, OSCAR. *The Christology of the New Testament.* Philadelphia: Westminster Press, 1959.

DAITZ, E. "The Picture Theory of Meaning," in Flew (*Essays*), pp. 53–74.

DENZINGER, HENRICUS and SCHÖNMETZER, ADOLFUS. *Encheridion Symbolorum Definitionum et Declarationum de Rebus Fidei et Morum.* Freiburg: Herder, 1963.

DESSAIN, CHARLES STEPHEN and BLEHL, VINCENT FERRER (ed.). *The Letters and Diaries of John Henry Newman,* Vol. XV, *The Achilli Trial, January 1852 to December 1853.* London: Nelson, 1964.

DIBELIUS, MARTIN. *An die Thessalonicher I, II, An die Philliper* (HNT;11). Tübingen: J. C. B. Mohr (Paul Siebeck), 1937.

———. *Botschaft und Geschichte, Gesammelte Aufsätze,* Vol. 2 (ed. G. Bornkamm, etc.). Tübingen: J. C. B. Mohr (Paul Siebeck), 1956.

"Die Christianisierung einer hellenistichen Formel," in above, pp. 14–29.

"Glaube und Mystik bei Paulus," as above, pp. 94–116.

"Paulus und die Mystik," as above, pp. 134–159.

———. *Die Formgeschichte des Evangeliums* (ed. G. Bornkamm). Tübingen: J. C. B. Mohr (Paul Siebeck), 1961.

———. *Die Pastoralbriefe* (Notes by H. Conzelmann), (HNT;13). Tübingen: J. C. B. Mohr (Paul Siebeck), 1955.

DOBSCHÜTZ, ERNST VON. *Ostern and Pfingsten, eine Studie zu I Korinther 15.* Leipzig: J. C. Hinrichs'sche Buchhandlung, 1903.

DODD, C. H. *The Apostolic Preaching and Its Developments, Three Lectures, with an Appendix on Eschatology and History.* London: Hodder and Stoughton, 1936.

———. "The Appearances of the Risen Christ: an Essay in Form-Criticism of the Gospels" in Nineham, D. E. (ed.). *Studies in the Gospels, Essays in Memory of R. H. Lightfoot,* pp. 9–35. Oxford: Basil Blackwell, 1955.

———. "The Mind of Paul: II" in his *New Testament Studies,* pp. 83–128. Manchester: Manchester University Press, 1954.

———. *The Parables of the Kingdom.* Digswell Place, Welwyn, Herts.: James Nisbett, 1961.

DOWNING, GERALD. *Has Christianity a Revelation?* (The Library of Philosophy and Theology.) London: SCM Press, 1964.

EHRHARDT, ARNOLD. "Christianity before The Apostles' Creed" in his *The Framework of The New Testament Stories,* pp. 151–199. Manchester: Manchester University Press, 1964.

EINSTEIN, ALFRED. *Mozart, His Character, His Work* (trans. by A. Mendel and N. Broder). London: Cassel, 1946.

FERRÉ, FREDERICK. *Language, Logic and God.* London: Eyre & Spottiswoode, 1962.

FLEW, ANTONY (ed.). *Essays in Conceptual Analysis.* London: Macmillan, 1963.
"Philosophy and Language," in above, pp. 1–20.

————. and MACINTYRE, ALASDAIR, ed.: *New Essays in Philosophical Theology.* London: SCM Press, 1963.

GRANT, FREDERICK C. *The Earliest Gospel.* New York: Abingdon-Cokesbury Press, 1943.

HAHN, FERDINAND. *Christologische Hoheitstitel, Ihre Geschichte im frühen Christentum* (FRLANT;83). Göttingen: Vandenhoeck & Ruprecht, 1963.

HAYAKAWA, S. I. *Language in Action.* New York: Harcourt, Brace, 1941.

HENKE, HEINRICH PHILIPP KONRAD. *Allgemeine Geschichte der christlichen Kirche nach der Zeitfolge* 4. Braunschweig: Verlag der Schulbuchhandlung, 1801.

HERBST, PETER. "The Nature of Facts," in Flew (*Essays*), pp. 134–156.

JEREMIAS, JOACHIM. *Die Gleichnisse Jesu.* Göttingen: Vandenhoeck & Ruprecht, 1962.

JOHNSON, JAMES M. *Letter from Rome,* "Behind the theological ferment," in *NCR,* August 11, 1965.

JÜNGERL, EBERHARD. "Das Gesetz zwischen Adam und Christus, Eine theologische Studie zu Röm 5, 12–21," pp. 42–74, in ZTK, 1963.

KAHLEFELD, HEINRICH. *Gleichnisse und Lehrstücke im Evangelium,* two volumes. Frankfurt: Josef Knecht, 1963.

————. *Der Jünger, Eine Auslegung der Rede Lk. 6, 20–49.* Frankfurt: Verlag Josef Knecht, 1962.

KÄSEMANN, ERNST. *Exegetische Versuche und Besinnungen,* Vol. 1. Göttingen: Vandenhoeck & Ruprecht, 1960.
"Amt und Gemeinde im Neuen Testament," pp. 109–134.
"Anliegen und Eigenart der paulinischen Abendmahlslehre," pp. 11–34.
"Begründet der neutestamentliche Kanon die Einheit der Kirche?", pp. 214–223.
"Das Problem des historischen Jesus," pp. 187–214.
"Eine Apologie der urchristlichen Eschatologie," pp. 135–157.

————. *Exegetische Versuche und Besinnungen,* Vol. 2, as above, 1964.
"Eine paulinische Variation des 'amor fati,' " pp. 223–239.
"Gottesgerechtigkeit bei Paulus," pp. 181–193.
"Neutestamentliche Fragen von Heute," pp. 11–31.
"Paulus und der Frühkatholizismus," pp. 239–252.
"Sackgassen im Streit um den historschen Jesus," pp. 31–68.

KRAMER, WERNER. *Christos Kyrios Gottessohn, Untersuchungen zu Gebrauch und Bedeutung der christologischen Bezeichnungen bei Paulus und den vorpaulinischen Gemeinden* (Abhandlungen zur Theologie des Alten and des Neuen Testamentes; 44). Zurich: Zwingli Verlag, 1963.

KÜMMEL, WERNER GEORG. *Das Neue Testament, Geschichte der Erforschung seiner Probleme* (Orbis Academicus, Problemgeschichten der Wissenschaft in Dokumenten und Darstellungen; III, 3). Freiburg-Munich: Verlag Karl Alber, 1958.

KUSS, OTTO. *Auslegung und Verkündigung,* Vol. 1, *Aufsätze zur Exegese des Neuen Testaments.* Regensburg: Verlag Friedrich Pustet, 1963.
"Die Heiden und die Werke des Gesetzes (Nach Röm 2, 14–16)," pp. 213–245.
"Enthusiasmus und Realismus bei Paulus," pp. 261–270."
"Kirchliches Amt und Freie Geistliche Vollmacht," pp. 271–280.
"Paulus über die Staatliche Gewalt," pp. 246–259.
"Zur Frage einer vor paulinischen Todestaufe," pp. 162–182.
"Zur paulinischen und nachpaulinische Tauflehre im Neuen Testament," pp. 121–150.
"Zur vorpaulinischen Tauflehre im Neuen Testament," pp. 98–120.

———. *Der Römerbrief.* Regensburg: Verlag Friedrich Pustet, 1957, 1959.

Lessings Werke (ed. J. Petersen, W. von Olshausen, etc.), Parts 22 and 23, *Theologische Schriften* III and IV (ed. L. Zscharnack). Berlin: Deutsches Verlagsbuchhaus Bong & Co., 1925.

LIETZMANN, HANS. *An die Korinther I·II* (notes by W. G. Kümmel) (HNT;9). Tübingen: J. C. B. Mohr (Paul Siebeck), 1949.

———. *Einführung in die Textgeschichte der Paulusbrief An die Römer* (HNT;3). Tübingen: J. C. B. Mohr (Paul Siebeck), 1919.

LINDARS, BARNABAS. *New Testament Apologetic, The Doctrinal Significance of the Old Testament Quotations.* London: SCM Press, 1961.

LORTZ, JOSEPH. *Die Reformation in Deutschland,* Vol. 1, *Voraussetzungen Aufbruch Erste Entscheidung.* Freiburg: Herder, 1962.

MALCOLM, NORMAN. *Ludwig Wittgenstein, A Memoir* (with a biographical sketch by G. H. v. Wright). London: Oxford University Press, 1958.

MARGIVAL, HENRI. "Richard Simon et la critique biblique au XVIIe siècle" in *Revue d'Histoire et de Littérature Religieuse,* Paris: I (1896), pp. I *seq.,* 159 *seq.;* II (1897), pp. 17 *seq.,* 223 *seq.,* 525 *seq.;* III (1898), pp. 117 *seq.,* 338 *seq.,* 508 *seq.;* IV (1899), pp. 123 *seq.,* 193 *seq.,* 435 *seq.,* 514 *seq.*

MICHEL, OTTO. *Der Brief an die Römer* (Meyer;4). Göttingen: Vandenhoeck & Ruprecht, 1963.

MOORE, GEORGE FOOT. *Judaism in the First Centuries of the Christian Era, The Age of the Tannaim,* Vol. 1. Cambridge: Harvard University Press, 1927.

MUSSET, ALFRED DE. *On ne badine pass avec l'amour.*

National Catholic Reporter, Kansas City.

NEWMAN, JOHN HENRY. *An Essay on the Development of Christian Doctrine.* London: Longmans, Green, 1894. For *Letters,* see Dessain.

Newsweek, New York.

OGDEN, C. K. and RICHARDS, I. A. *The Meaning of Meaning, A Study of The Influence of Language upon Thought and of The Science of Symbolism* (with essays by B. Malinowsky and F. G. Crookshank). London: Routledge & Kegan Paul, 1960.

ORIZET, LOUIS. *Les Vins de France* (Que-Sais-Je, Le Point des Connaissances Actuelles; 208). Paris: Presses Universitaires de France, 1964.

PFURTNER, STEPHEN. *Luther and Aquinas on Salvation.* New York: Sheed & Ward, 1964.

PITCHER, GEORGE (ed.). *Truth* (Contemporary Perspectives in Philosophy Series). Englewood Cliffs: Prentice-Hall, 1964.

QUINE, WILLARD VAN ORMAN. *From a Logical Point of View, 9 Logico-Philosophical Essays.* New York and Evanston: Harper & Row, Harper Torchbooks, 1963.
"Meaning in Linguistics," pp. 47–64.
"On What There Is," pp. 1–19.
"Two Dogmas of Empiricism," pp. 20–46.

———. *Word and Object.* Cambridge: The M.I.T. Press, 1964.

RAMSEY, IAN T. *Christian Discourse, Some Logical Explorations.* London: Oxford University Press, 1965.

———. *Models and Mystery.* London: Oxford University Press, 1964.

———. *On Being Sure in Religion.* London: The Athlone Press, 1963.

———. *Religious Language, An Empirical Placing of Theological Phrases.* New York: Macmillan, 1963.

RESE, MARTIN. "Überprüfung einiger Thesen von Joachim Jeremias zum Thema des Gottesknechtes im Judentum," in ZTK, 1963, pp. 21–41.

ROBINSON, JAMES M. *A New Quest of the Historical Jesus* (Studies in Biblical Theology;25). London: SCM Press, 1966.

SCHLIER, HEINRICH. *Der Brief an die Galater* (Meyer;7). Göttingen: Vandenhoeck & Ruprecht, 1962.

———. "Die Ordnung der Kirche nach den Pastoralbriefen" in his *Die Zeit der Kirche, Exegetische Aufsätze und Vorträge,* pp. 129–147. Freiburg: Herder, 1962.

SCHMIEDEL, P. W. "Resurrection- and Ascension-Narratives" in *Encyclopaedia Biblica,* Vol. 4 (ed. T. K. Cheyne and J. Sutherland Black), columns 4039–4087. London: Adam and Charles Black, 1903.

SCHOTT, ERNEST F. *The Varieties of New Testament Religion.* New York: Charles Scribner's Sons, 1943.

SEEBERG, ALFRED. *Der Katechismus der Urchristenheit.* Leipzig: A. Deichert'sche Verlagsbuchhandlung Nachf (George Böhme), 1903.

SHORT, ROBERT. *The Gospel According to Peanuts.* Richmond, Va.: John Knox Press, 1965.

SIMON, RICHARD. *Histoire Critique des principeaux Commentateurs du Nouveau Testament depuis le commencement du Christianisme jusques à notre tems: avec une Dissertation Critique sur les principaux Actes Manuscrits qui ont été citez dans les trois Parties de cet Ouvrage.* Rotterdam: Chez Reinier Leers, 1693.

SMART, J. J. C. "The Existence of God," in Flew (*New*), pp. 28–46.

———. "Metaphysics, Logic, and Theology," as above, pp. 12–27.

Time, New York.

TÖDT, H. E. *The Son of Man in the Synoptic Tradition.* Philadelphia: Westminster Press, 1965.

TURNER, NIGEL. *Syntax,* Vol. 3 of Moulton, James Hope: *A Grammar of New Testament Greek.* Edinburgh: T. and T. Clark, 1963.

TYRRELL, GEORGE. *Christianity at the Crossroads.* London: Longmans, Green, 1910.

ULLMANN, STEPHEN. *The Principles of Semantics* (Glasgow University Publications;84). Oxford: Basil Blackwell, 1963.

————. *Semantics, An Introduction to the Science of Meaning.* Oxford: Basil Blackwell, 1964.

VIELHAUER, PHILIPP. *Aufsätze zum Neuen Testament* (Theologische Bücherei, Neudrucke und Berichte aus dem 20. Jahrhundert, Neues Testament;31). Munich: Chr. Kaiser Verlag, 1965.
"Gottereich und Menschensohn in der Verkündigung Jesu," in above, pp. 55–91.
"Jesus und der Menschensohn, zur Diskussion mit Heinz Edvard Tödt und Edvard Schweizer," as above, pp. 92–140.

WARD, MAISIE. *Unfinished Business.* London; New York: Sheed & Ward, 1964.

WEINREICH, URIEL. "On the Semantic Structure of Language" in Greenberg, Joseph H. (ed.): *Universals of Language, Report of a Conference held at Dobbs Ferry, New York, April 13–15, 1961,* pp. 142–216. Cambridge: The M.I.T. Press, 1966.

WEISS, JOHANNES. *Der erste Korintherbrief* (Meyer;5). Göttingen: Vandenhoeck & Ruprecht, 1910.

WILCKENS, ULRICH. *Die Missionsreden der Apostelgeschichte, Form- und Traditionsgeschichtliche Untersuchungen* (Wissentschaftliche Monographien zum Alten and Neuen Testament;5). Neukirchen: Neukirchener Verlag, 1961.

ZIFF, PAUL. *Semantic Analysis.* Ithaca: Cornell University Press, 1960.